L'ALCHEMIST

THE COMPLETE FOUR-PANEL COMICS

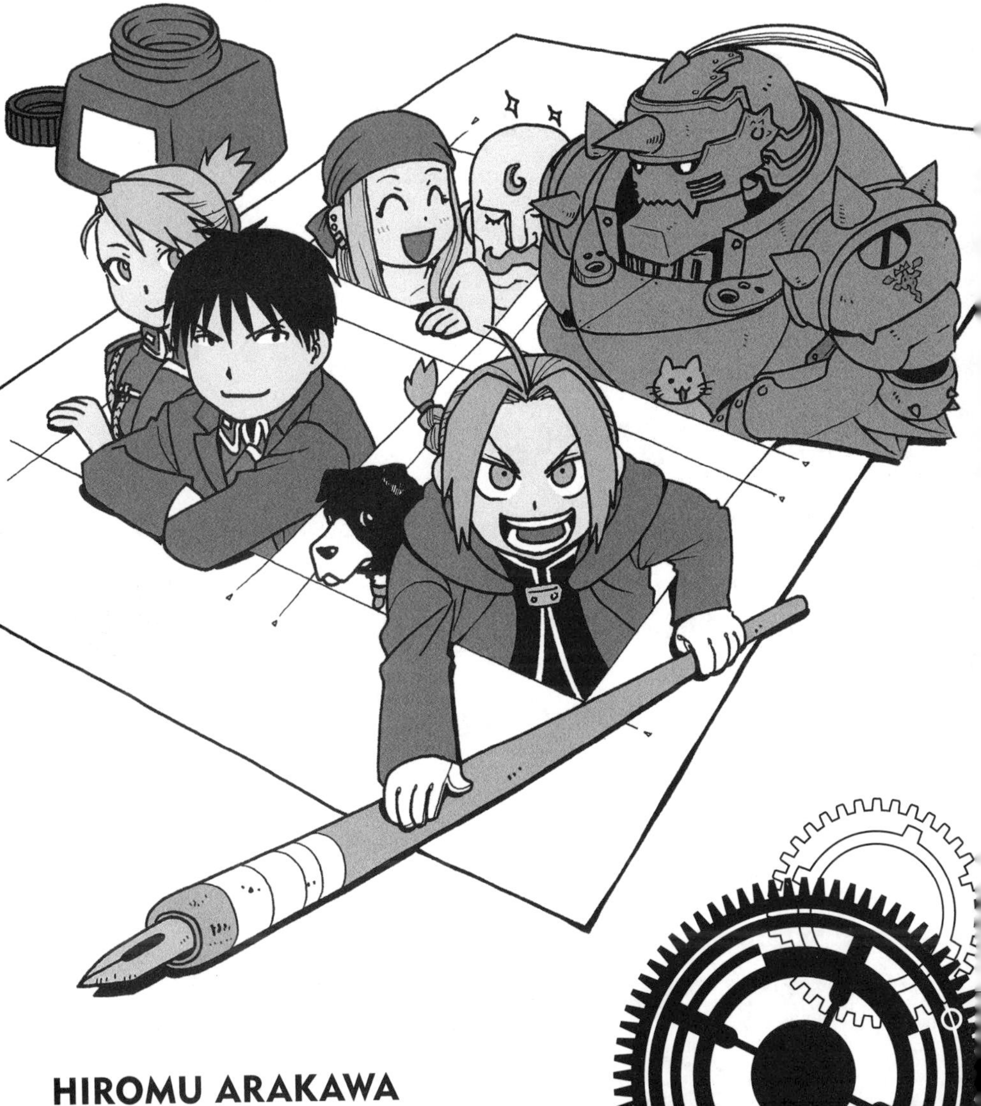

HIROMU ARAKAWA

CONTENTS

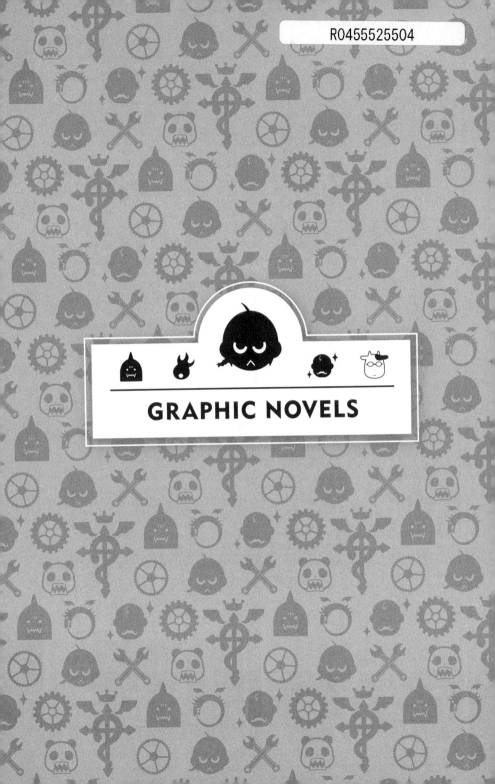

GRAPHIC NOVELS

ALCHEMISTS IN FULLMETAL

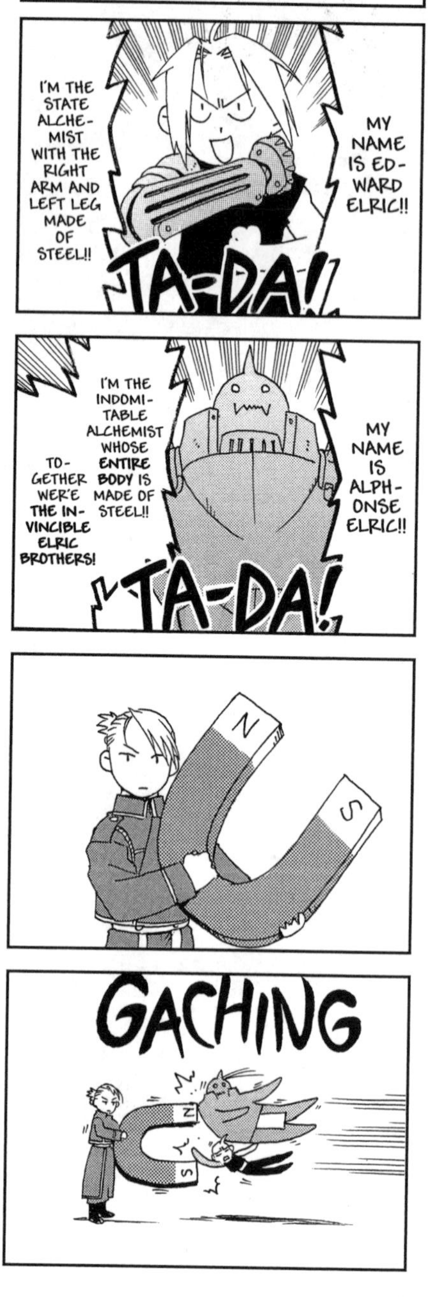
MY NAME IS EDWARD ELRIC!!
I'M THE STATE ALCHEMIST WITH THE RIGHT ARM AND LEFT LEG MADE OF STEEL!!
TA-DA!
MY NAME IS ALPHONSE ELRIC!!
I'M THE INDOMITABLE ALCHEMIST WHOSE ENTIRE BODY IS MADE OF STEEL!!
TOGETHER WE'RE THE INVINCIBLE ELRIC BROTHERS!
TA-DA!
GACHING

COPPER ALCHEMIST

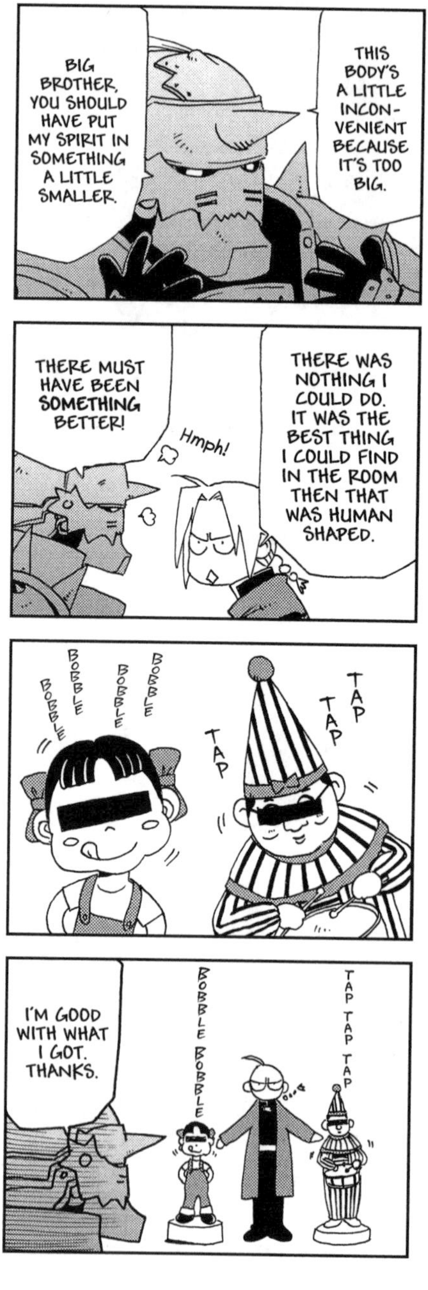
THIS BODY'S A LITTLE INCONVENIENT BECAUSE IT'S TOO BIG.
BIG BROTHER, YOU SHOULD HAVE PUT MY SPIRIT IN SOMETHING A LITTLE SMALLER.
THERE WAS NOTHING I COULD DO. IT WAS THE BEST THING I COULD FIND IN THE ROOM THEN THAT WAS HUMAN SHAPED.
Hmph!
THERE MUST HAVE BEEN SOMETHING BETTER!
TAP TAP TAP
BOBBLE BOBBLE BOBBLE BOBBLE
TAP TAP TAP TAP
BOBBLE BOBBLE
I'M GOOD WITH WHAT I GOT. THANKS.

FULLMETAL ALCHEMIST: COMPLETE

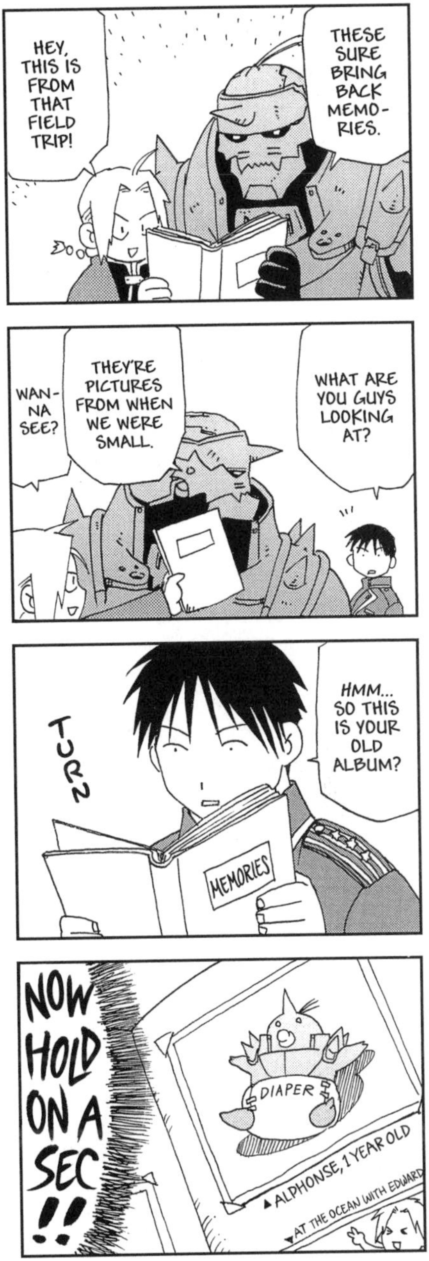
THESE SURE BRING BACK MEMO-RIES.
HEY, THIS IS FROM THAT FIELD TRIP!
WHAT ARE YOU GUYS LOOKING AT?
THEY'RE PICTURES FROM WHEN WE WERE SMALL.
WAN-NA SEE?
HMM... SO THIS IS YOUR OLD ALBUM?
MEMORIES
TURN
DIAPER
▲ALPHONSE, 1 YEAR OLD
▼AT THE OCEAN WITH EDWARD
NOW HOLD ON A SEC!!

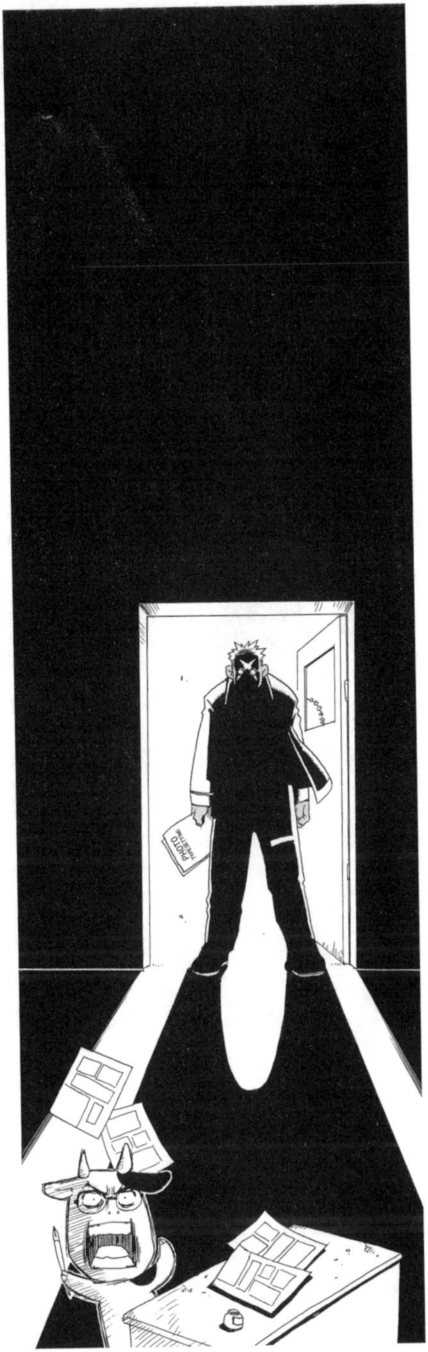

POPULARITY EMPIRE

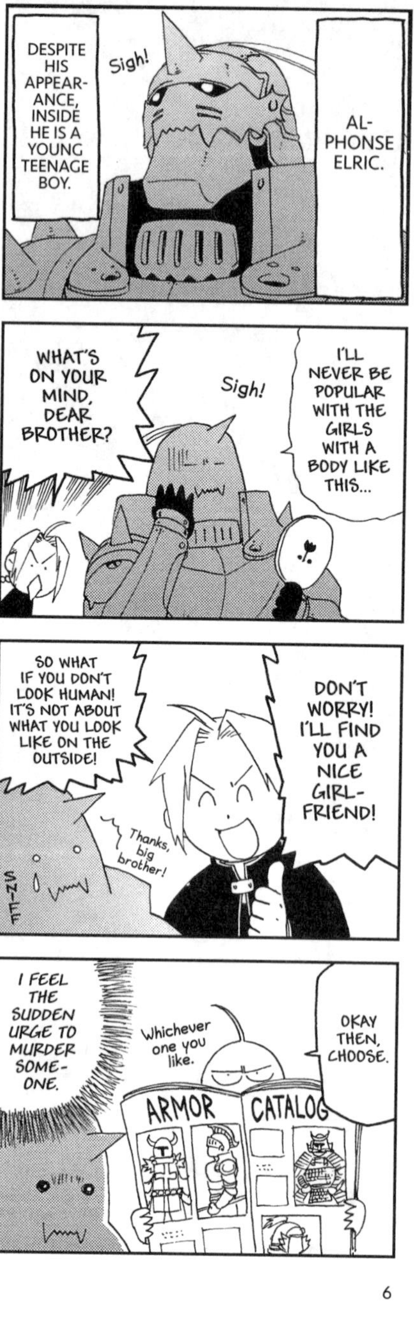
ALPHONSE ELRIC.
Sigh!
DESPITE HIS APPEARANCE, INSIDE HE IS A YOUNG TEENAGE BOY.
I'LL NEVER BE POPULAR WITH THE GIRLS WITH A BODY LIKE THIS...
Sigh!
WHAT'S ON YOUR MIND, DEAR BROTHER?
DON'T WORRY! I'LL FIND YOU A NICE GIRLFRIEND!
SO WHAT IF YOU DON'T LOOK HUMAN! IT'S NOT ABOUT WHAT YOU LOOK LIKE ON THE OUTSIDE!
Thanks, big brother!
SNIFF
OKAY THEN, CHOOSE.
Whichever one you like.
I FEEL THE SUDDEN URGE TO MURDER SOMEONE.
ARMOR CATALOG

FIRST, DO SOMETHING ABOUT THE LOINCLOTH

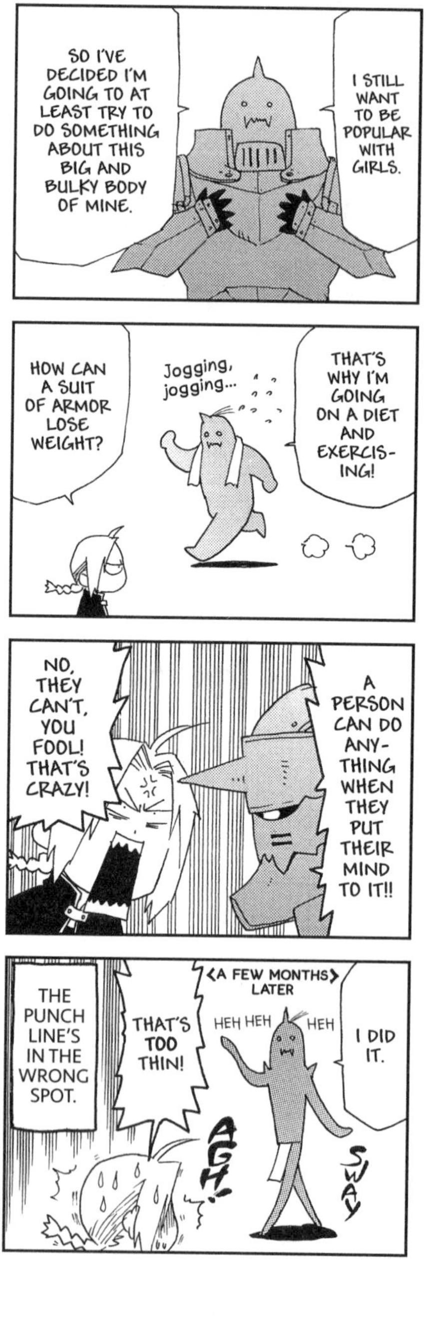
I STILL WANT TO BE POPULAR WITH GIRLS.
SO I'VE DECIDED I'M GOING TO AT LEAST TRY TO DO SOMETHING ABOUT THIS BIG AND BULKY BODY OF MINE.
THAT'S WHY I'M GOING ON A DIET AND EXERCISING!
Jogging, jogging...
HOW CAN A SUIT OF ARMOR LOSE WEIGHT?
A PERSON CAN DO ANYTHING WHEN THEY PUT THEIR MIND TO IT!!
NO, THEY CAN'T, YOU FOOL! THAT'S CRAZY!
I DID IT.
‹A FEW MONTHS› LATER
HEH HEH HEH
SWAY
THAT'S TOO THIN!
AGH!
THE PUNCH LINE'S IN THE WRONG SPOT.

THE PITIFUL TRUTH

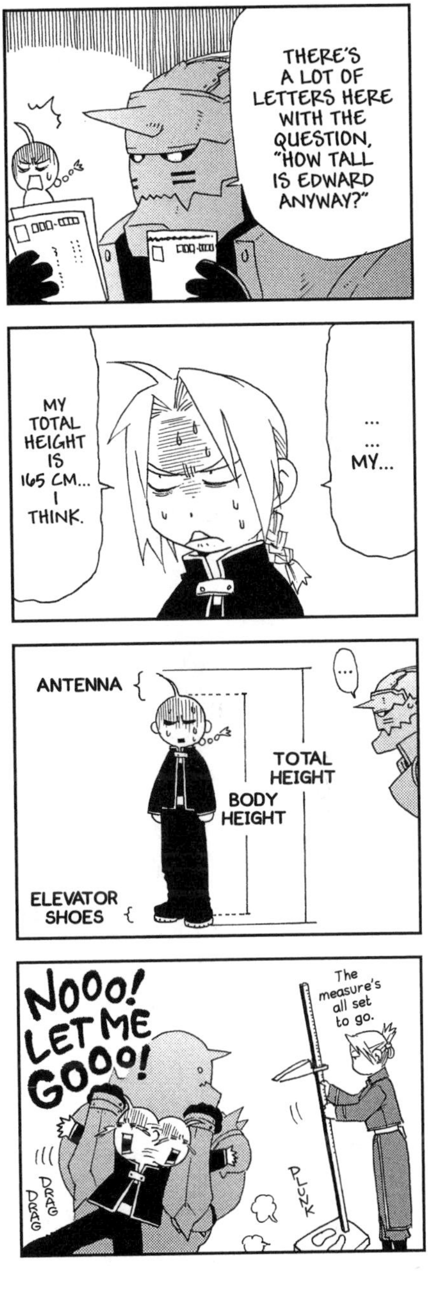
THERE'S A LOT OF LETTERS HERE WITH THE QUESTION, "HOW TALL IS EDWARD ANYWAY?"
... ... MY...
MY TOTAL HEIGHT IS 165 CM... I THINK.
...
TOTAL HEIGHT
BODY HEIGHT
ANTENNA
ELEVATOR SHOES
The measure's all set to go.
PLUNK
NOOO! LET ME GOOO!
DRAG DRAG

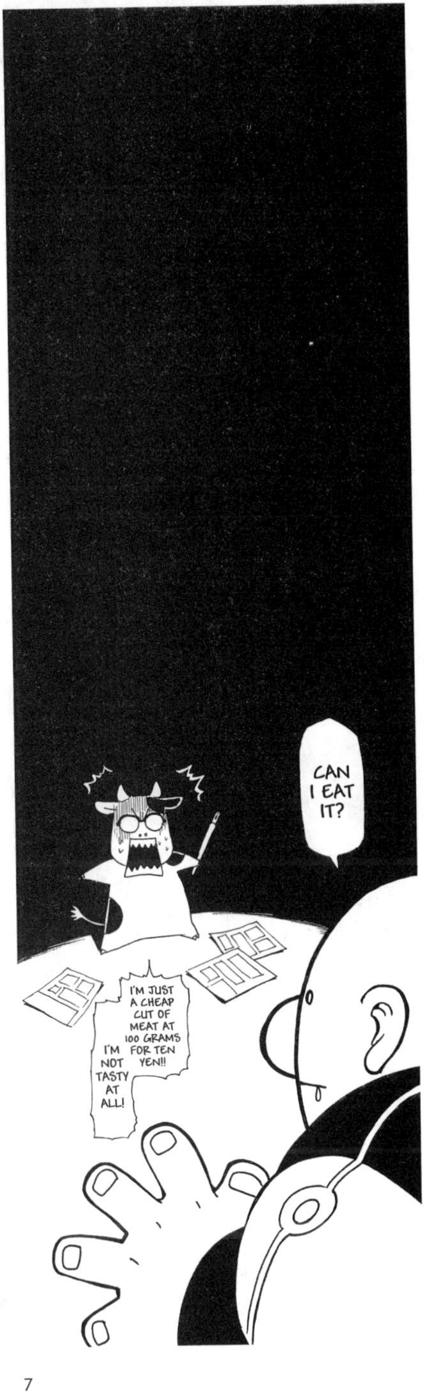
CAN I EAT IT?
I'M JUST A CHEAP CUT OF MEAT AT 100 GRAMS FOR TEN YEN!! I'M NOT TASTY AT ALL!

THE AMBITIOUS ALCHEMIST

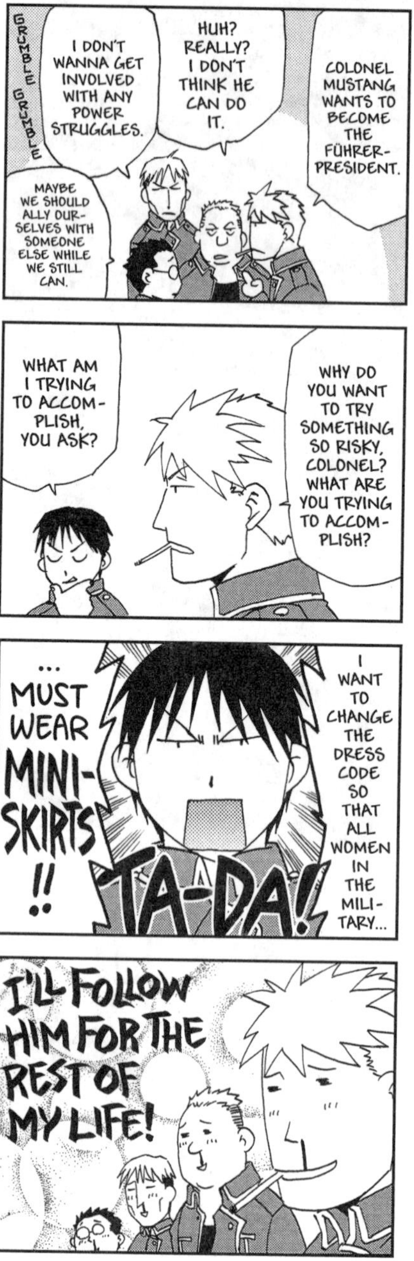
COLONEL MUSTANG WANTS TO BECOME THE FÜHRER-PRESIDENT.
HUH? REALLY? I DON'T THINK HE CAN DO IT.
I DON'T WANNA GET INVOLVED WITH ANY POWER STRUGGLES.
GRUMBLE GRUMBLE
MAYBE WE SHOULD ALLY OURSELVES WITH SOMEONE ELSE WHILE WE STILL CAN.
WHY DO YOU WANT TO TRY SOMETHING SO RISKY, COLONEL? WHAT ARE YOU TRYING TO ACCOMPLISH?
WHAT AM I TRYING TO ACCOMPLISH, YOU ASK?
I WANT TO CHANGE THE DRESS CODE SO THAT ALL WOMEN IN THE MILITARY...
TA-DA!
... MUST WEAR MINI-SKIRTS!!
I'LL FOLLOW HIM FOR THE REST OF MY LIFE!

AL'S BIG HAIRSTYLE STRATEGY

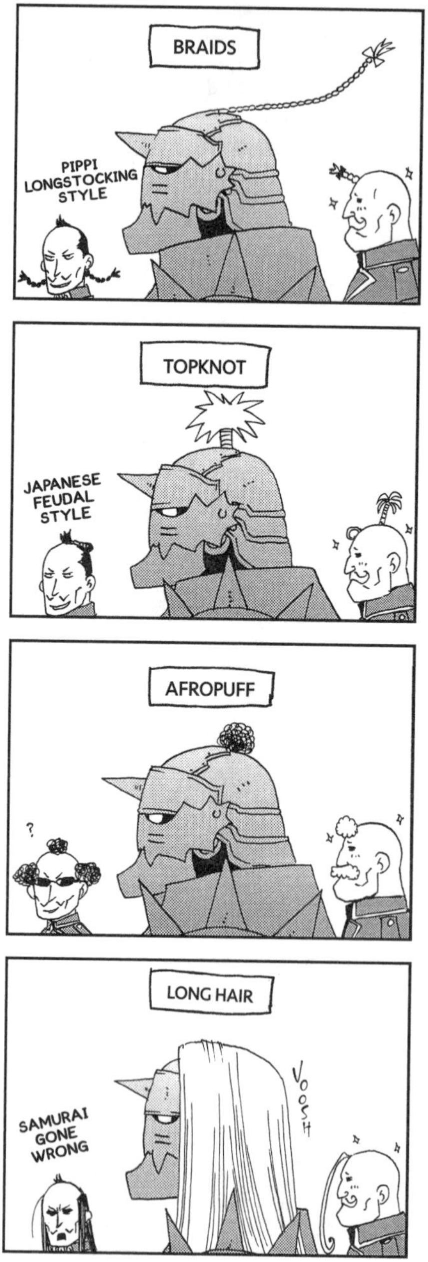
BRAIDS
PIPPI LONGSTOCKING STYLE
TOPKNOT
JAPANESE FEUDAL STYLE
AFROPUFF
?
LONG HAIR
VOOSH
SAMURAI GONE WRONG

I MADE PINAKO'S HAIRSTYLE LIKE THIS JUST SO I COULD DO THIS JOKE (SERIOUSLY!)

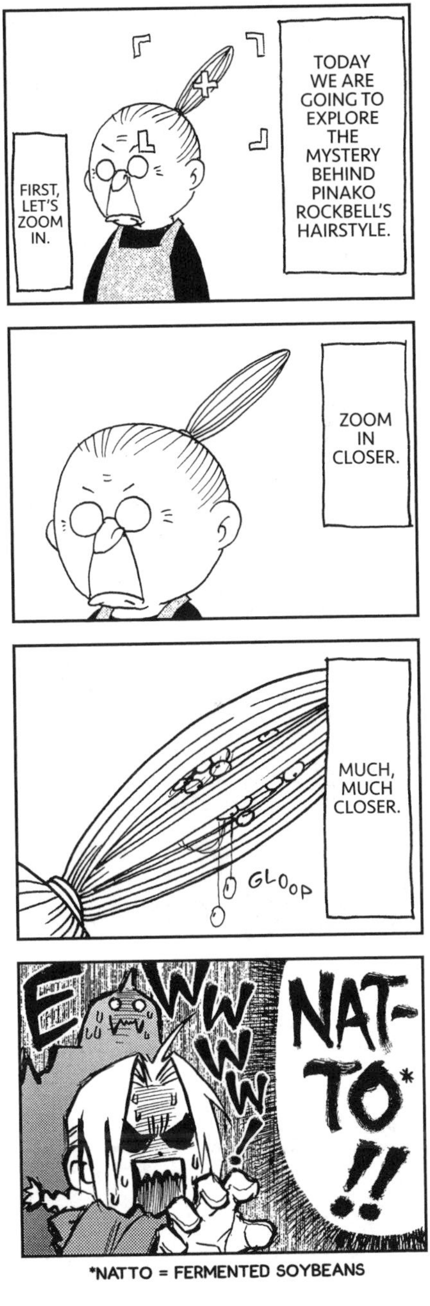
TODAY WE ARE GOING TO EXPLORE THE MYSTERY BEHIND PINAKO ROCKBELL'S HAIRSTYLE.
FIRST, LET'S ZOOM IN.
ZOOM IN CLOSER.
MUCH, MUCH CLOSER.
GLOOP
NAT-TO*!!
EWWWWWW!

*NATTO = FERMENTED SOYBEANS

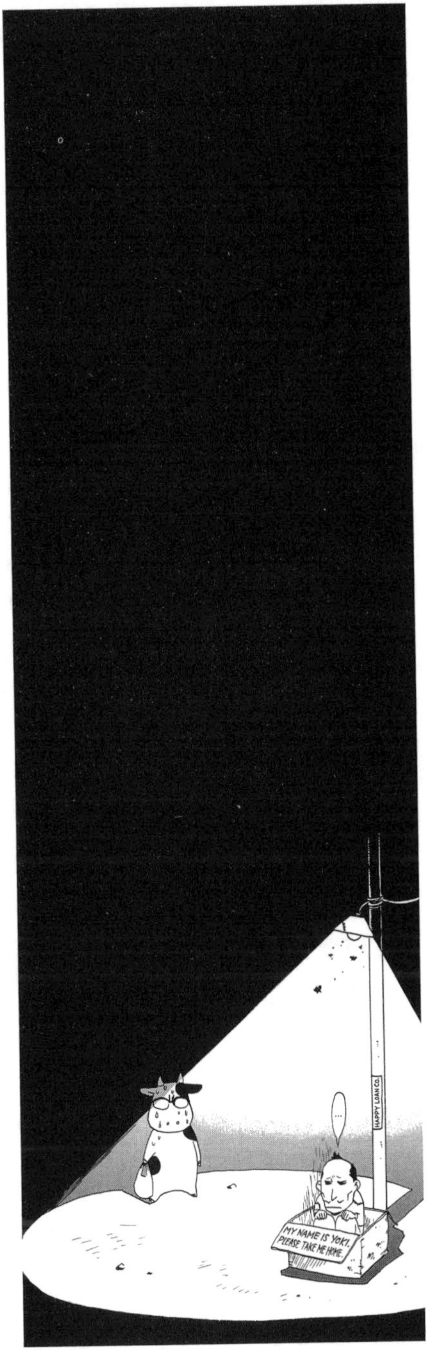
...
HAPPY LOAN CO.
MY NAME IS YOKI. PLEASE TAKE ME HOME.

CAT

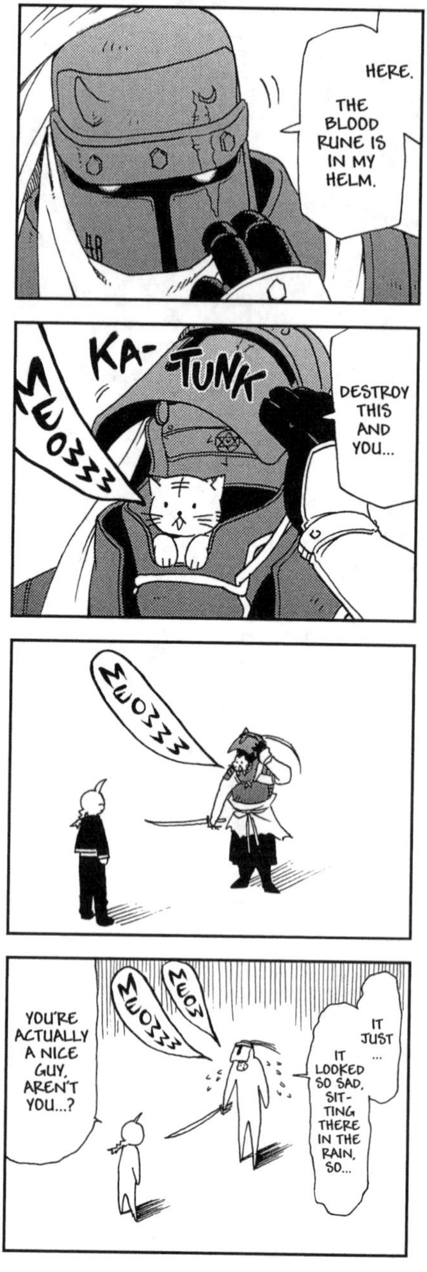
HERE.
THE BLOOD RUNE IS IN MY HELM.
DESTROY THIS AND YOU...
KA-TUNK
MEOWWW
MEOWWW
IT JUST ...
IT LOOKED SO SAD, SITTING THERE IN THE RAIN, SO...
MEOW
MEOWWW
YOU'RE ACTUALLY A NICE GUY, AREN'T YOU...?

CAT: EPISODE 2

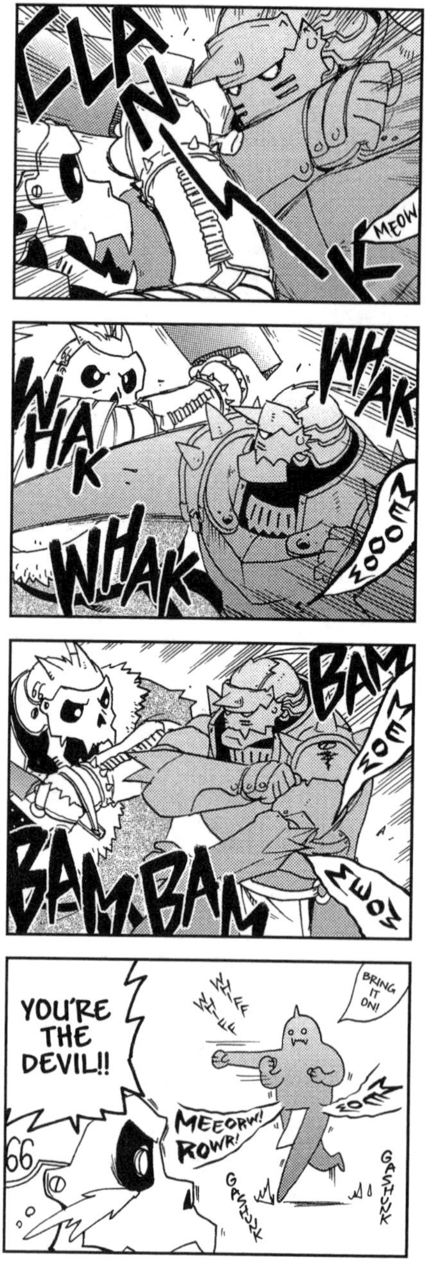
CLANK
MEOW
WHAK
MEOOOW
WHAK
WHAK
BAM
MEOW
BAM BAM
MEOW
BRING IT ON!
WHIFF
WHIFF
MEOW
YOU'RE THE DEVIL!!
MEEORW! ROWR!
GASHUNK
GASHUNK

SOMEBODY STOP THEM

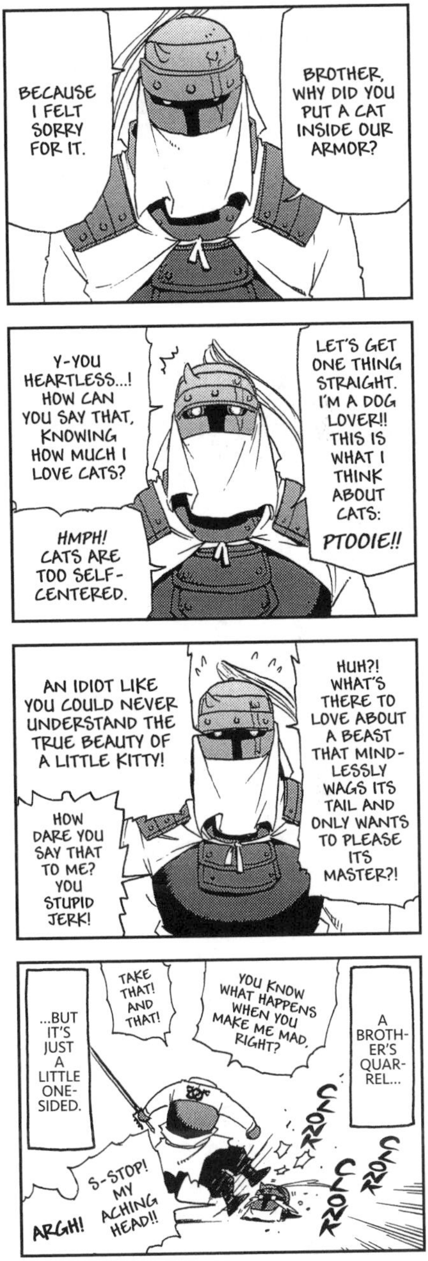
BROTHER, WHY DID YOU PUT A CAT INSIDE OUR ARMOR?
BECAUSE I FELT SORRY FOR IT.
LET'S GET ONE THING STRAIGHT. I'M A DOG LOVER!! THIS IS WHAT I THINK ABOUT CATS: PTOOIE!!
Y-YOU HEARTLESS...! HOW CAN YOU SAY THAT, KNOWING HOW MUCH I LOVE CATS?
HMPH! CATS ARE TOO SELF-CENTERED.
HUH?! WHAT'S THERE TO LOVE ABOUT A BEAST THAT MINDLESSLY WAGS ITS TAIL AND ONLY WANTS TO PLEASE ITS MASTER?!
AN IDIOT LIKE YOU COULD NEVER UNDERSTAND THE TRUE BEAUTY OF A LITTLE KITTY!
HOW DARE YOU SAY THAT TO ME? YOU STUPID JERK!
A BROTHER'S QUARREL...
YOU KNOW WHAT HAPPENS WHEN YOU MAKE ME MAD, RIGHT?
TAKE THAT! AND THAT!
...BUT IT'S JUST A LITTLE ONE-SIDED.
CLONK CLONK
CLONK CLONK
S-STOP! MY ACHING HEAD!!
ARGH!

MIRACLE HAIR

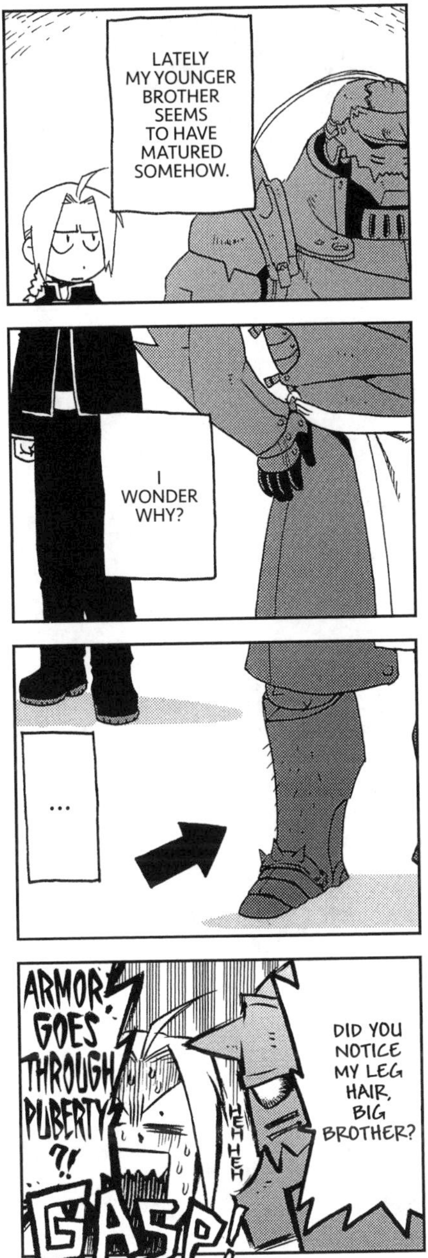
LATELY MY YOUNGER BROTHER SEEMS TO HAVE MATURED SOMEHOW.
I WONDER WHY?
...
DID YOU NOTICE MY LEG HAIR, BIG BROTHER?
HEH HEH
ARMOR GOES THROUGH PUBERTY?!
GASP!

THE AMBITIOUS ALCHEMIST: PART 2

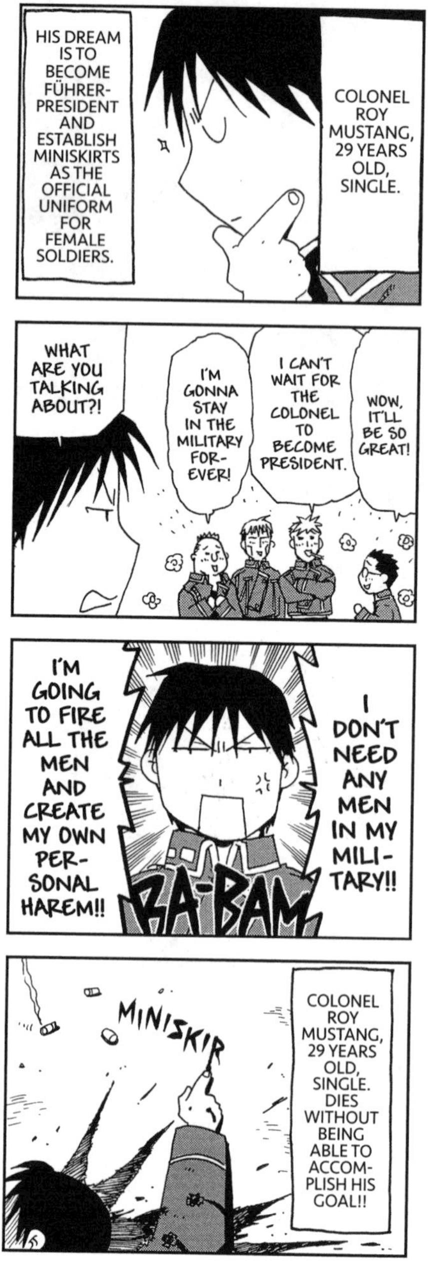
COLONEL ROY MUSTANG, 29 YEARS OLD, SINGLE.
HIS DREAM IS TO BECOME FÜHRER-PRESIDENT AND ESTABLISH MINISKIRTS AS THE OFFICIAL UNIFORM FOR FEMALE SOLDIERS.
WOW, IT'LL BE SO GREAT!
I CAN'T WAIT FOR THE COLONEL TO BECOME PRESIDENT.
I'M GONNA STAY IN THE MILITARY FOREVER!
WHAT ARE YOU TALKING ABOUT?!
I DON'T NEED ANY MEN IN MY MILITARY!!
I'M GOING TO FIRE ALL THE MEN AND CREATE MY OWN PERSONAL HAREM!!
BA-BAM
COLONEL ROY MUSTANG, 29 YEARS OLD, SINGLE. DIES WITHOUT BEING ABLE TO ACCOMPLISH HIS GOAL!!
MINISKIR

A MAN'S DIGNITY

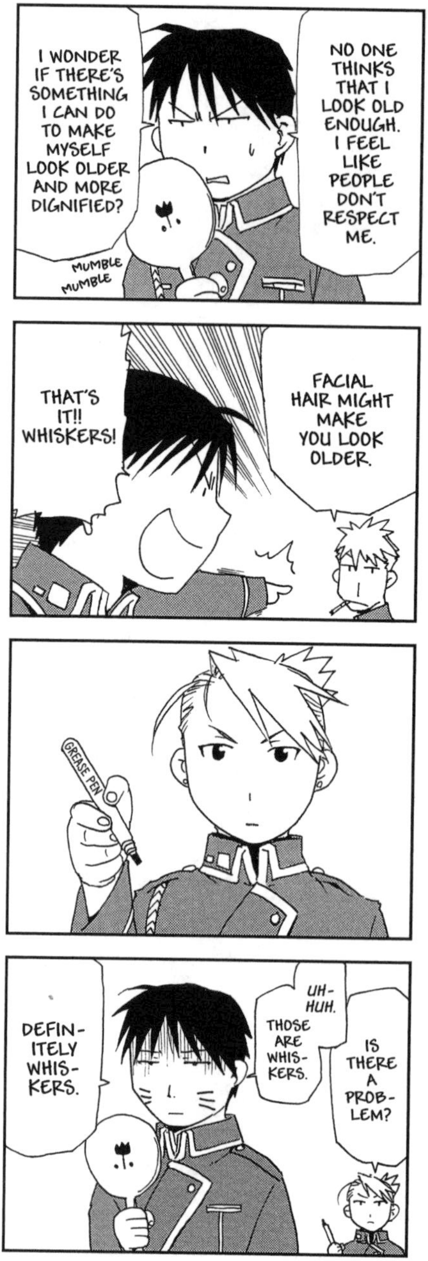
NO ONE THINKS THAT I LOOK OLD ENOUGH. I FEEL LIKE PEOPLE DON'T RESPECT ME.
I WONDER IF THERE'S SOMETHING I CAN DO TO MAKE MYSELF LOOK OLDER AND MORE DIGNIFIED?
MUMBLE MUMBLE
FACIAL HAIR MIGHT MAKE YOU LOOK OLDER.
THAT'S IT!! WHISKERS!
GREASE PEN
IS THERE A PROBLEM?
UH-HUH. THOSE ARE WHISKERS.
DEFINITELY WHISKERS.

MAYBE THE LOINCLOTH IS THE PROBLEM?

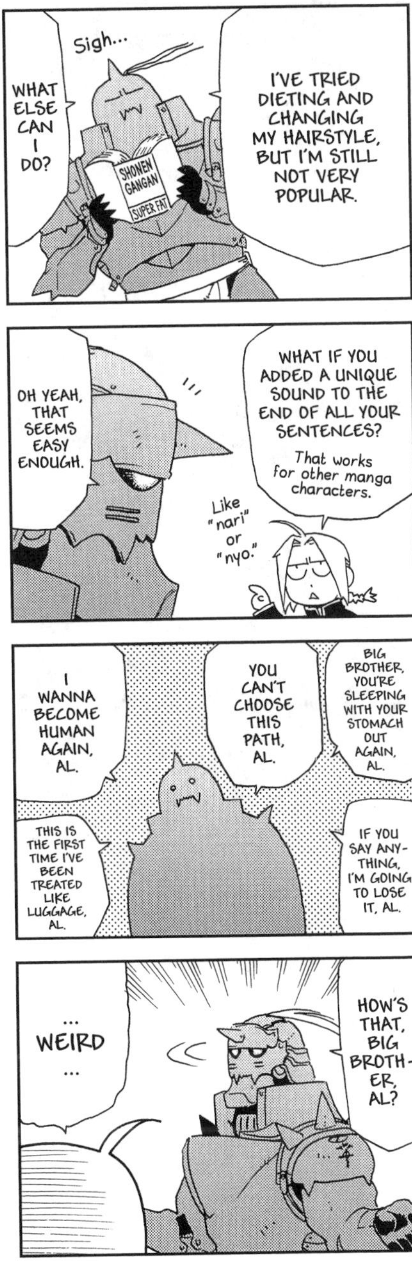
I'VE TRIED DIETING AND CHANGING MY HAIRSTYLE, BUT I'M STILL NOT VERY POPULAR.
Sigh...
SHONEN GANGAN SUPER FAT
WHAT ELSE CAN I DO?
WHAT IF YOU ADDED A UNIQUE SOUND TO THE END OF ALL YOUR SENTENCES?
That works for other manga characters.
Like "nari" or "nyo."
OH YEAH, THAT SEEMS EASY ENOUGH.
BIG BROTHER, YOU'RE SLEEPING WITH YOUR STOMACH OUT AGAIN, AL.
YOU CAN'T CHOOSE THIS PATH, AL.
I WANNA BECOME HUMAN AGAIN, AL.
IF YOU SAY ANY-THING, I'M GOING TO LOSE IT, AL.
THIS IS THE FIRST TIME I'VE BEEN TREATED LIKE LUGGAGE, AL.
HOW'S THAT, BIG BROTH-ER, AL?
... WEIRD ...

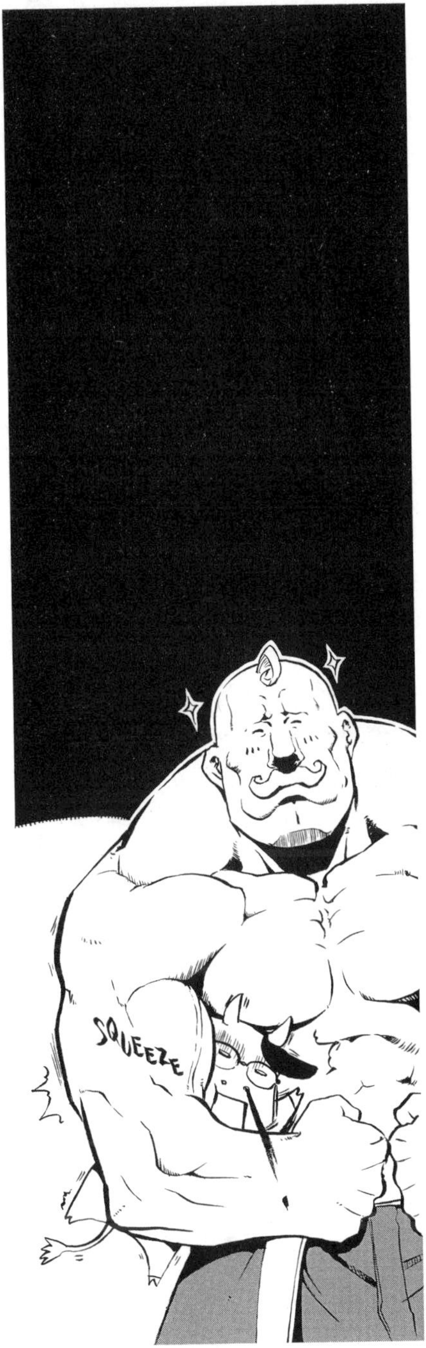
SQUEEZE

IT WAS A GREASE PEN, REMEMBER

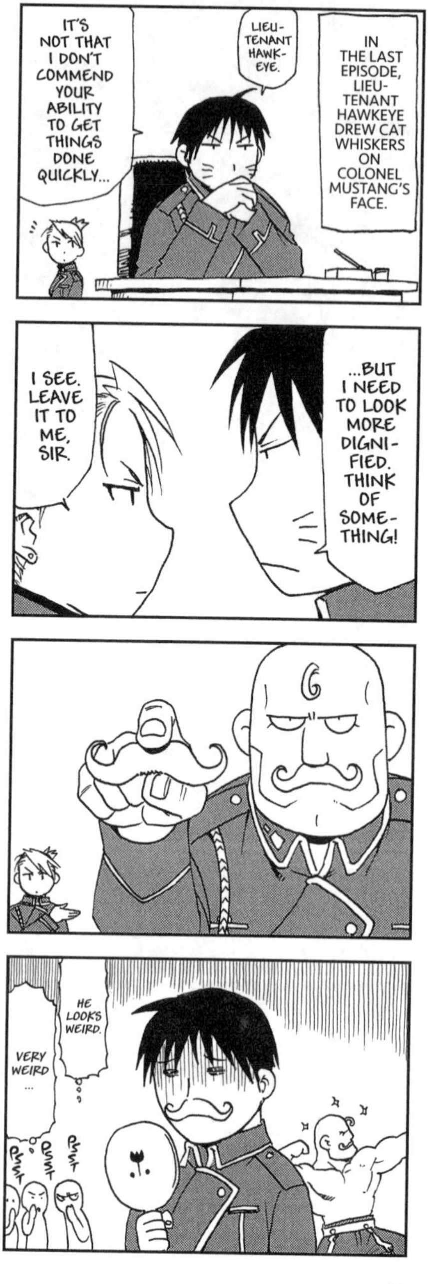
IN THE LAST EPISODE, LIEUTENANT HAWKEYE DREW CAT WHISKERS ON COLONEL MUSTANG'S FACE.
LIEUTENANT HAWKEYE.
IT'S NOT THAT I DON'T COMMEND YOUR ABILITY TO GET THINGS DONE QUICKLY...
...BUT I NEED TO LOOK MORE DIGNIFIED. THINK OF SOMETHING!
I SEE. LEAVE IT TO ME, SIR.
HE LOOKS WEIRD.
VERY WEIRD ...
PSST
PSST
PSST

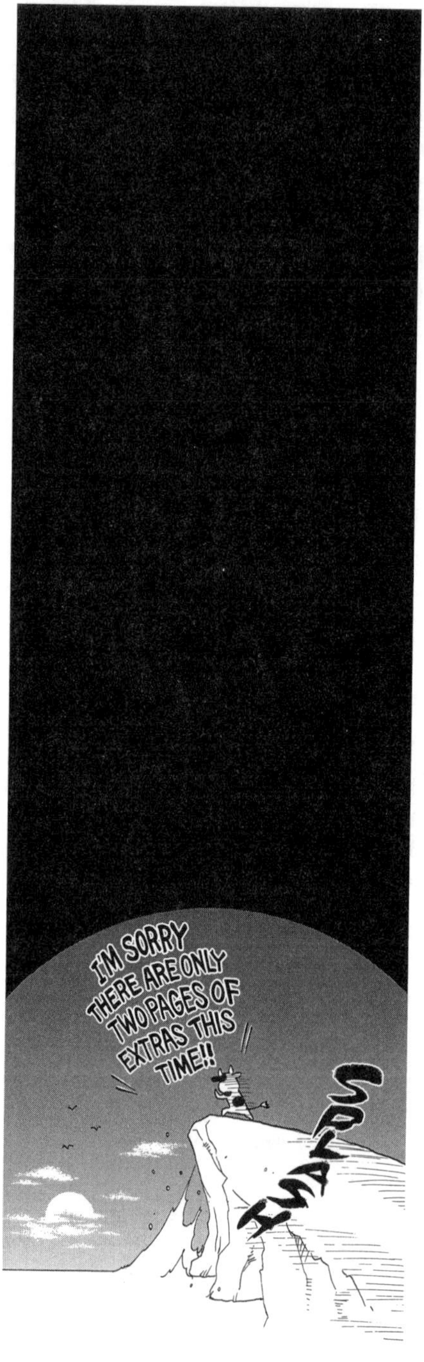
I'M SORRY THERE ARE ONLY TWO PAGES OF EXTRAS THIS TIME!!
SPLASH

I COULDN'T GO TO THE OCEAN THIS YEAR

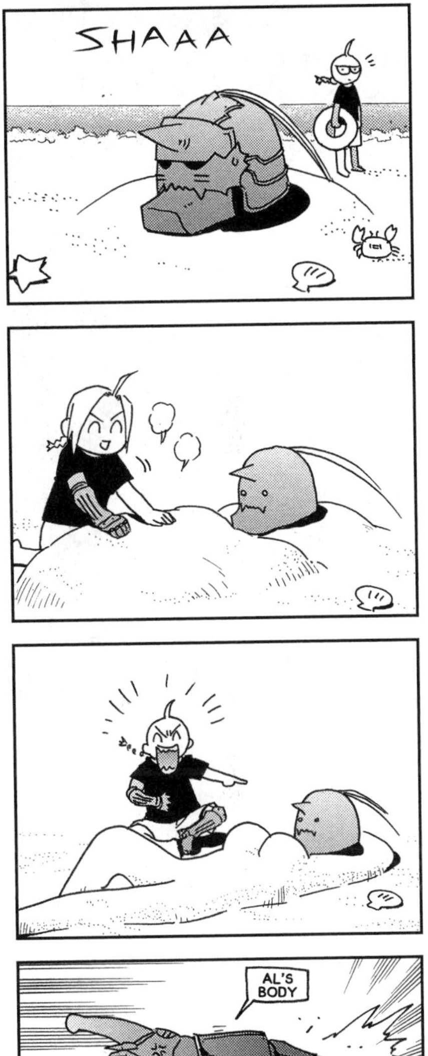
SHAAA
AL'S BODY

YOU TOO?

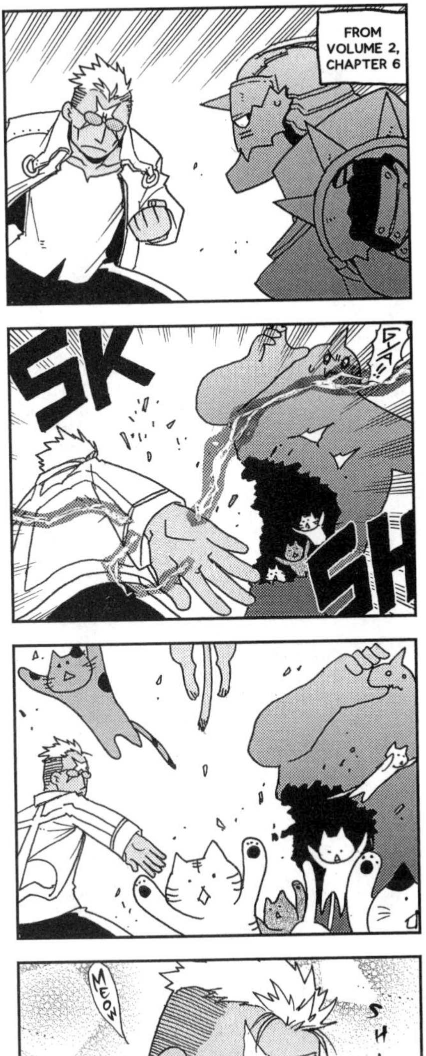
FROM VOLUME 2, CHAPTER 6
SK
SH
MEOW
SHIMMER

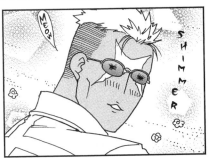

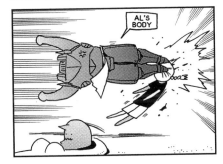

EARS, EARS, EARS

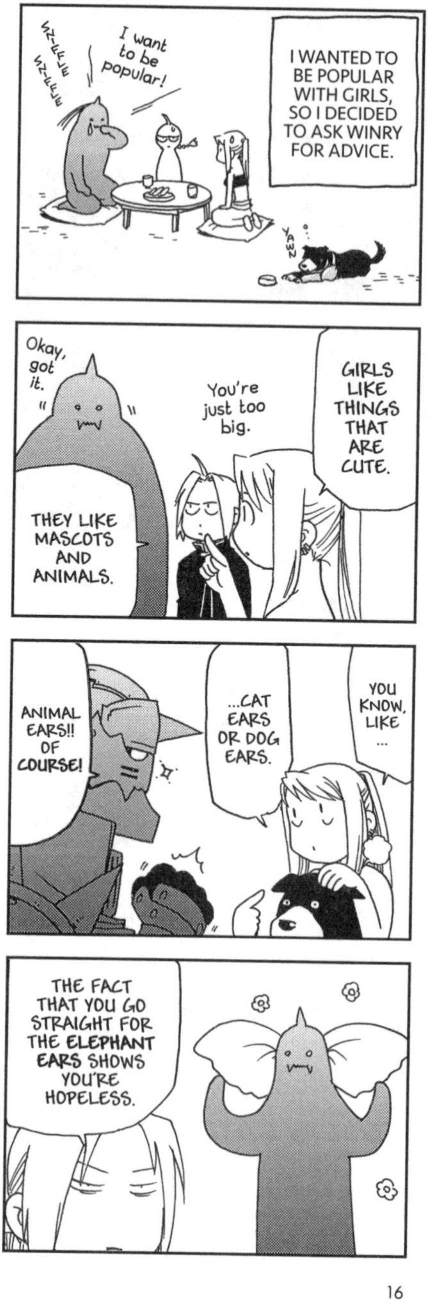
I WANTED TO BE POPULAR WITH GIRLS, SO I DECIDED TO ASK WINRY FOR ADVICE.
I want to be popular!
SNIFFLE SNIFFLE
YAWN
GIRLS LIKE THINGS THAT ARE CUTE.
You're just too big.
Okay, got it.
THEY LIKE MASCOTS AND ANIMALS.
YOU KNOW, LIKE ...
...CAT EARS OR DOG EARS.
ANIMAL EARS!! OF COURSE!
THE FACT THAT YOU GO STRAIGHT FOR THE ELEPHANT EARS SHOWS YOU'RE HOPELESS.

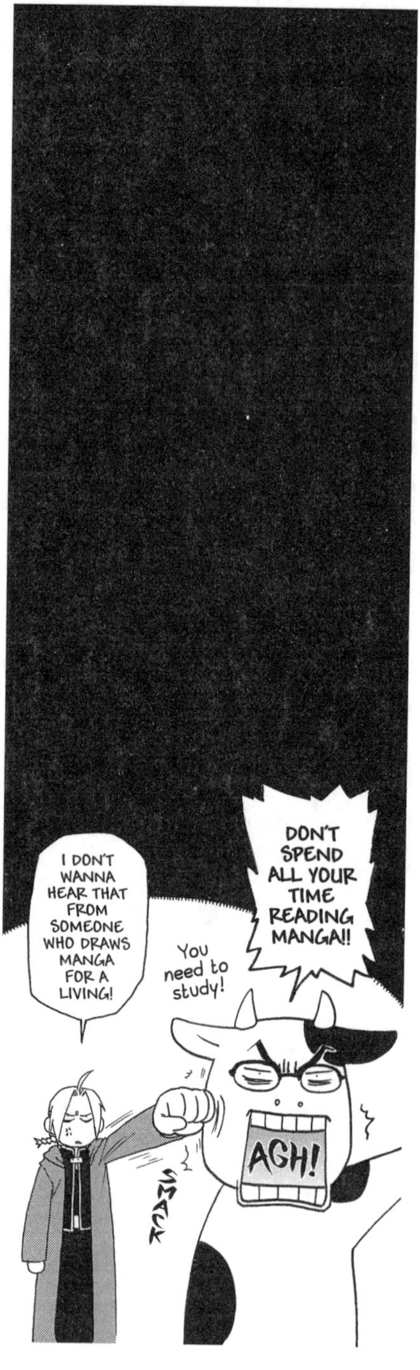
DON'T SPEND ALL YOUR TIME READING MANGA!!
You need to study!
I DON'T WANNA HEAR THAT FROM SOMEONE WHO DRAWS MANGA FOR A LIVING!
AGH!
SMACK

CRUEL GIRL

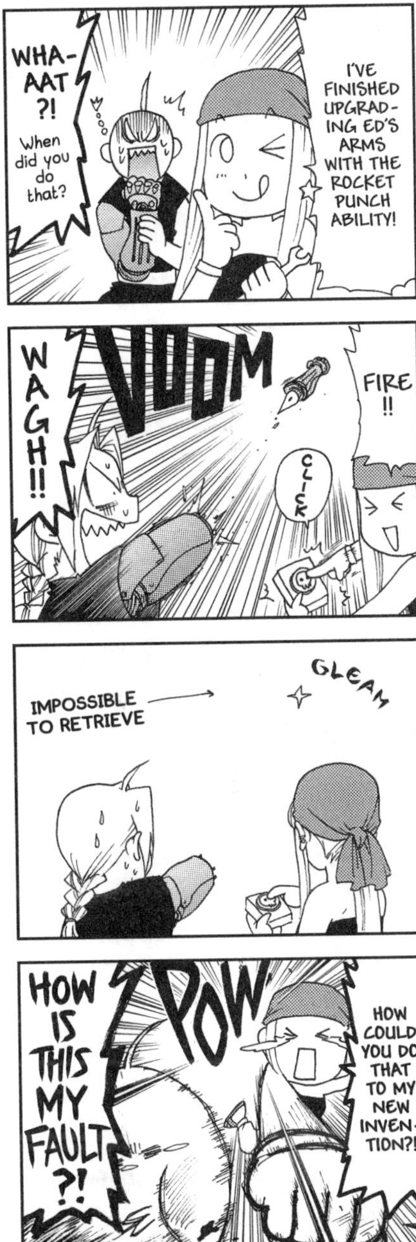
I'VE FINISHED UPGRAD-ING ED'S ARMS WITH THE ROCKET PUNCH ABILITY!
WHA-AAT?!
When did you do that?
FIRE!!
CLICK
VOOM
WAGH!!
GLEAM
IMPOSSIBLE TO RETRIEVE
HOW COULD YOU DO THAT TO MY NEW INVEN-TION?!
POW
HOW IS THIS MY FAULT?!

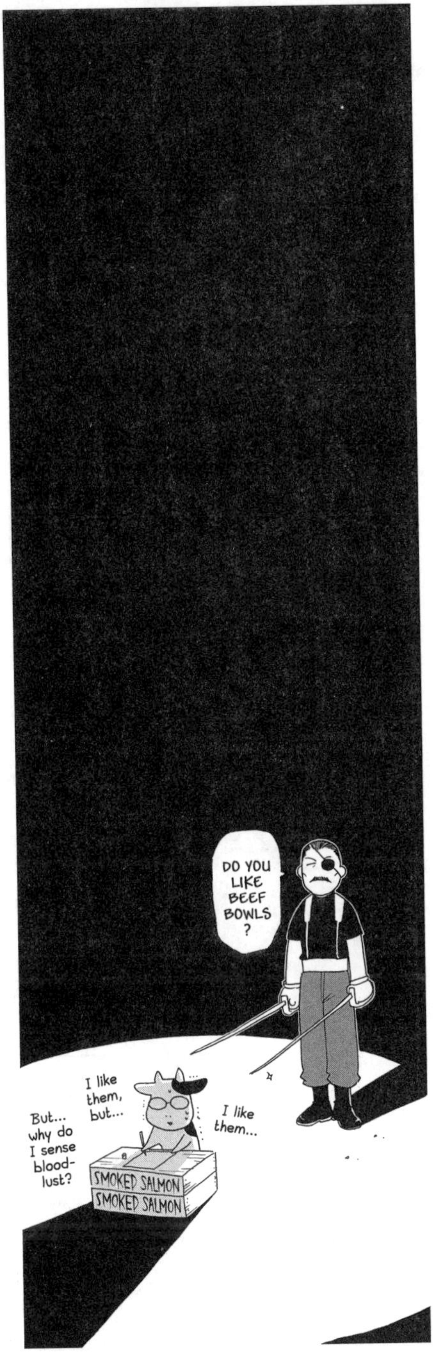
DO YOU LIKE BEEF BOWLS?
I like them...
I like them, but...
But... why do I sense blood-lust?
SMOKED SALMON
SMOKED SALMON

MEAT, MEAT, ARMOR, MEAT, MEAT

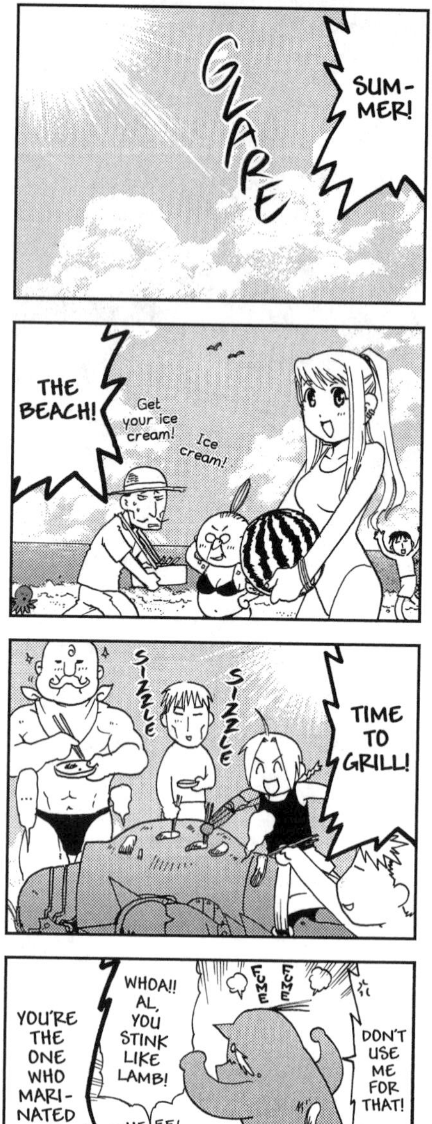
SUMMER!
GLARE
THE BEACH!
Get your ice cream!
Ice cream!
TIME TO GRILL!
SIZZLE
SIZZLE
DON'T USE ME FOR THAT!
FUME
FUME
WHOA!! AL, YOU STINK LIKE LAMB!
YOU'RE THE ONE WHO MARINATED ME WITH GARLIC!!
WHEEE!

THE WONDERFUL WORLD OF DOGS

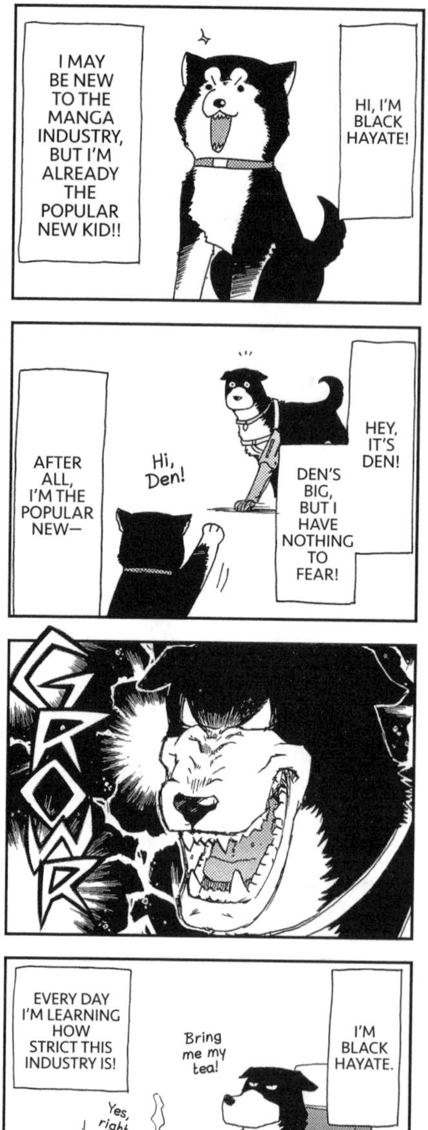
HI, I'M BLACK HAYATE!
I MAY BE NEW TO THE MANGA INDUSTRY, BUT I'M ALREADY THE POPULAR NEW KID!!
HEY, IT'S DEN!
DEN'S BIG, BUT I HAVE NOTHING TO FEAR!
Hi, Den!
AFTER ALL, I'M THE POPULAR NEW—
GROWR
I'M BLACK HAYATE.
Bring me my tea!
EVERY DAY I'M LEARNING HOW STRICT THIS INDUSTRY IS!
Yes, right away!

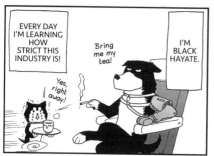

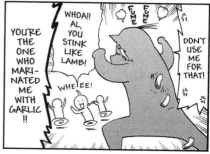

DEATH TRAP

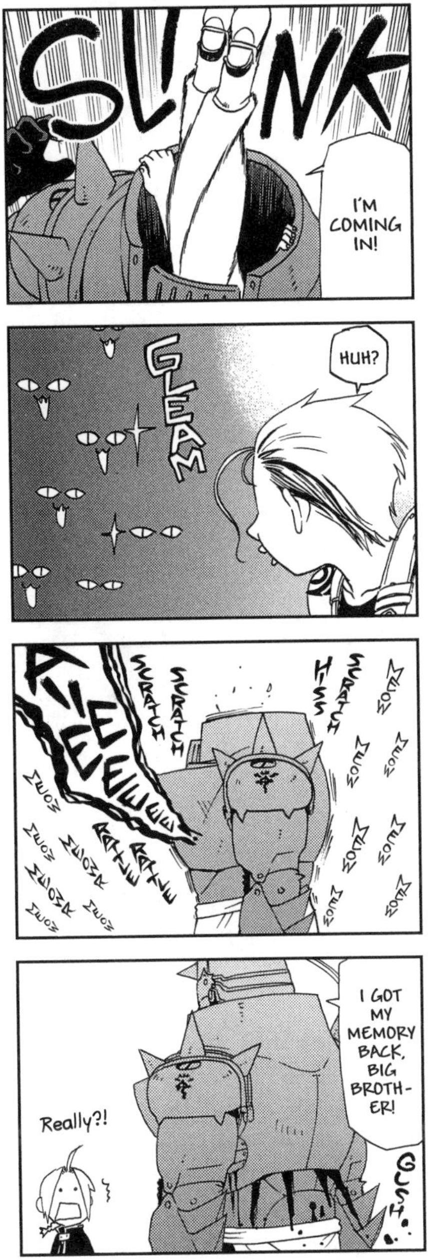
SLINK
I'M COMING IN!
HUH?
GLEAM
AIEEEEEEE
SCRATCH
SCRATCH
HISS
SCRATCH
RATTLE
RATTLE
I GOT MY MEMORY BACK, BIG BROTHER!
GUSH
Really?!

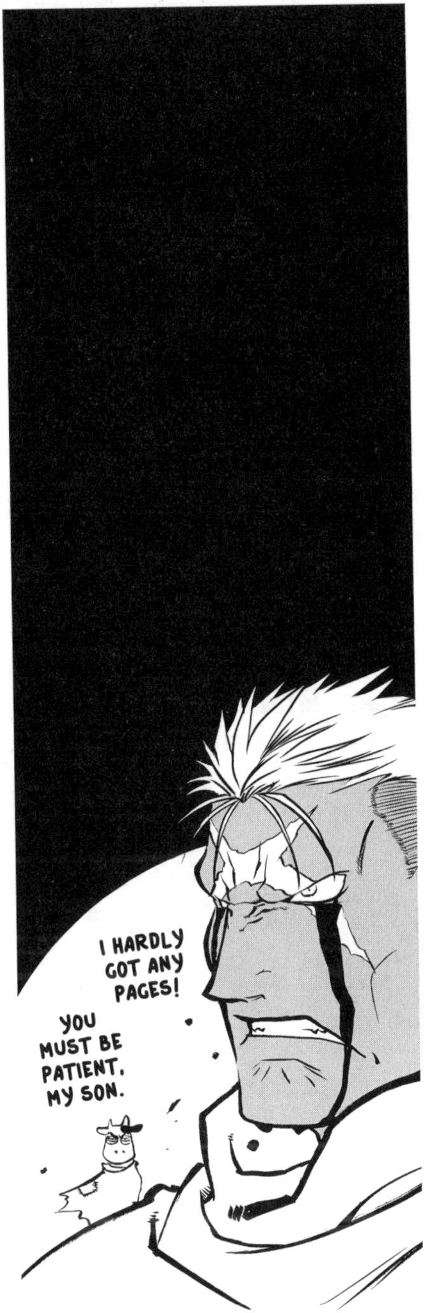
I HARDLY GOT ANY PAGES!
YOU MUST BE PATIENT, MY SON.

CRAMPED

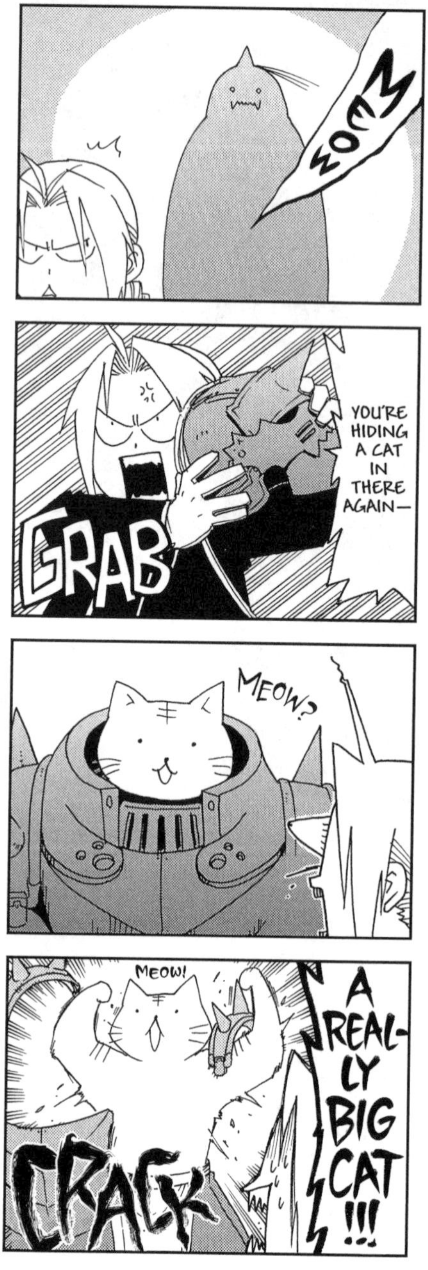
WOOM
YOU'RE HIDING A CAT IN THERE AGAIN—
GRAB
MEOW?
A REALLY BIG CAT!!!
MEOW!
CRACK

A BAD SOLUTION

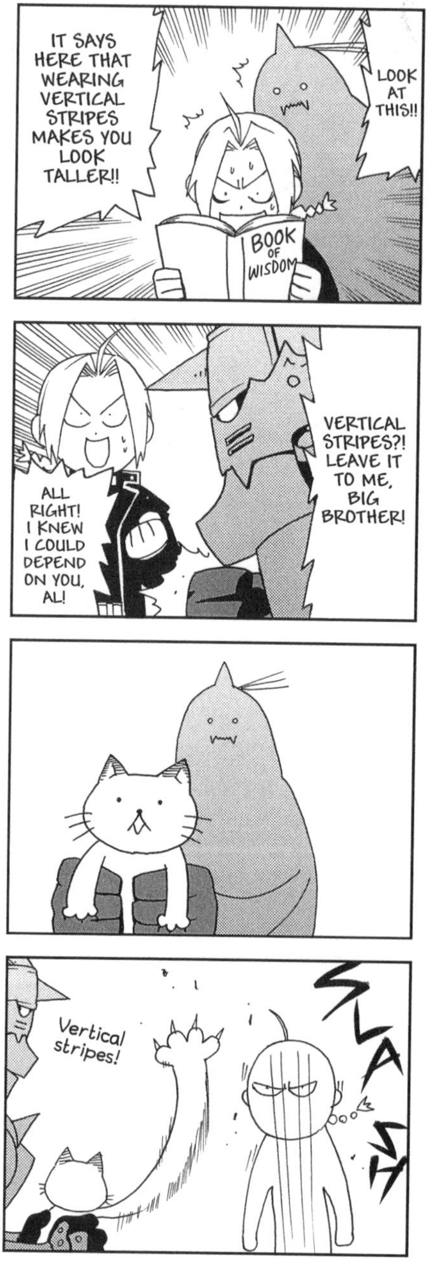
LOOK AT THIS!!
IT SAYS HERE THAT WEARING VERTICAL STRIPES MAKES YOU LOOK TALLER!!
BOOK OF WISDOM
VERTICAL STRIPES?! LEAVE IT TO ME, BIG BROTHER!
ALL RIGHT! I KNEW I COULD DEPEND ON YOU, AL!
SLASH
Vertical stripes!

LIFE LINE

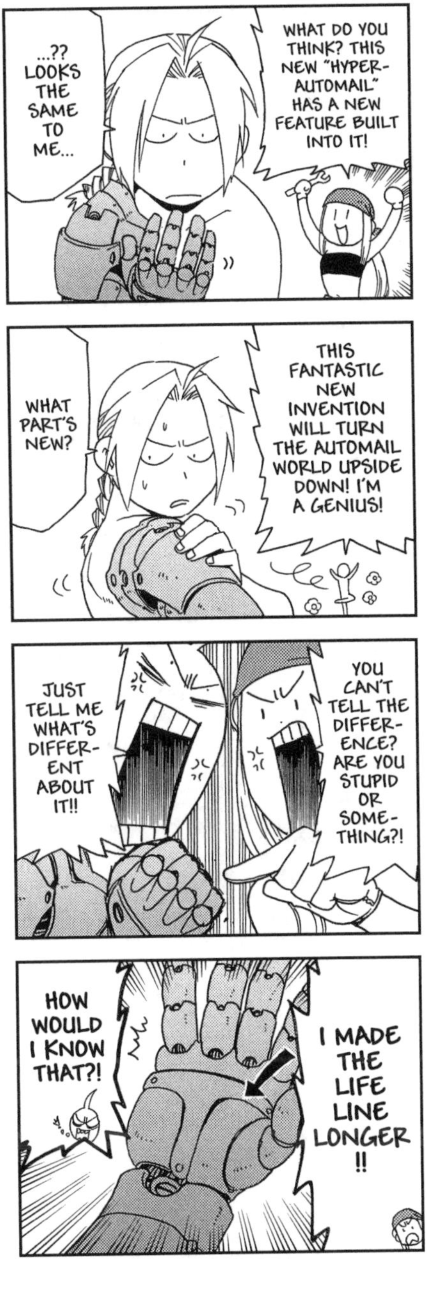
WHAT DO YOU THINK? THIS NEW "HYPER-AUTOMAIL" HAS A NEW FEATURE BUILT INTO IT!
...?? LOOKS THE SAME TO ME...
THIS FANTASTIC NEW INVENTION WILL TURN THE AUTOMAIL WORLD UPSIDE DOWN! I'M A GENIUS!
WHAT PART'S NEW?
YOU CAN'T TELL THE DIFFERENCE? ARE YOU STUPID OR SOMETHING?!
JUST TELL ME WHAT'S DIFFERENT ABOUT IT!!
I MADE THE LIFE LINE LONGER!!
HOW WOULD I KNOW THAT?!

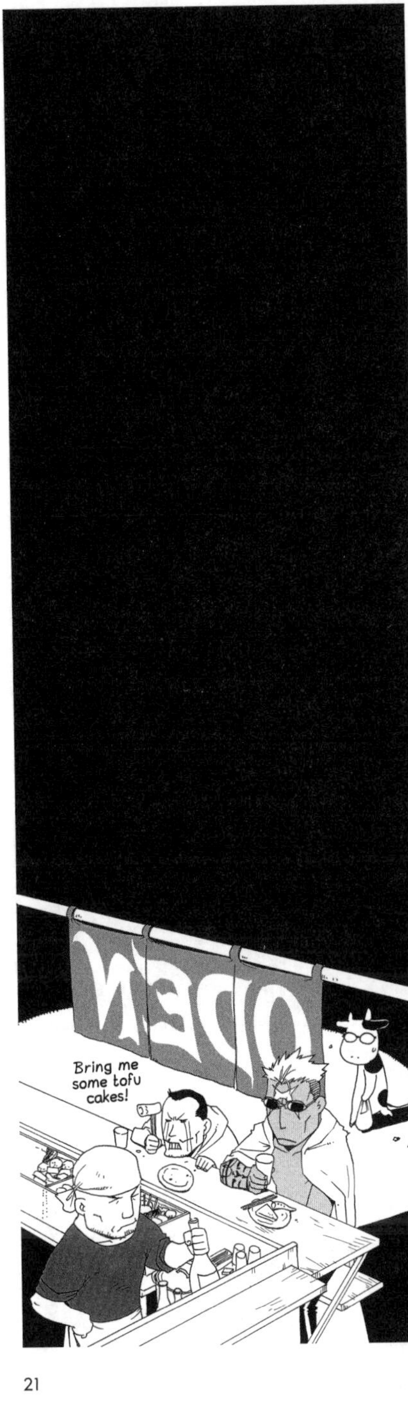
Bring me some tofu cakes!

IF ED AND AL'S SITUATIONS WERE REVERSED

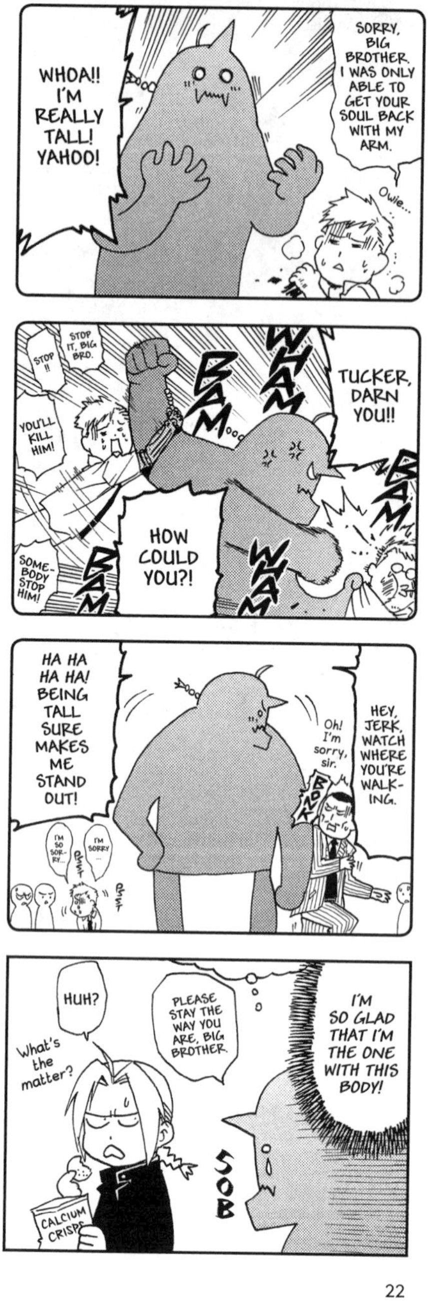
SORRY, BIG BROTHER. I WAS ONLY ABLE TO GET YOUR SOUL BACK WITH MY ARM.
Owie...
WHOA!! I'M REALLY TALL! YAHOO!
TUCKER, DARN YOU!!
WHAM
BAM
BAM
WHAM
STOP IT, BIG BRO.
STOP!!
YOU'LL KILL HIM!
HOW COULD YOU?!
BAM
SOMEBODY STOP HIM!
HEY, JERK, WATCH WHERE YOU'RE WALKING.
Oh! I'm sorry, sir.
BONK
HA HA HA HA! BEING TALL SURE MAKES ME STAND OUT!
I'M SORRY...
I'M SO SORRY...
I'M SO GLAD THAT I'M THE ONE WITH THIS BODY!
SOB
PLEASE STAY THE WAY YOU ARE, BIG BROTHER.
HUH?
What's the matter?
CALCIUM CRISPS

HOHENHEIM THE UNJUST

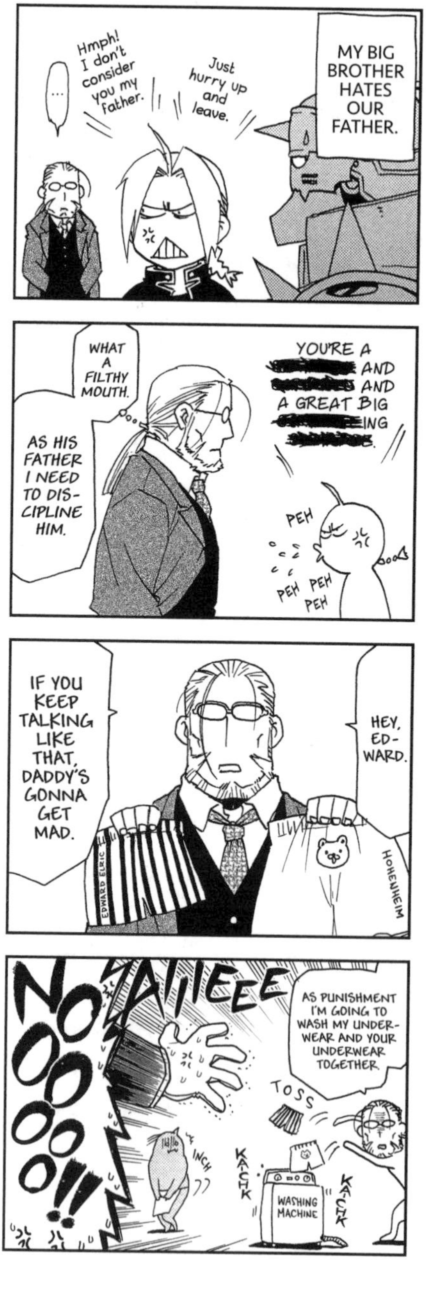
MY BIG BROTHER HATES OUR FATHER.
Just hurry up and leave.
Hmph! I don't consider you my father.
...
YOU'RE A [redacted] AND [redacted] AND A GREAT BIG [redacted]ING [redacted].
WHAT A FILTHY MOUTH.
AS HIS FATHER I NEED TO DISCIPLINE HIM.
PEH
PEH PEH
PEH
HEY, EDWARD.
IF YOU KEEP TALKING LIKE THAT, DADDY'S GONNA GET MAD.
HOHENHEIM
EDWARD ELRIC
AS PUNISHMENT I'M GOING TO WASH MY UNDERWEAR AND YOUR UNDERWEAR TOGETHER.
AIIIEEE
NOOOOOOO!!
TOSS
KACHK
KACHK
INCH
WASHING MACHINE

HAWKEYE'S CODE NAMES

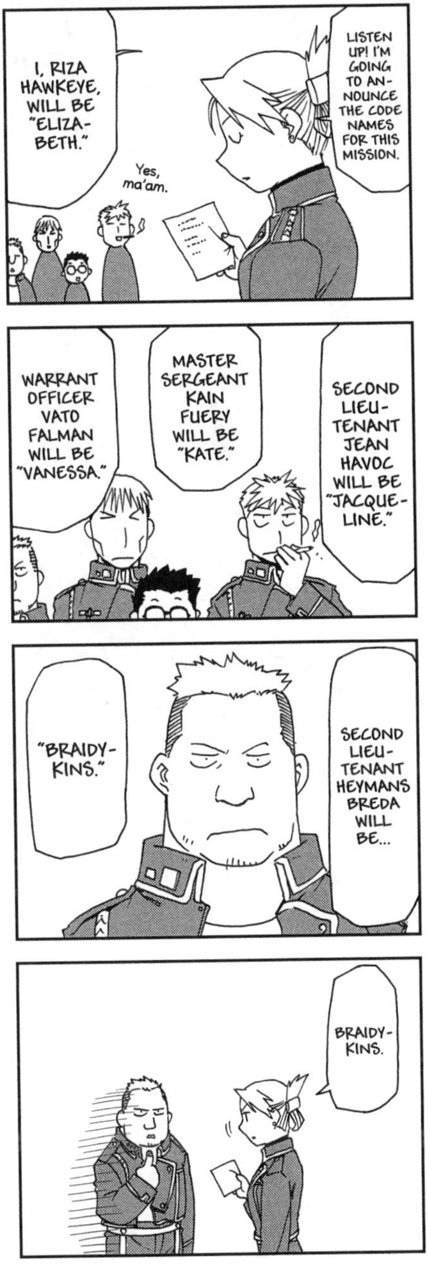
LISTEN UP! I'M GOING TO AN-NOUNCE THE CODE NAMES FOR THIS MISSION.
I, RIZA HAWKEYE, WILL BE "ELIZA-BETH."
Yes, ma'am.
SECOND LIEU-TENANT JEAN HAVOC WILL BE "JACQUE-LINE."
MASTER SERGEANT KAIN FUERY WILL BE "KATE."
WARRANT OFFICER VATO FALMAN WILL BE "VANESSA."
SECOND LIEU-TENANT HEYMANS BREDA WILL BE...
"BRAIDY-KINS."
BRAIDY-KINS.

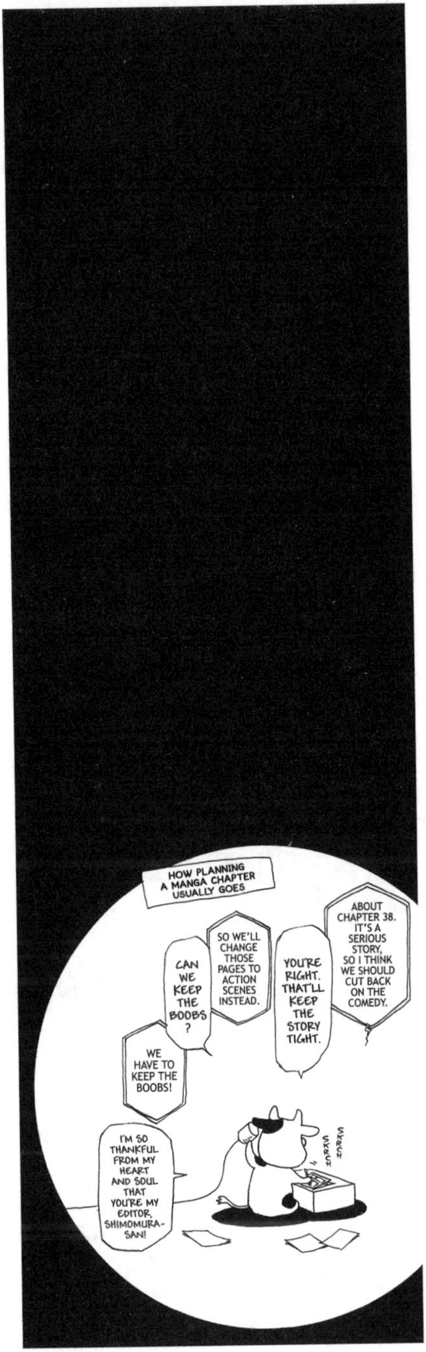
HOW PLANNING A MANGA CHAPTER USUALLY GOES
ABOUT CHAPTER 38. IT'S A SERIOUS STORY, SO I THINK WE SHOULD CUT BACK ON THE COMEDY.
YOU'RE RIGHT. THAT'LL KEEP THE STORY TIGHT.
SO WE'LL CHANGE THOSE PAGES TO ACTION SCENES INSTEAD.
CAN WE KEEP THE BOOBS?
WE HAVE TO KEEP THE BOOBS!
I'M SO THANKFUL FROM MY HEART AND SOUL THAT YOU'RE MY EDITOR, SHIMOMURA-SAN!

RETURN OF THE BASTARD (GIFT INCLUDED)

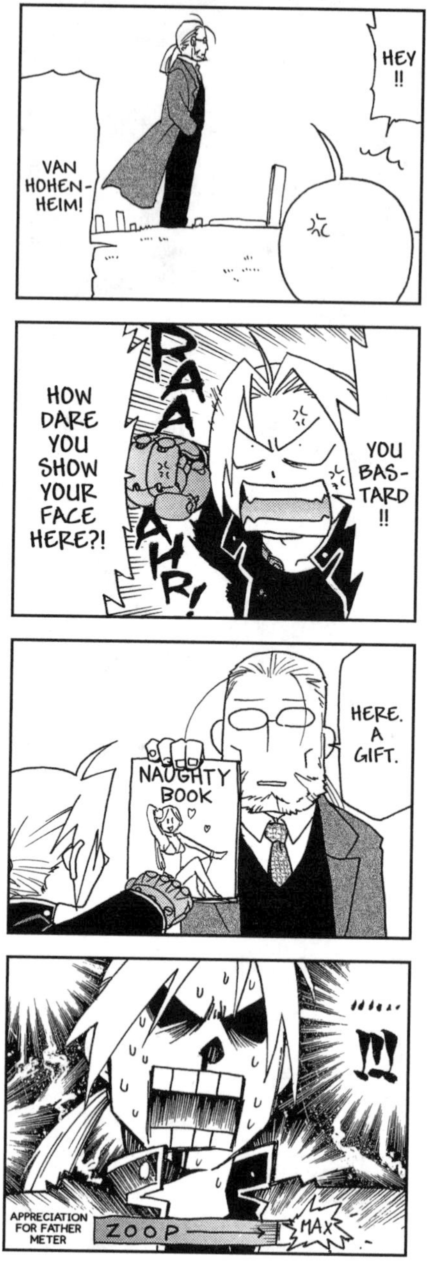
HEY !!
VAN HOHEN-HEIM!
RAAAHR!
YOU BAS-TARD !!
HOW DARE YOU SHOW YOUR FACE HERE?!
HERE. A GIFT.
NAUGHTY BOOK
......
!!!
APPRECIATION FOR FATHER METER
ZOOP
MAX

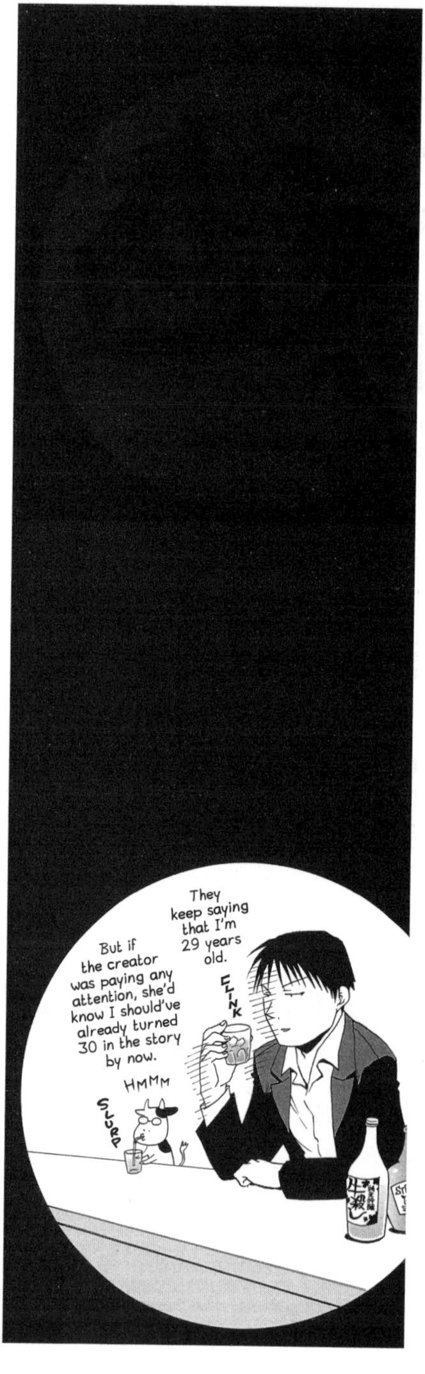
They keep saying that I'm 29 years old.
But if the creator was paying any attention, she'd know I should've already turned 30 in the story by now.
CLINK
HMMM
SLURP

ANTI-HOMUNCULUS SECRET WEAPON!

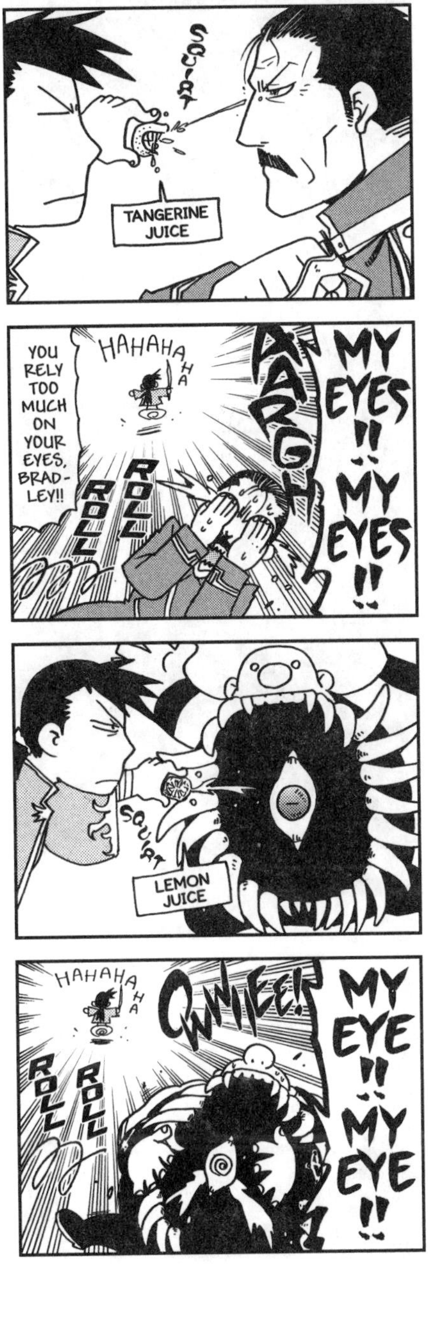
SQUIRT
TANGERINE JUICE
MY EYES!! MY EYES!!
AARGH
HAHAHAHA
YOU RELY TOO MUCH ON YOUR EYES, BRADLEY!!
ROLL
ROLL
SQUIRT
LEMON JUICE
MY EYE!! MY EYE!!
OWIEE!!
HAHAHAHA
ROLL
ROLL

STOP IT...

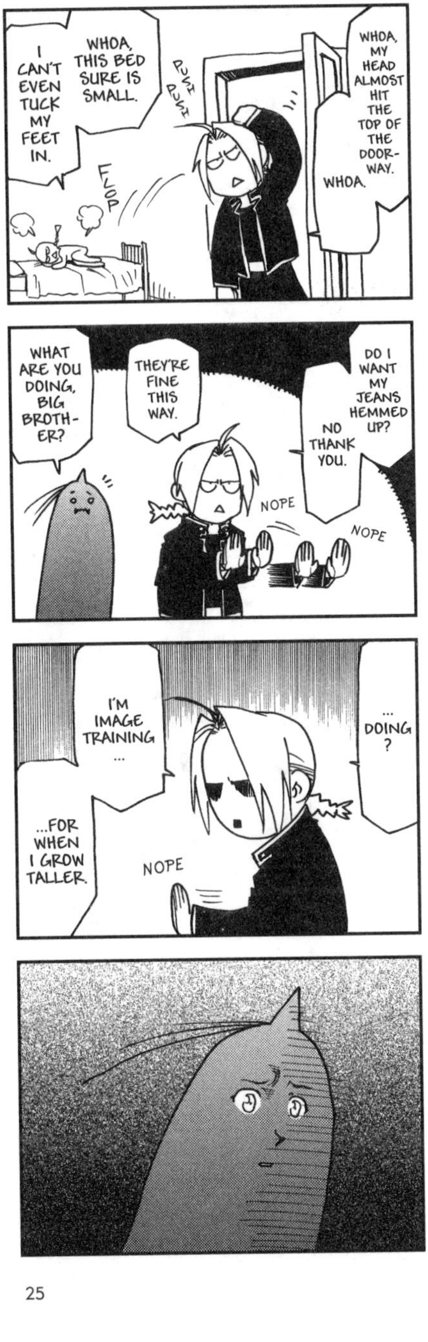
WHOA, MY HEAD ALMOST HIT THE TOP OF THE DOORWAY.
WHOA.
PUSH PUSH
WHOA, THIS BED SURE IS SMALL.
I CAN'T EVEN TUCK MY FEET IN.
FLOP
DO I WANT MY JEANS HEMMED UP?
NO THANK YOU.
NOPE
NOPE
THEY'RE FINE THIS WAY.
WHAT ARE YOU DOING, BIG BROTHER?
...DOING?
I'M IMAGE TRAINING...
...FOR WHEN I GROW TALLER.
NOPE

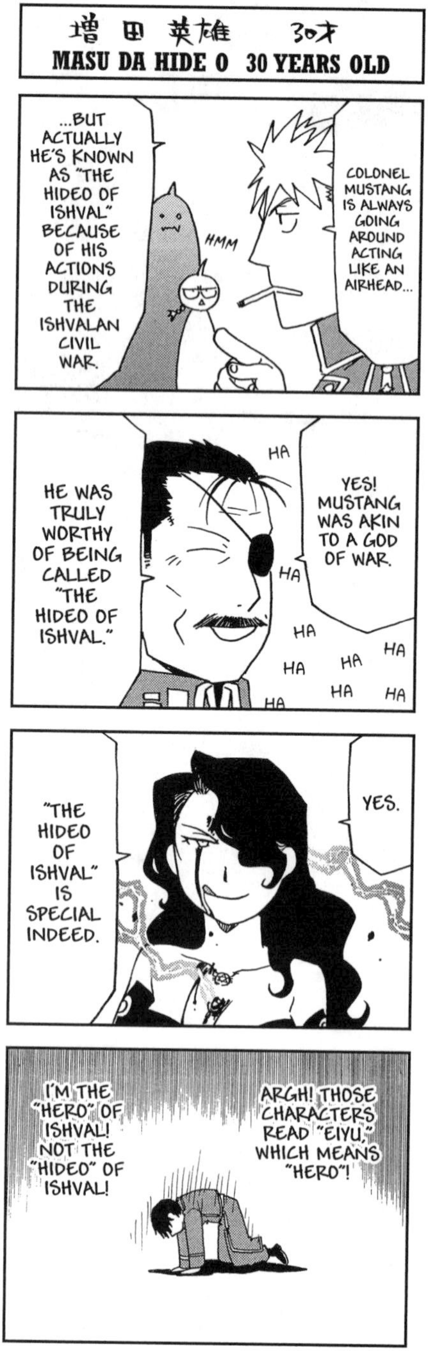
増田英雄 30才
MASU DA HIDE O 30 YEARS OLD
COLONEL MUSTANG IS ALWAYS GOING AROUND ACTING LIKE AN AIRHEAD...
HMM
...BUT ACTUALLY HE'S KNOWN AS "THE HIDEO OF ISHVAL" BECAUSE OF HIS ACTIONS DURING THE ISHVALAN CIVIL WAR.
YES! MUSTANG WAS AKIN TO A GOD OF WAR.
HA HA HA HA HA HA HA HA HA
HE WAS TRULY WORTHY OF BEING CALLED "THE HIDEO OF ISHVAL."
YES.
"THE HIDEO OF ISHVAL" IS SPECIAL INDEED.
ARGH! THOSE CHARACTERS READ "EIYU," WHICH MEANS "HERO"!
I'M THE "HERO" OF ISHVAL! NOT THE "HIDEO" OF ISHVAL!

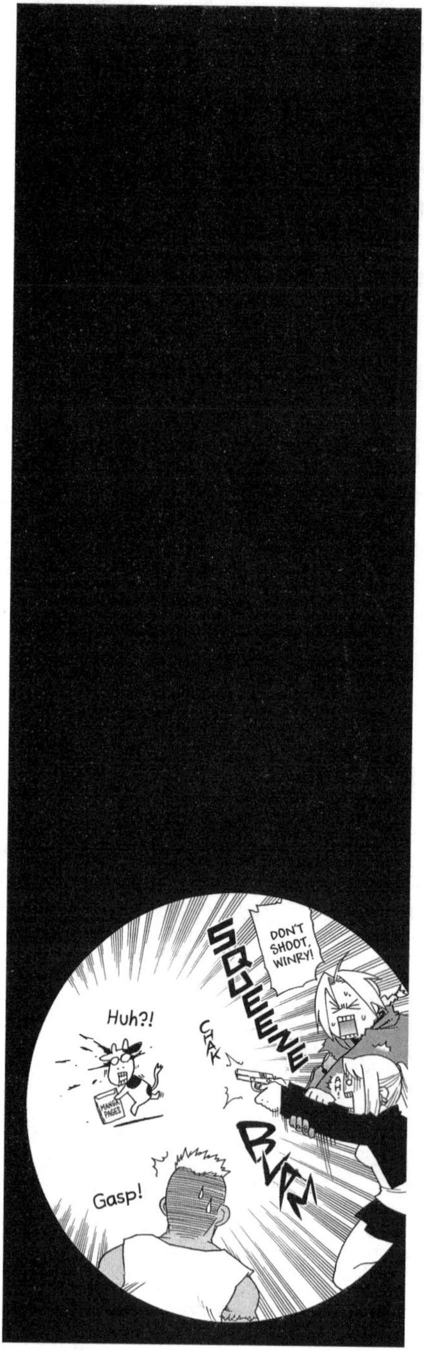
DON'T SHOOT, WINRY!
AH!
CHAK
Huh?!
MANGA PAGES
Gasp!

THE GOLDEN AGE

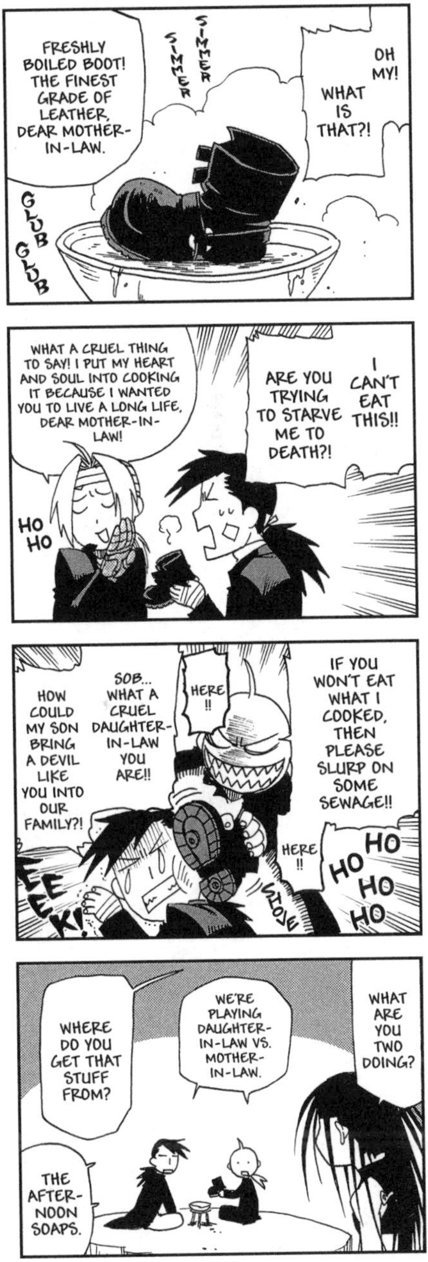
OH MY! WHAT IS THAT?!
SIMMER SIMMER
FRESHLY BOILED BOOT! THE FINEST GRADE OF LEATHER, DEAR MOTHER-IN-LAW.
GLUB GLUB
I CAN'T EAT THIS!!
ARE YOU TRYING TO STARVE ME TO DEATH?!
WHAT A CRUEL THING TO SAY! I PUT MY HEART AND SOUL INTO COOKING IT BECAUSE I WANTED YOU TO LIVE A LONG LIFE, DEAR MOTHER-IN-LAW!
HO HO
IF YOU WON'T EAT WHAT I COOKED, THEN PLEASE SLURP ON SOME SEWAGE!!
HERE!!
SOB... WHAT A CRUEL DAUGHTER-IN-LAW YOU ARE!!
HOW COULD MY SON BRING A DEVIL LIKE YOU INTO OUR FAMILY?!
HERE!!
HO HO HO HO
SHOVE
EEEK!
WHAT ARE YOU TWO DOING?
WE'RE PLAYING DAUGHTER-IN-LAW VS. MOTHER-IN-LAW.
WHERE DO YOU GET THAT STUFF FROM?
THE AFTERNOON SOAPS.

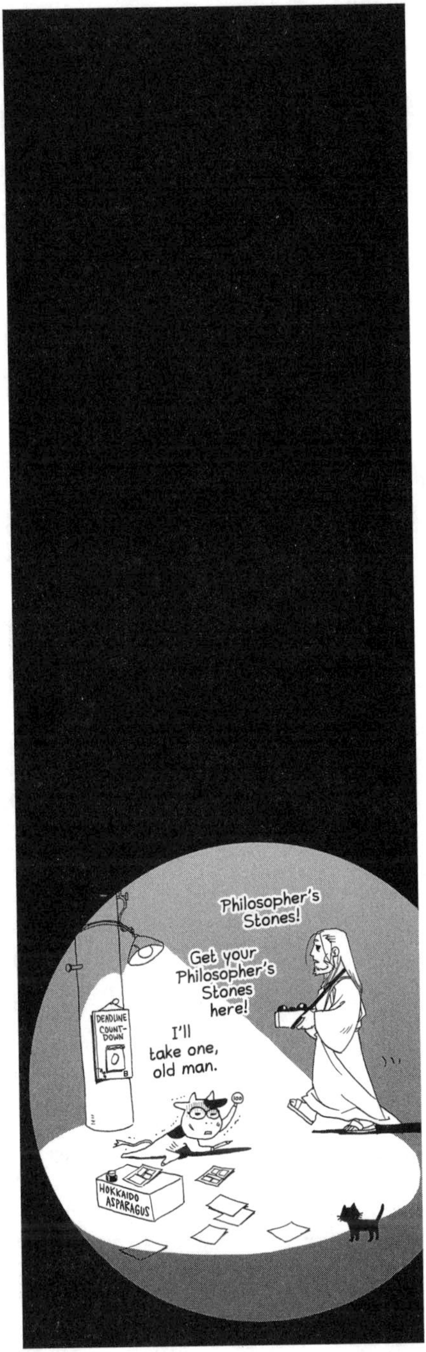
Philosopher's Stones!
Get your Philosopher's Stones here!
I'll take one, old man.
DEADLINE COUNT-DOWN
0
HOKKAIDO ASPARAGUS

MY BROTHER 60 YEARS YOUNGER

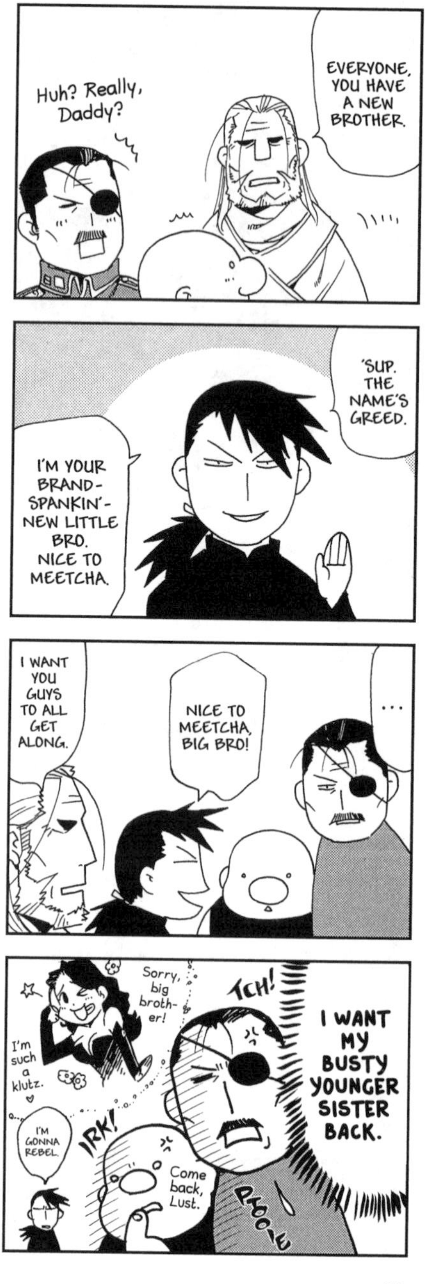
EVERYONE, YOU HAVE A NEW BROTHER.
Huh? Really, Daddy?
'SUP. THE NAME'S GREED.
I'M YOUR BRAND-SPANKIN'-NEW LITTLE BRO. NICE TO MEETCHA.
...
NICE TO MEETCHA, BIG BRO!
I WANT YOU GUYS TO ALL GET ALONG.
I WANT MY BUSTY YOUNGER SISTER BACK.
TCH!
Sorry, big brother!
I'm such a klutz.
IRK!
I'M GONNA REBEL.
Come back, Lust.
PTOOIE

DO THEY STILL SELL SHAMPOO HATS?

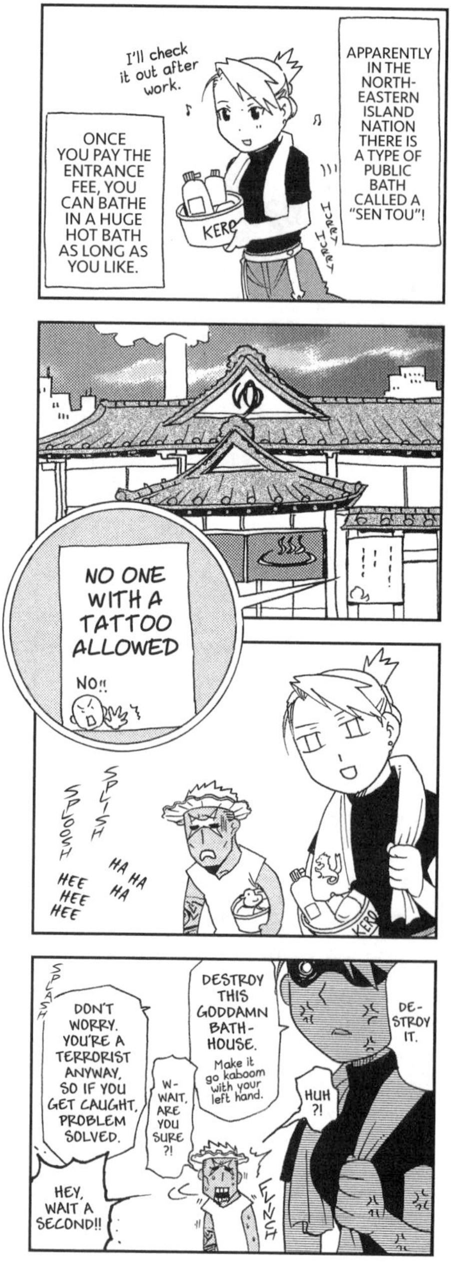
APPARENTLY IN THE NORTH-EASTERN ISLAND NATION THERE IS A TYPE OF PUBLIC BATH CALLED A "SEN TOU"!
I'll check it out after work.
HURRY HURRY
KERO
ONCE YOU PAY THE ENTRANCE FEE, YOU CAN BATHE IN A HUGE HOT BATH AS LONG AS YOU LIKE.
NO ONE WITH A TATTOO ALLOWED
NO!!
SPLISH
SPLOOSH
HA HA HA
HEE HEE HEE
KERO
DE-STROY IT.
HUH?!
DESTROY THIS GODDAMN BATH-HOUSE.
Make it go kaboom with your left hand.
DON'T WORRY. YOU'RE A TERRORIST ANYWAY, SO IF YOU GET CAUGHT, PROBLEM SOLVED.
W-WAIT, ARE YOU SURE?!
FLINCH
SPLASH
HEY, WAIT A SECOND!!

EDWARD AND THE MAGIC LAMP

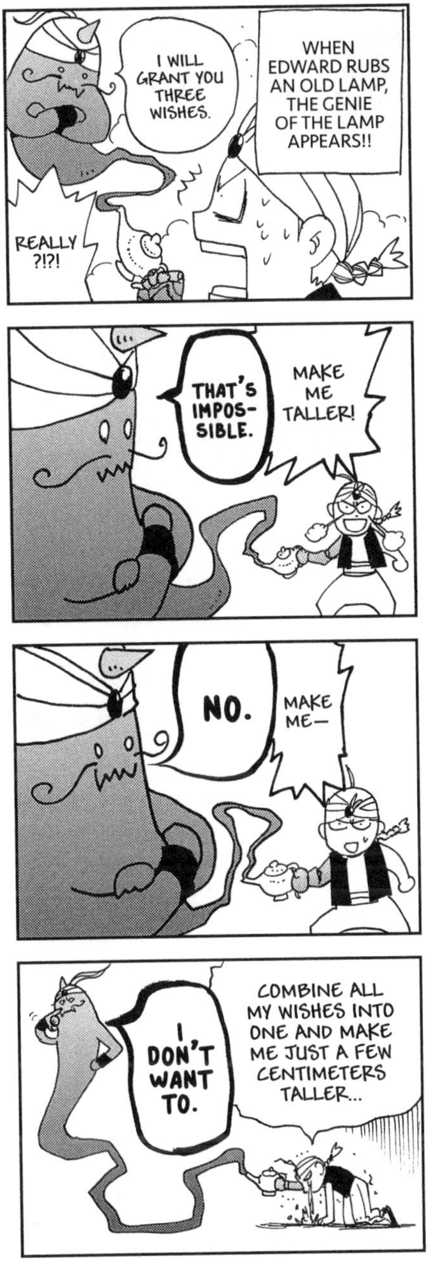
WHEN EDWARD RUBS AN OLD LAMP, THE GENIE OF THE LAMP APPEARS!!
I WILL GRANT YOU THREE WISHES.
REALLY ?!?!
MAKE ME TALLER!
THAT'S IMPOSSIBLE.
MAKE ME—
NO.
COMBINE ALL MY WISHES INTO ONE AND MAKE ME JUST A FEW CENTIMETERS TALLER...
I DON'T WANT TO.

FOR YOUR EYES

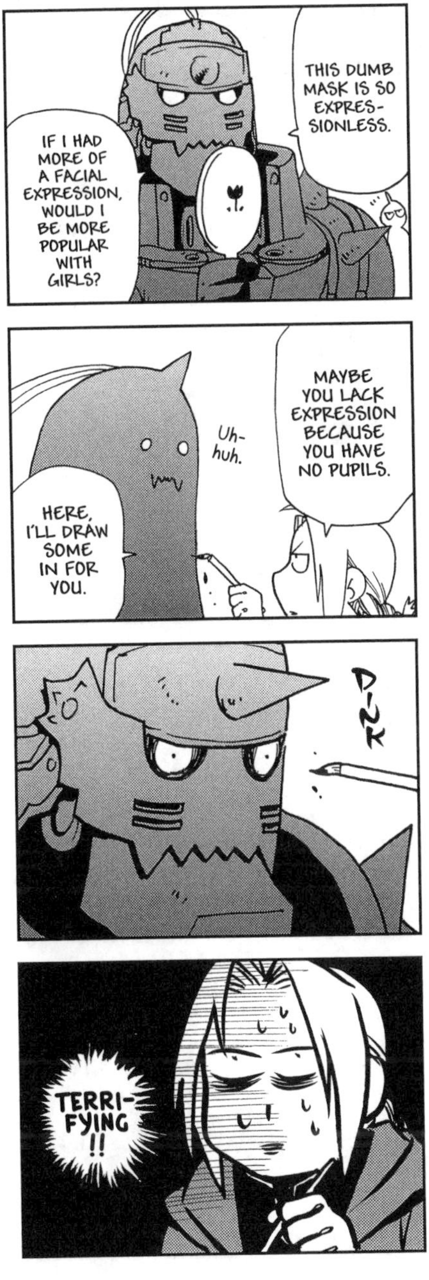
THIS DUMB MASK IS SO EXPRESSIONLESS.
IF I HAD MORE OF A FACIAL EXPRESSION, WOULD I BE MORE POPULAR WITH GIRLS?
MAYBE YOU LACK EXPRESSION BECAUSE YOU HAVE NO PUPILS.
Uh-huh.
HERE, I'LL DRAW SOME IN FOR YOU.
DINK
TERRIFYING!!

OLDER BROTHER'S WISH

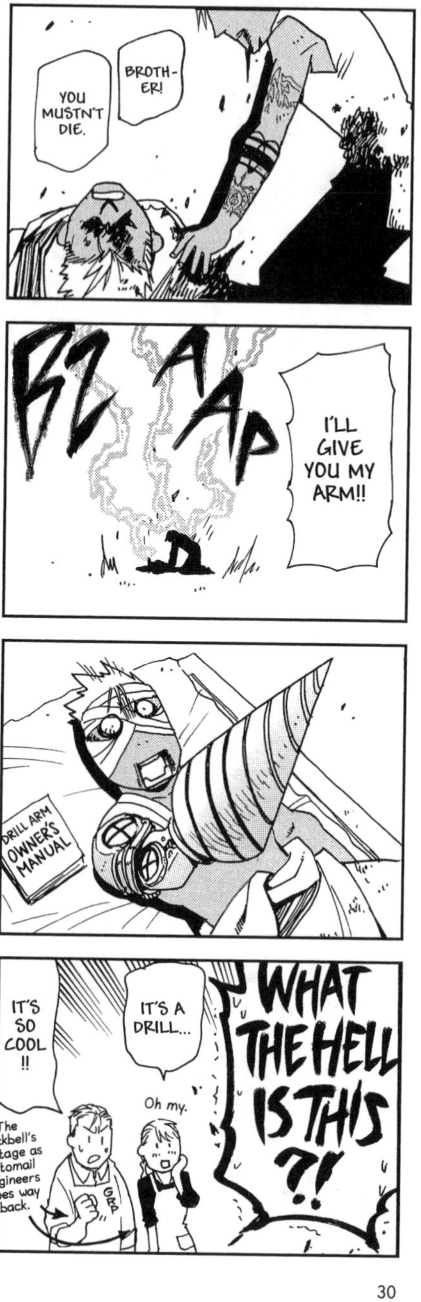
BROTH-ER!
YOU MUSTN'T DIE.
I'LL GIVE YOU MY ARM!!
BZAAAP
DRILL ARM OWNER'S MANUAL
WHAT THE HELL IS THIS?!
IT'S A DRILL...
IT'S SO COOL!!
Oh my.
The Rockbell's heritage as automail engineers goes way back.
GRP

PLEASE LET ME USE YOUR RESTROOM!

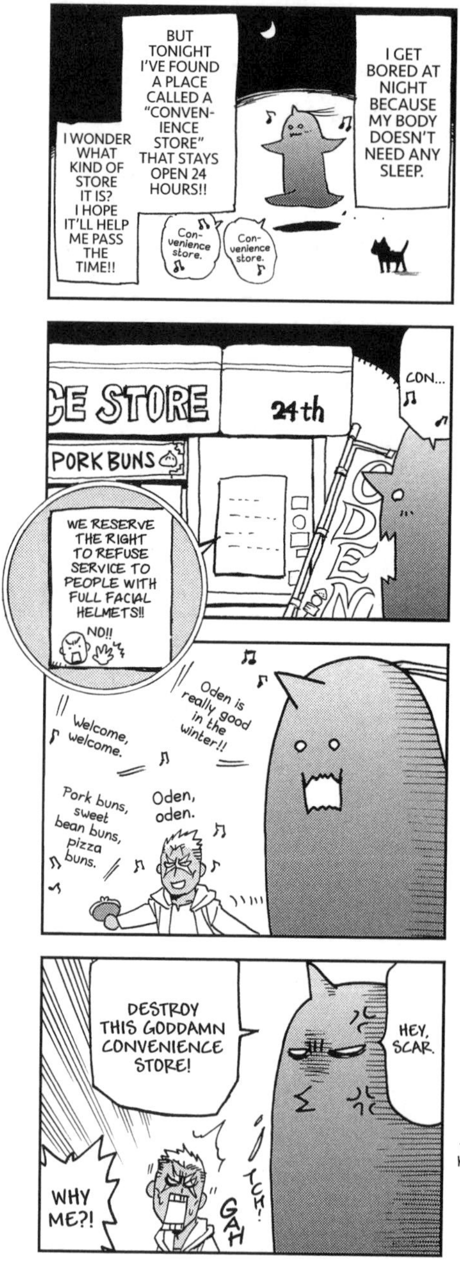
I GET BORED AT NIGHT BECAUSE MY BODY DOESN'T NEED ANY SLEEP.
BUT TONIGHT I'VE FOUND A PLACE CALLED A "CONVEN-IENCE STORE" THAT STAYS OPEN 24 HOURS!!
I WONDER WHAT KIND OF STORE IT IS? I HOPE IT'LL HELP ME PASS THE TIME!!
Con-venience store.
Con-venience store.
CON...
24th
CE STORE
PORK BUNS
ODEN
WE RESERVE THE RIGHT TO REFUSE SERVICE TO PEOPLE WITH FULL FACIAL HELMETS!!
NO!!
Oden is really good in the winter!!
Welcome, welcome.
Oden, oden.
Pork buns, sweet bean buns, pizza buns.
HEY, SCAR.
DESTROY THIS GODDAMN CONVENIENCE STORE!
TCH!
GAH
WHY ME?!

ADDITIONAL FEE REQUIRED IF YOU WANT TO SEE MORE

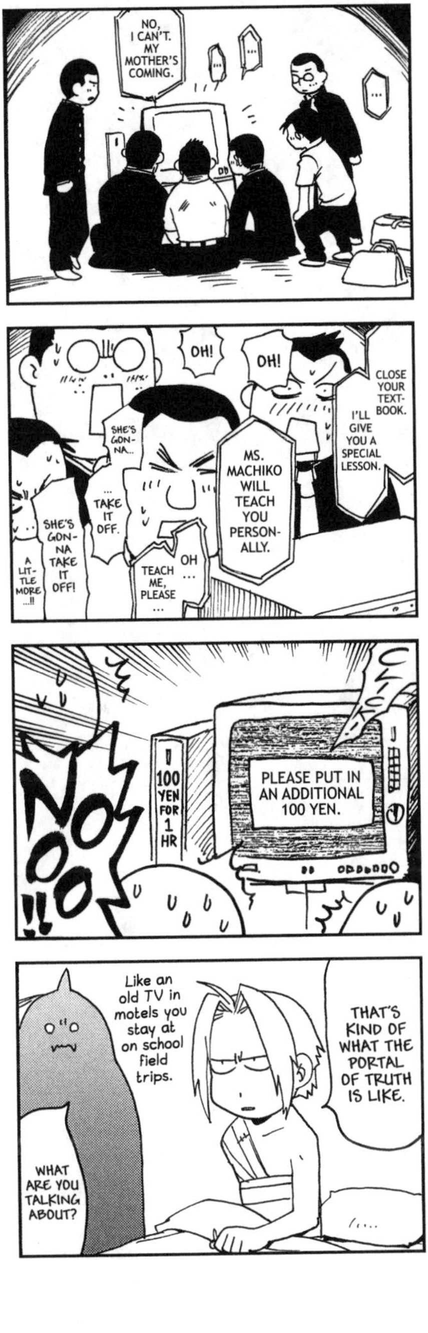
NO, I CAN'T. MY MOTHER'S COMING.
...
...
...
CLOSE YOUR TEXT-BOOK. I'LL GIVE YOU A SPECIAL LESSON.
OH!
OH!
MS. MACHIKO WILL TEACH YOU PERSON-ALLY.
SHE'S GON-NA...
... TAKE IT OFF.
OH ...
TEACH ME, PLEASE ...
SHE'S GON-NA TAKE IT OFF!
A LIT-TLE MORE ...!!
CLICK
PLEASE PUT IN AN ADDITIONAL 100 YEN.
100 YEN FOR 1 HR
NOOOO!!
THAT'S KIND OF WHAT THE PORTAL OF TRUTH IS LIKE.
Like an old TV in motels you stay at on school field trips.
WHAT ARE YOU TALKING ABOUT?

HARD-BOILED

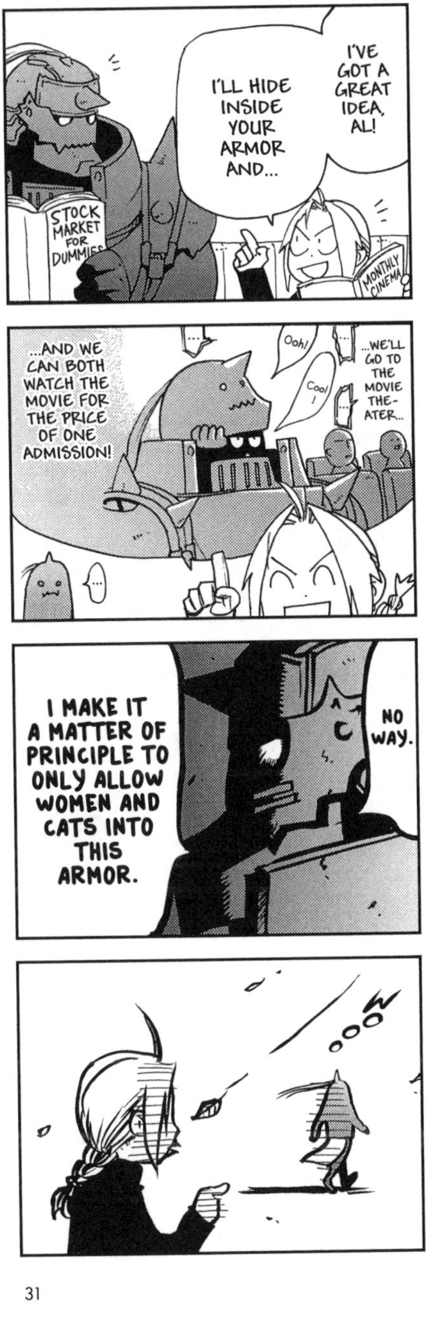
I'VE GOT A GREAT IDEA, AL!
I'LL HIDE INSIDE YOUR ARMOR AND...
STOCK MARKET FOR DUMMIES
MONTHLY CINEMA
...WE'LL GO TO THE MOVIE THE-ATER...
Ooh!
Cool!
...
...
...AND WE CAN BOTH WATCH THE MOVIE FOR THE PRICE OF ONE ADMISSION!
...
NO WAY.
I MAKE IT A MATTER OF PRINCIPLE TO ONLY ALLOW WOMEN AND CATS INTO THIS ARMOR.

HUMAN VS. ARTIFICIAL HUMAN

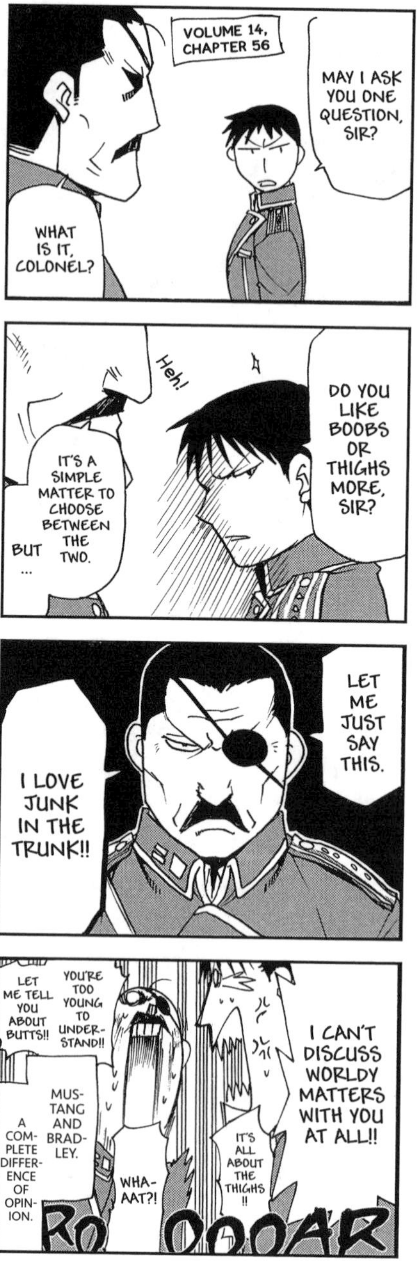
VOLUME 14, CHAPTER 56
MAY I ASK YOU ONE QUESTION, SIR?
WHAT IS IT, COLONEL?
DO YOU LIKE BOOBS OR THIGHS MORE, SIR?
Heh!
IT'S A SIMPLE MATTER TO CHOOSE BETWEEN THE TWO.
BUT ...
LET ME JUST SAY THIS.
I LOVE JUNK IN THE TRUNK!!
I CAN'T DISCUSS WORLDY MATTERS WITH YOU AT ALL!!
YOU'RE TOO YOUNG TO UNDERSTAND!!
LET ME TELL YOU ABOUT BUTTS!!
IT'S ALL ABOUT THE THIGHS !!
MUSTANG AND BRADLEY.
WHA-AAT?!
A COMPLETE DIFFERENCE OF OPINION.
ROOOOAR

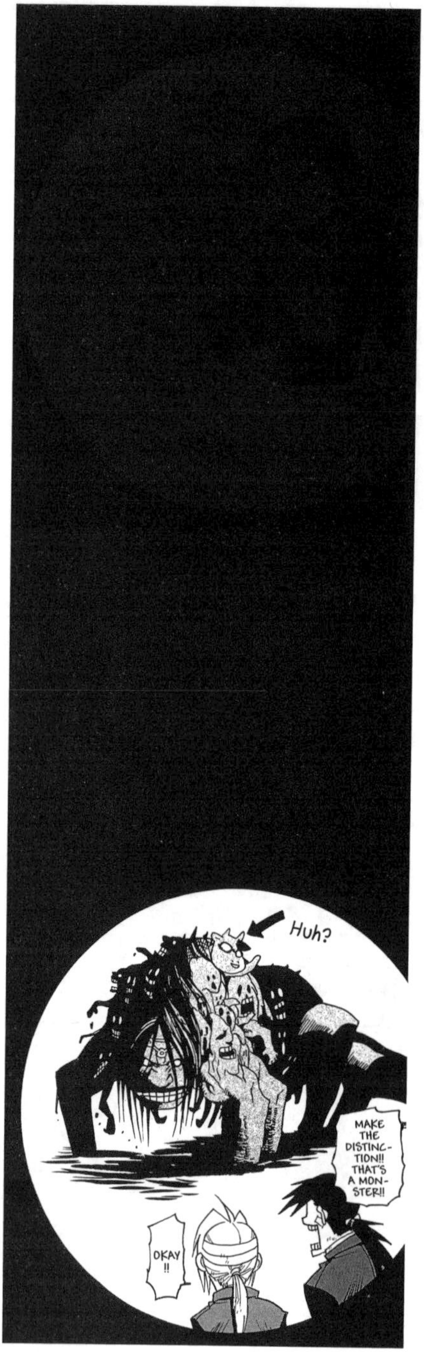
Huh?
MAKE THE DISTINCTION!! THAT'S A MONSTER!!
OKAY !!

EDWARD AND THE MAGIC LAMP: PART 2

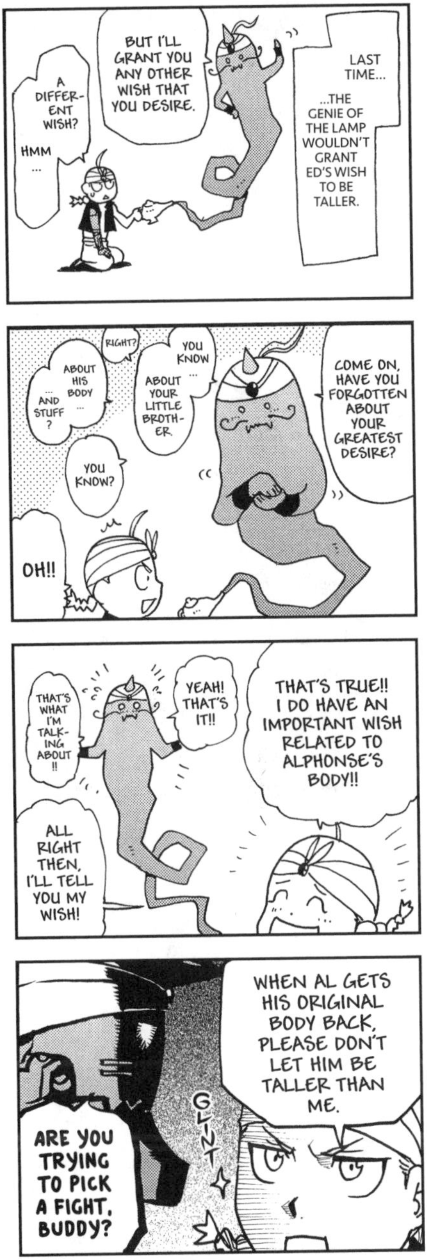
LAST TIME... ...THE GENIE OF THE LAMP WOULDN'T GRANT ED'S WISH TO BE TALLER.
BUT I'LL GRANT YOU ANY OTHER WISH THAT YOU DESIRE.
A DIFFERENT WISH? HMM ...
COME ON, HAVE YOU FORGOTTEN ABOUT YOUR GREATEST DESIRE?
YOU KNOW ...
RIGHT?
ABOUT YOUR LITTLE BROTHER
ABOUT HIS BODY ...
... AND STUFF ?
YOU KNOW?
OH!!
THAT'S TRUE!! I DO HAVE AN IMPORTANT WISH RELATED TO ALPHONSE'S BODY!!
YEAH! THAT'S IT!!
THAT'S WHAT I'M TALKING ABOUT !!
ALL RIGHT THEN, I'LL TELL YOU MY WISH!
WHEN AL GETS HIS ORIGINAL BODY BACK, PLEASE DON'T LET HIM BE TALLER THAN ME.
GLINT
ARE YOU TRYING TO PICK A FIGHT, BUDDY?

SECRETS ARE REVEALED

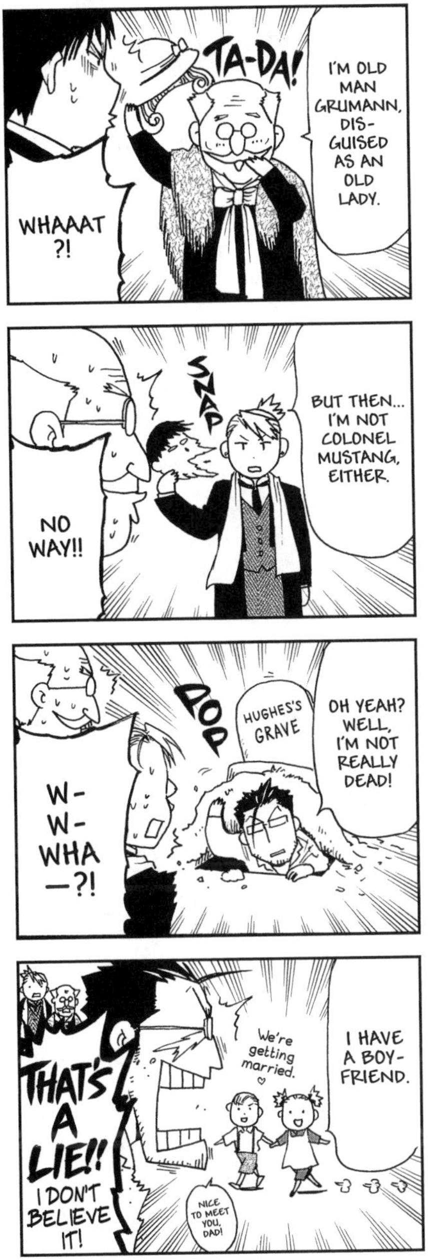
I'M OLD MAN GRUMANN, DISGUISED AS AN OLD LADY.
TA-DA!
WHAAAT ?!
BUT THEN... I'M NOT COLONEL MUSTANG, EITHER.
SNAP
NO WAY!!
OH YEAH? WELL, I'M NOT REALLY DEAD!
HUGHES'S GRAVE
POP
W-W-WHA—?!
I HAVE A BOYFRIEND.
We're getting married.
NICE TO MEET YOU, DAD!
THAT'S A LIE!! I DON'T BELIEVE IT!

MATERIALS ON LOCATION

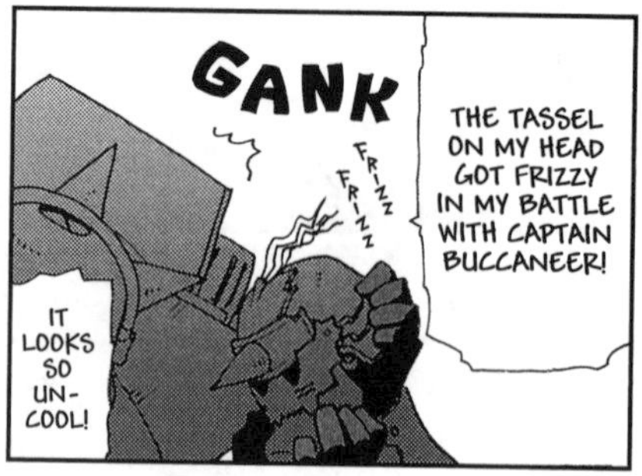
THE TASSEL ON MY HEAD GOT FRIZZY IN MY BATTLE WITH CAPTAIN BUCCANEER!
GANK
FRIZZ FRIZZ
IT LOOKS SO UN-COOL!

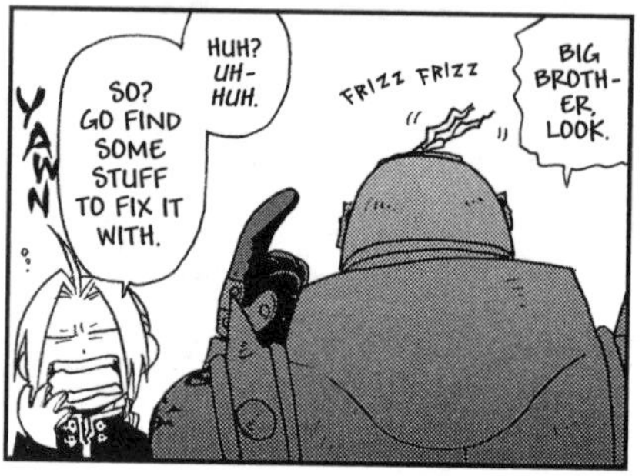
BIG BROTH-ER, LOOK.
FRIZZ FRIZZ
HUH? UH-HUH.
SO? GO FIND SOME STUFF TO FIX IT WITH.
YAWN

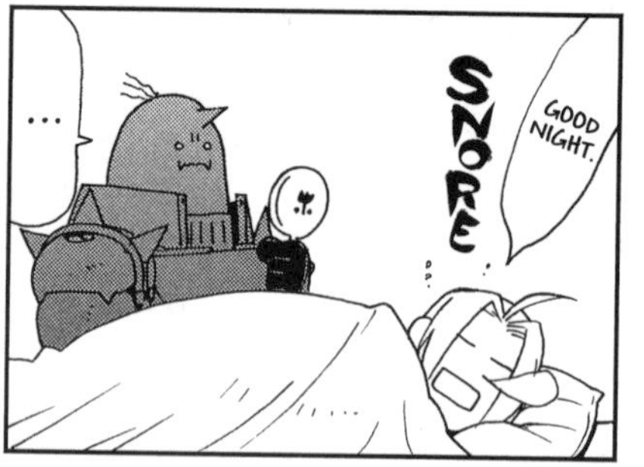
GOOD NIGHT.
SNORE
...

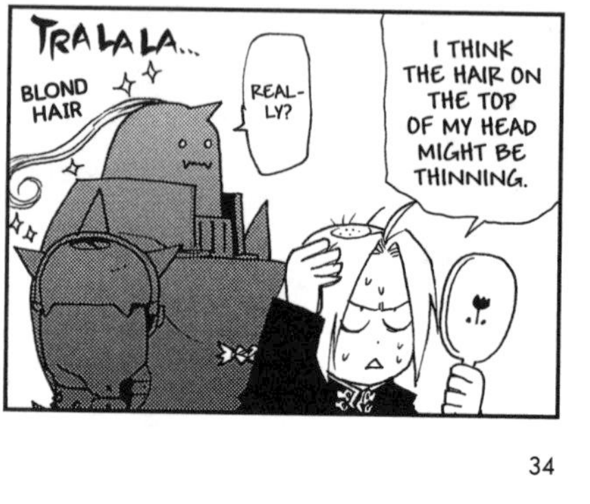
I THINK THE HAIR ON THE TOP OF MY HEAD MIGHT BE THINNING.
REAL-LY?
BLOND HAIR
TRALALA...

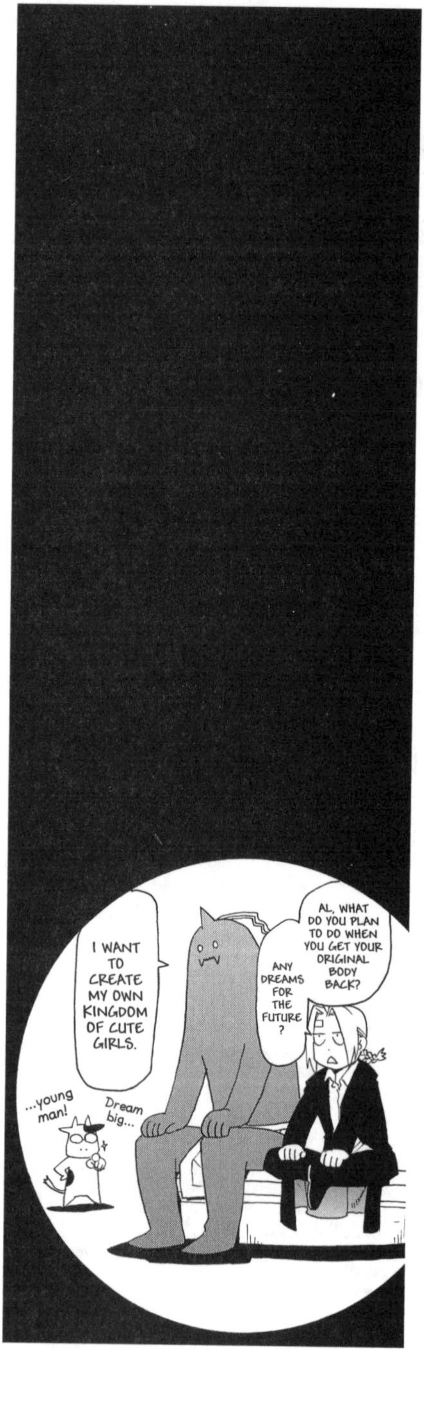
AL, WHAT DO YOU PLAN TO DO WHEN YOU GET YOUR ORIGINAL BODY BACK?
ANY DREAMS FOR THE FUTURE?
I WANT TO CREATE MY OWN KINGDOM OF CUTE GIRLS.
Dream big...
...young man!

EDWARD AND THE MAGIC LAMP: PART 3

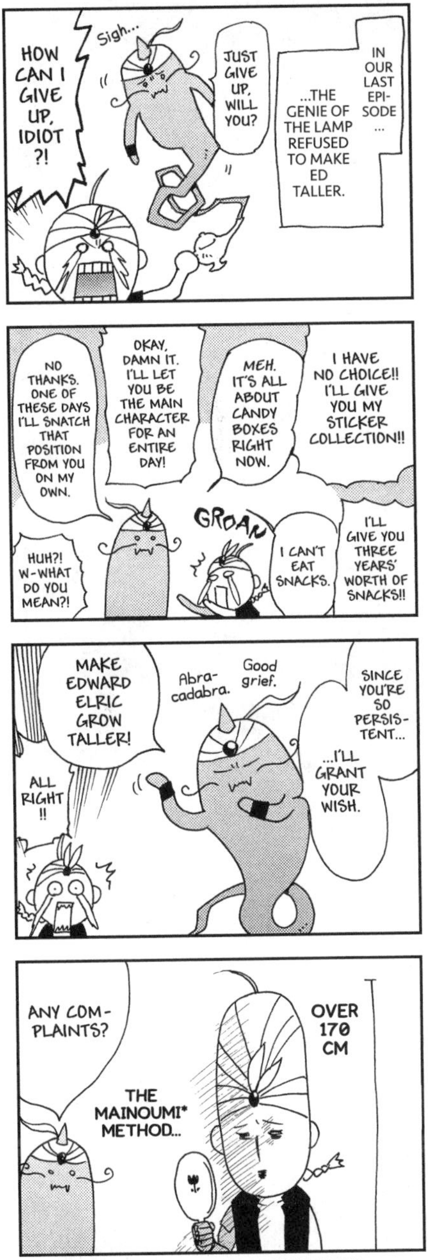
IN OUR LAST EPI-SODE ...
...THE GENIE OF THE LAMP REFUSED TO MAKE ED TALLER.
JUST GIVE UP, WILL YOU?
Sigh...
HOW CAN I GIVE UP, IDIOT ?!
I HAVE NO CHOICE!! I'LL GIVE YOU MY STICKER COLLECTION!!
MEH. IT'S ALL ABOUT CANDY BOXES RIGHT NOW.
OKAY, DAMN IT. I'LL LET YOU BE THE MAIN CHARACTER FOR AN ENTIRE DAY!
NO THANKS. ONE OF THESE DAYS I'LL SNATCH THAT POSITION FROM YOU ON MY OWN.
I'LL GIVE YOU THREE YEARS' WORTH OF SNACKS!!
I CAN'T EAT SNACKS.
GROAN
HUH?! W-WHAT DO YOU MEAN?!
SINCE YOU'RE SO PERSIS-TENT...
Good grief.
Abra-cadabra.
MAKE EDWARD ELRIC GROW TALLER!
...I'LL GRANT YOUR WISH.
ALL RIGHT !!
OVER 170 CM
ANY COM-PLAINTS?
THE MAINOUMI* METHOD...

*MAINOUMI IS A SUMO WRESTLER WHO IMPLANTED SILICONE IN HIS HEAD TO MEET SUMO HEIGHT REQUIREMENTS.

HAVOC AND THE MAGIC BOING

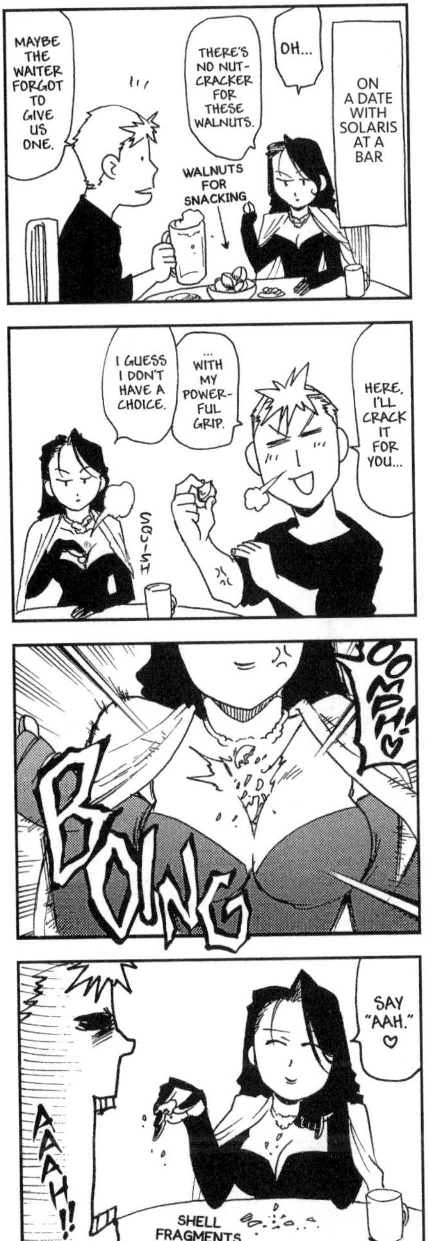
ON A DATE WITH SOLARIS AT A BAR
OH...
THERE'S NO NUT-CRACKER FOR THESE WALNUTS.
MAYBE THE WAITER FORGOT TO GIVE US ONE.
WALNUTS FOR SNACKING
HERE, I'LL CRACK IT FOR YOU...
...WITH MY POWER-FUL GRIP.
I GUESS I DON'T HAVE A CHOICE.
SQUISH
BOOMPH!♡
BOING
SAY "AAH." ♡
AAAH!!
SHELL FRAGMENTS

A DAY IN THE LIFE OF FATHER

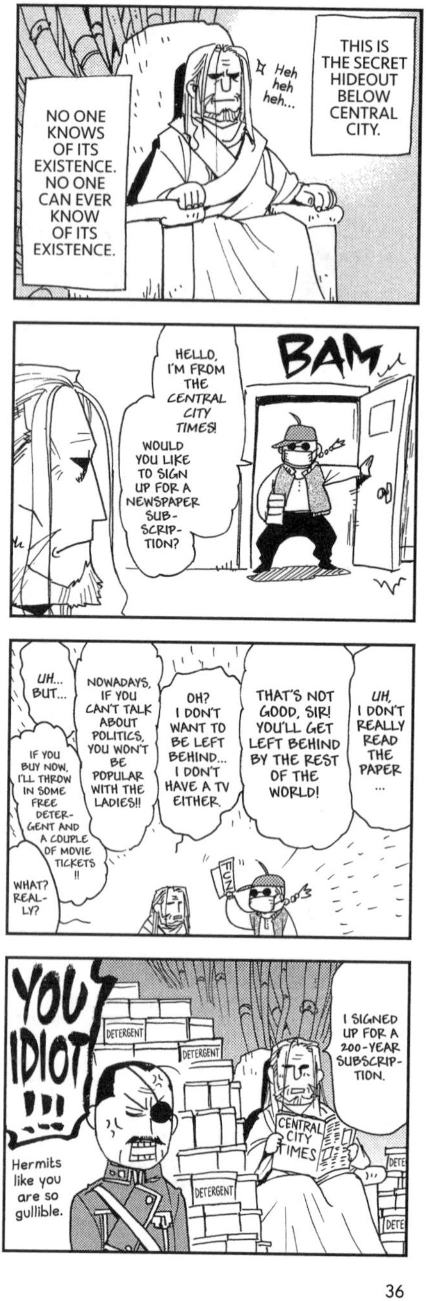
THIS IS THE SECRET HIDEOUT BELOW CENTRAL CITY.
Heh heh heh...
NO ONE KNOWS OF ITS EXISTENCE. NO ONE CAN EVER KNOW OF ITS EXISTENCE.
BAM
HELLO, I'M FROM THE CENTRAL CITY TIMES!
WOULD YOU LIKE TO SIGN UP FOR A NEWSPAPER SUB-SCRIP-TION?
UH, I DON'T REALLY READ THE PAPER ...
THAT'S NOT GOOD, SIR! YOU'LL GET LEFT BEHIND BY THE REST OF THE WORLD!
OH? I DON'T WANT TO BE LEFT BEHIND... I DON'T HAVE A TV EITHER.
NOWADAYS, IF YOU CAN'T TALK ABOUT POLITICS, YOU WON'T BE POPULAR WITH THE LADIES!!
UH... BUT...
IF YOU BUY NOW, I'LL THROW IN SOME FREE DETER-GENT AND A COUPLE OF MOVIE TICKETS !!
WHAT? REAL-LY?
FUN
I SIGNED UP FOR A 200-YEAR SUBSCRIP-TION.
CENTRAL CITY TIMES
DETERGENT
DETERGENT
DETERGENT
YOU IDIOT!!!
Hermits like you are so gullible.

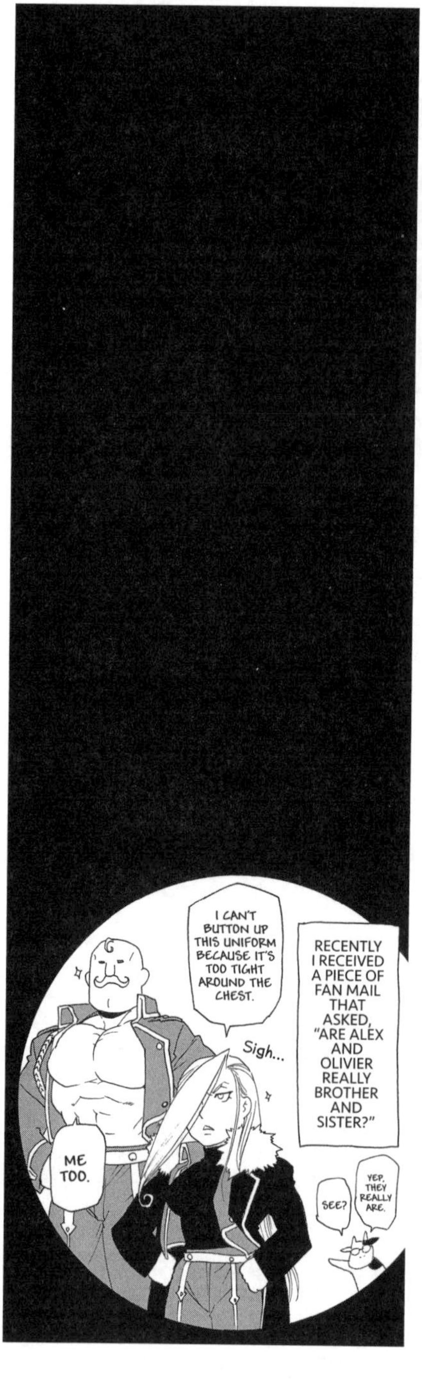
RECENTLY I RECEIVED A PIECE OF FAN MAIL THAT ASKED, "ARE ALEX AND OLIVIER REALLY BROTHER AND SISTER?"
I CAN'T BUTTON UP THIS UNIFORM BECAUSE IT'S TOO TIGHT AROUND THE CHEST.
Sigh...
ME TOO.
YEP, THEY REALLY ARE.
SEE?

“BAYATE” THE FAITHFUL DOG

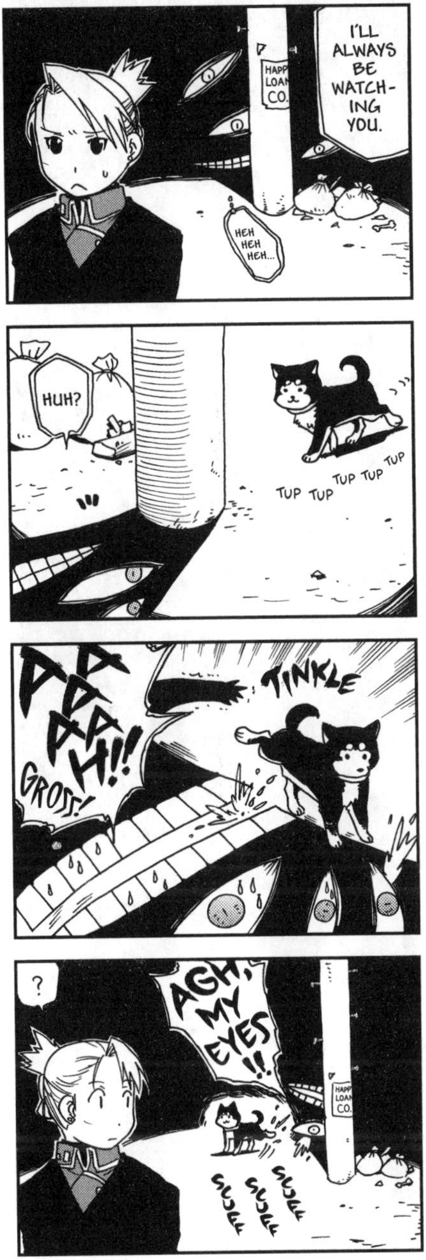
I'LL ALWAYS BE WATCHING YOU.
HEH HEH HEH...
HUH?
TUP TUP TUP TUP TUP
TINKLE
AAAAH!!
GROSS!
?
AGH, MY EYES!!
SNIFF SNIFF SNIFF

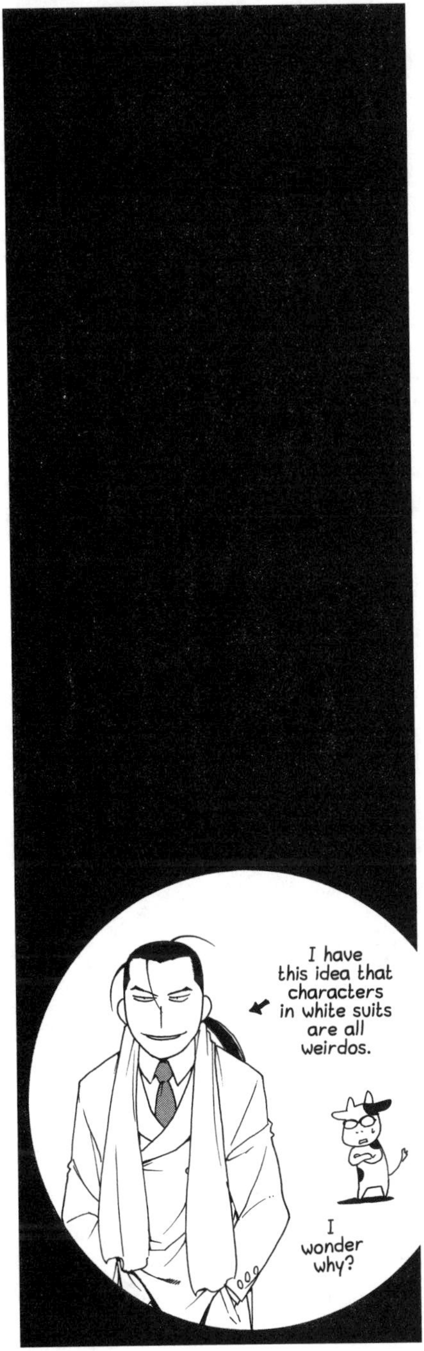
I have this idea that characters in white suits are all weirdos.
I wonder why?

AN ENDANGERED SPECIES

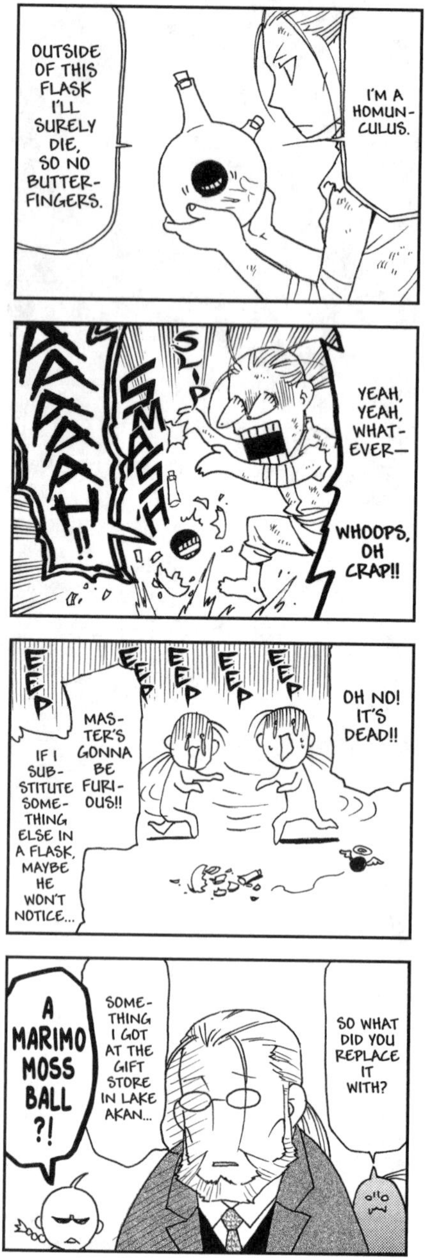
I'M A HOMUNCULUS.
OUTSIDE OF THIS FLASK I'LL SURELY DIE, SO NO BUTTERFINGERS.
YEAH, YEAH, WHATEVER—
WHOOPS, OH CRAP!!
SLIP
SMASH
AAAAAH!!
OH NO! IT'S DEAD!!
EEP
EEP
EEP
EEP
EEP
MASTER'S GONNA BE FURIOUS!!
IF I SUBSTITUTE SOMETHING ELSE IN A FLASK, MAYBE HE WON'T NOTICE...
SO WHAT DID YOU REPLACE IT WITH?
SOMETHING I GOT AT THE GIFT STORE IN LAKE AKAN...
A MARIMO MOSS BALL?!

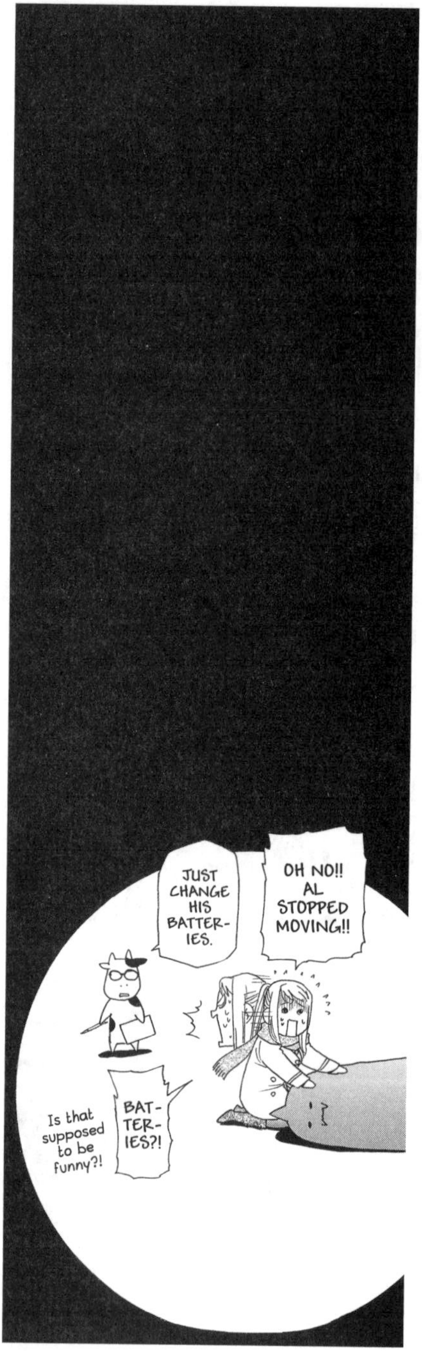
OH NO!! AL STOPPED MOVING!!
JUST CHANGE HIS BATTERIES.
BATTERIES?!
Is that supposed to be funny?!

WHAT IF?

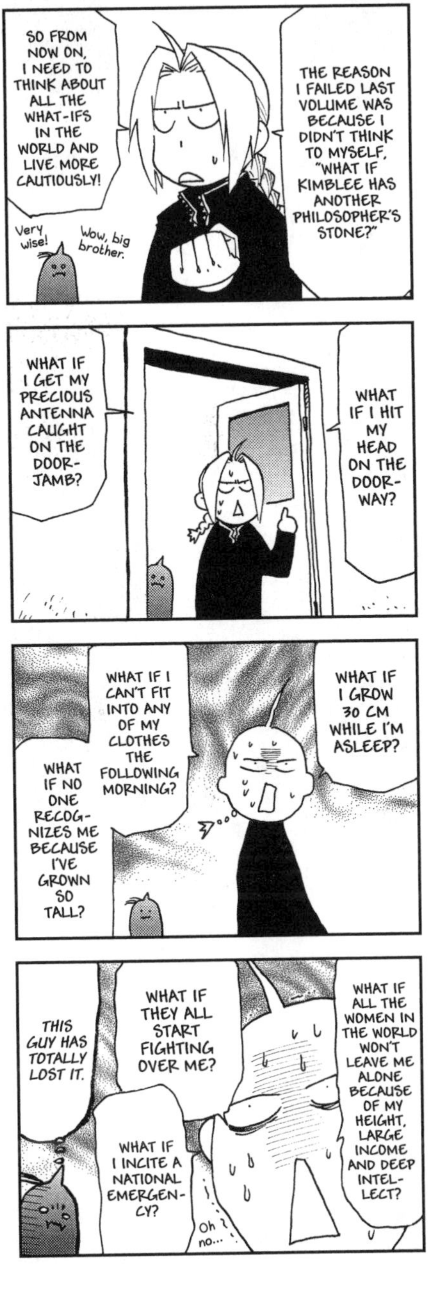
THE REASON I FAILED LAST VOLUME WAS BECAUSE I DIDN'T THINK TO MYSELF, "WHAT IF KIMBLEE HAS ANOTHER PHILOSOPHER'S STONE?"
SO FROM NOW ON, I NEED TO THINK ABOUT ALL THE WHAT-IFS IN THE WORLD AND LIVE MORE CAUTIOUSLY!
Wow, big brother.
Very wise!
WHAT IF I HIT MY HEAD ON THE DOOR-WAY?
WHAT IF I GET MY PRECIOUS ANTENNA CAUGHT ON THE DOOR-JAMB?
WHAT IF I GROW 30 CM WHILE I'M ASLEEP?
WHAT IF I CAN'T FIT INTO ANY OF MY CLOTHES THE FOLLOWING MORNING?
WHAT IF NO ONE RECOG-NIZES ME BECAUSE I'VE GROWN SO TALL?
WHAT IF ALL THE WOMEN IN THE WORLD WON'T LEAVE ME ALONE BECAUSE OF MY HEIGHT, LARGE INCOME AND DEEP INTEL-LECT?
WHAT IF THEY ALL START FIGHTING OVER ME?
THIS GUY HAS TOTALLY LOST IT.
WHAT IF I INCITE A NATIONAL EMERGEN-CY?
Oh no...

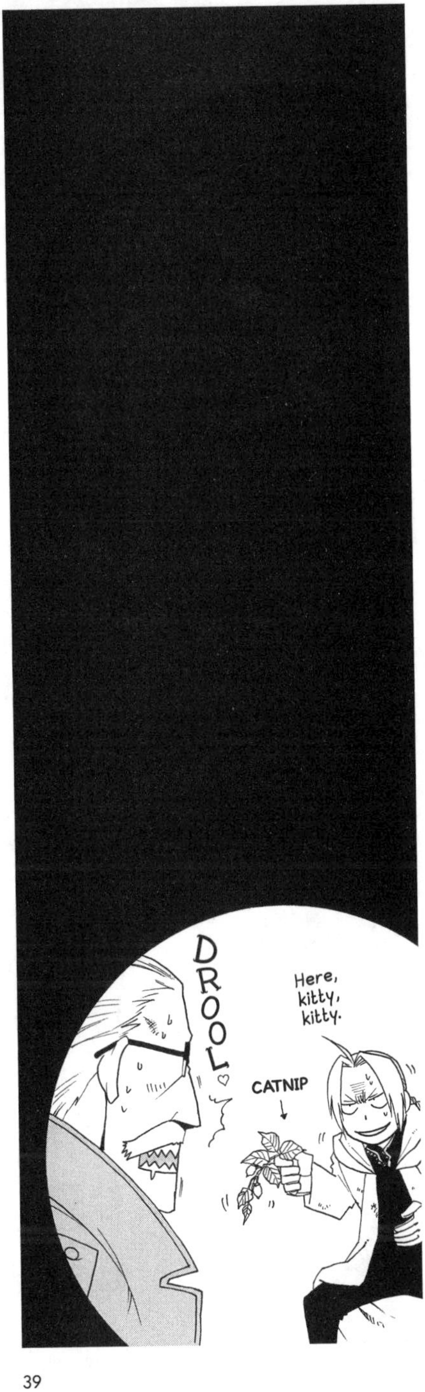
Here, kitty, kitty.
CATNIP
DROOL♡

FREEDOM

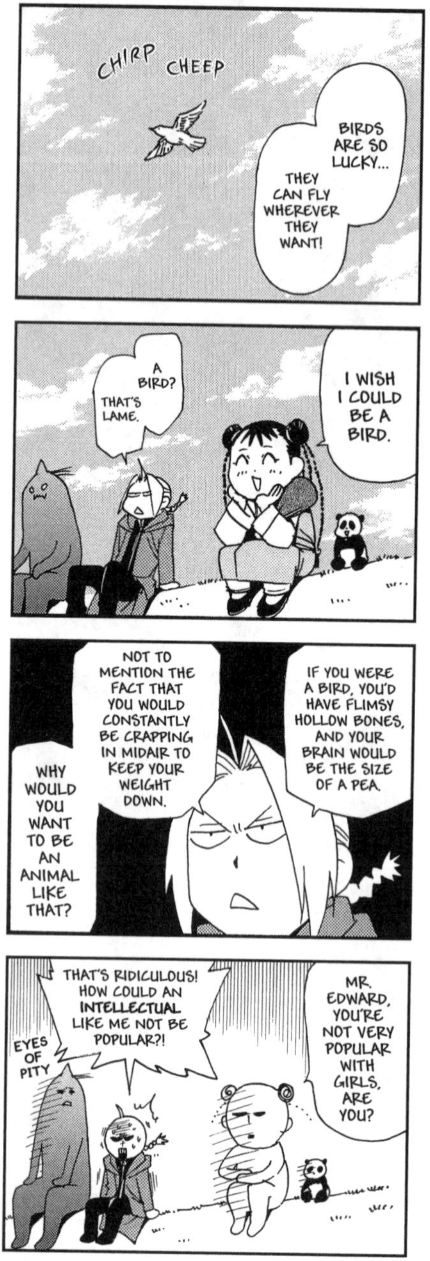
CHIRP CHEEP
BIRDS ARE SO LUCKY... THEY CAN FLY WHEREVER THEY WANT!
I WISH I COULD BE A BIRD.
A BIRD? THAT'S LAME.
IF YOU WERE A BIRD, YOU'D HAVE FLIMSY HOLLOW BONES, AND YOUR BRAIN WOULD BE THE SIZE OF A PEA.
NOT TO MENTION THE FACT THAT YOU WOULD CONSTANTLY BE CRAPPING IN MIDAIR TO KEEP YOUR WEIGHT DOWN.
WHY WOULD YOU WANT TO BE AN ANIMAL LIKE THAT?
MR. EDWARD, YOU'RE NOT VERY POPULAR WITH GIRLS, ARE YOU?
THAT'S RIDICULOUS! HOW COULD AN INTELLECTUAL LIKE ME NOT BE POPULAR?!
EYES OF PITY

THE GREAT "GET POPULAR" PLAN

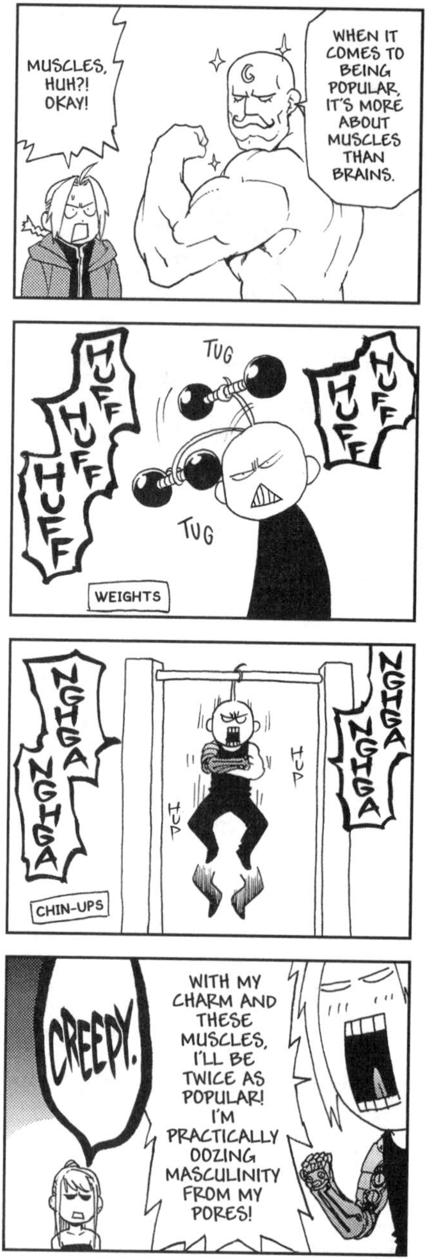
WHEN IT COMES TO BEING POPULAR, IT'S MORE ABOUT MUSCLES THAN BRAINS.
MUSCLES, HUH?! OKAY!
HUFF HUFF
TUG
TUG
HUFF HUFF HUFF
WEIGHTS
NGHGA NGHGA
HUP
HUP
NGHGA NGHGA NGHGA
CHIN-UPS
WITH MY CHARM AND THESE MUSCLES, I'LL BE TWICE AS POPULAR! I'M PRACTICALLY OOZING MASCULINITY FROM MY PORES!
CREEPY.

HAWKEYE'S HOMECOMING

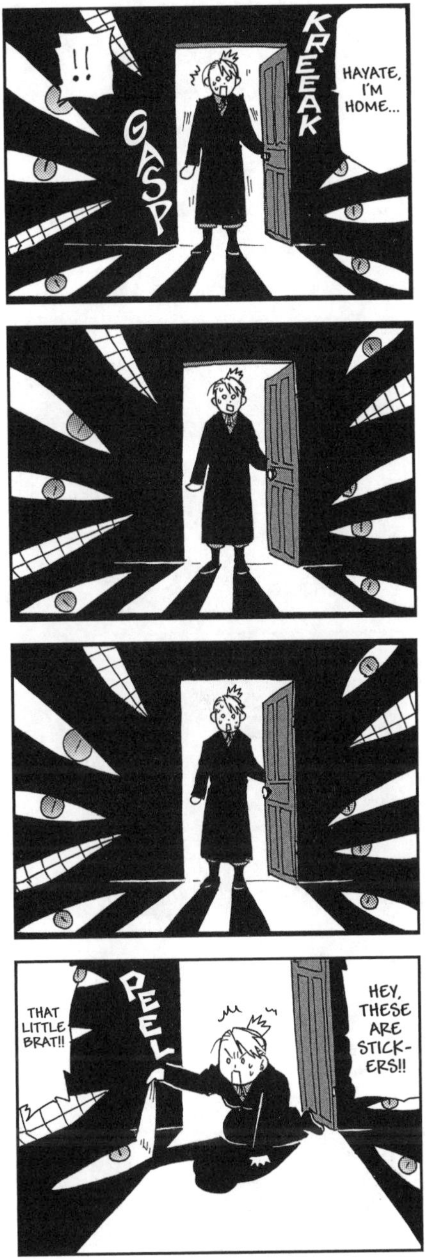
HAYATE, I'M HOME...
KREEAK
!!
GASP
PEEL
HEY, THESE ARE STICKERS!!
THAT LITTLE BRAT!!

MUGGER

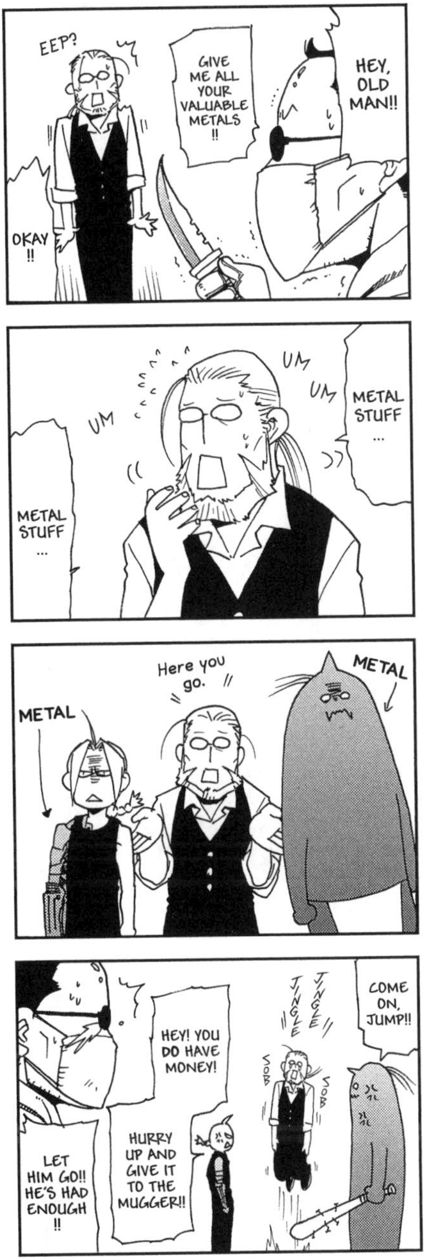
HEY, OLD MAN!!
GIVE ME ALL YOUR VALUABLE METALS!!
EEP?
OKAY!!
METAL STUFF ...
UM
UM
UM
METAL STUFF ...
METAL
Here you go.
METAL
COME ON, JUMP!!
JINGLE
JINGLE
SOB
SOB
HEY! YOU DO HAVE MONEY!
HURRY UP AND GIVE IT TO THE MUGGER!!
LET HIM GO!! HE'S HAD ENOUGH!!

EXTREME HOMUNCULUS

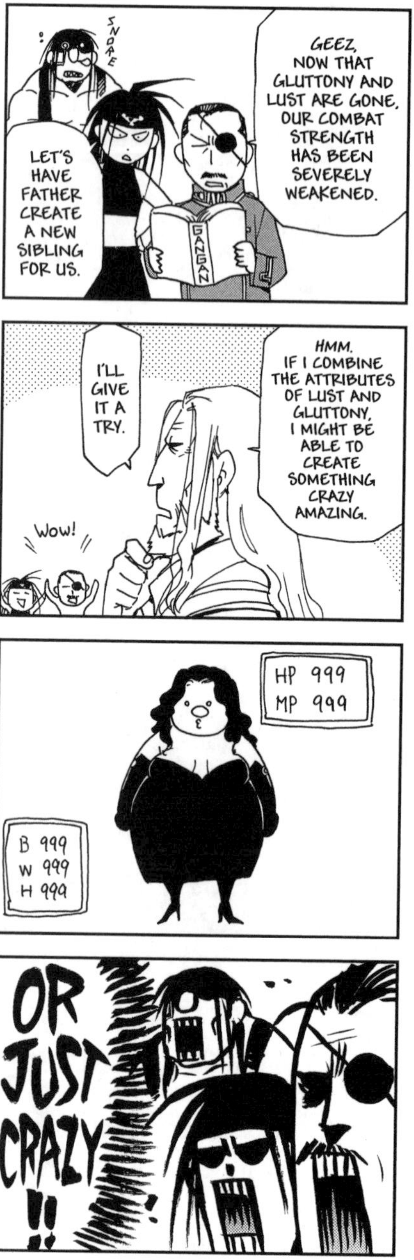
GEEZ, NOW THAT GLUTTONY AND LUST ARE GONE, OUR COMBAT STRENGTH HAS BEEN SEVERELY WEAKENED.
SNORE
LET'S HAVE FATHER CREATE A NEW SIBLING FOR US.
GANGAN
HMM. IF I COMBINE THE ATTRIBUTES OF LUST AND GLUTTONY, I MIGHT BE ABLE TO CREATE SOMETHING CRAZY AMAZING.
I'LL GIVE IT A TRY.
WOW!
HP 999
MP 999
B 999
W 999
H 999
OR JUST CRAZY!!

HERO FOR A DAY

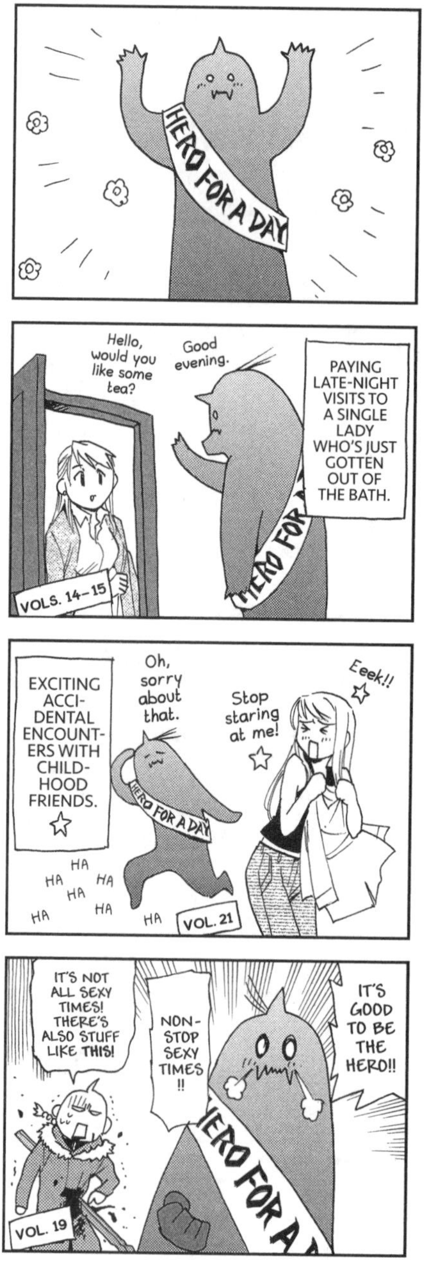
HERO FOR A DAY
PAYING LATE-NIGHT VISITS TO A SINGLE LADY WHO'S JUST GOTTEN OUT OF THE BATH.
Good evening.
Hello, would you like some tea?
VOLS. 14–15
Eeek!!
Stop staring at me!
Oh, sorry about that.
EXCITING ACCI-DENTAL ENCOUNT-ERS WITH CHILD-HOOD FRIENDS. ☆
HERO FOR A DAY
HA HA HA HA HA HA HA
VOL. 21
IT'S GOOD TO BE THE HERO!!
NON-STOP SEXY TIMES!!
IT'S NOT ALL SEXY TIMES! THERE'S ALSO STUFF LIKE **THIS**!
VOL. 19

ROACH MOTEL

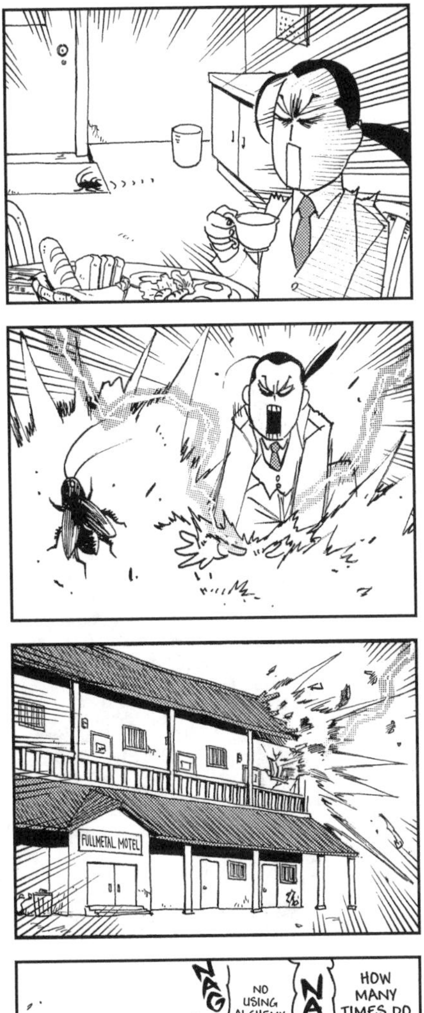
FULLMETAL MOTEL
HOW MANY TIMES DO I HAVE TO TELL YOU, MR. KIMBLEE?!
NAG
NO USING ALCHEMY ON ROACHES!
NAG
Sorry, ma'am.
NAG

FORTUNES

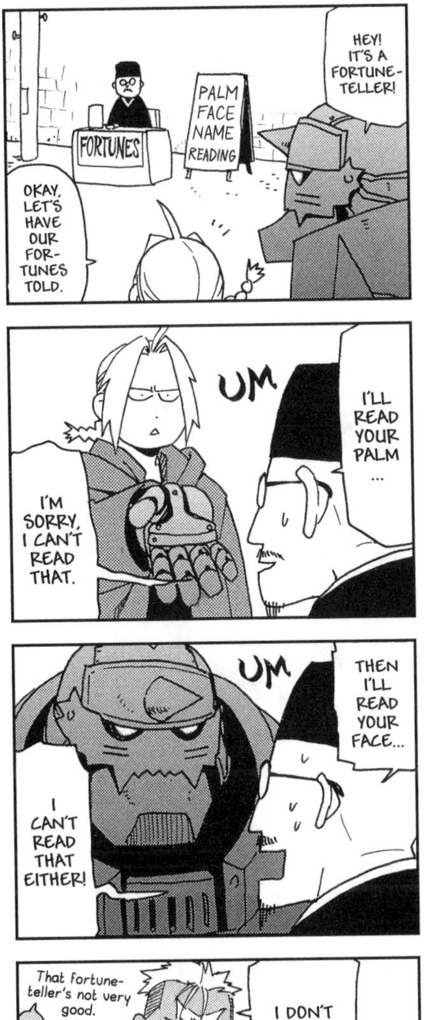
HEY! IT'S A FORTUNE-TELLER!
PALM FACE NAME READING
FORTUNES
OKAY, LET'S HAVE OUR FORTUNES TOLD.
UM
I'LL READ YOUR PALM...
I'M SORRY, I CAN'T READ THAT.
THEN I'LL READ YOUR FACE...
UM
I CAN'T READ THAT EITHER!
NAME...
UM
I DON'T NEED TO TELL YOU MY NAME, JERK!!
WHY DID YOU GUYS EVEN COME HERE?!
That fortune-teller's not very good.

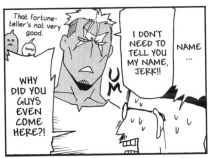

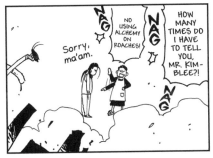

THE DANGERS OF OVEREATING

GOBBLE!!
WAAH!
HEH HEH HEH. I'VE ACQUIRED GLUTTONY'S ABILITIES.
MUNCH MUNCH
MUNCH
NOW I HAVE THE ADVANTAGE...
CHUBBA
I THINK YOU'VE MADE A MISTAKE.

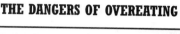

FULLMETAL SCIENCE KIDS!

TODAY YOU CAN HAVE SOME JUICE FOR SNACK TIME.
DON'T SPILL IT...
HEY!!
AL GOT MORE THAN I DID!
NO WAY.
YES WAY!! GO GET THE GRADUATED CYLINDERS FROM HOHENHEIM'S ROOM!!
SEE? AL, YOU GOT 1.4 MILLILITERS MORE THAN ME!!
YOUR LINE OF SIGHT HAS TO BE LEVEL WITH THE SURFACE OF THE WATER!
BIG BROTHER, YOU'RE SHORT. THAT'S WHY YOUR LINE OF SIGHT IS WRONG!
I'M LOOKING AT IT THE RIGHT WAY, STUPID!!
I-IT'S CUBICAL EXPANSION!! MY SEAT IS IN THE SUNLIGHT, SO THE TEMPERATURE OF THE JUICE INCREASED AND CAUSED THE VOLUME TO INCREASE TOO!!
RAR
THAT'S IMPOSSIBLE!! THE RATE OF CUBICAL EXPANSION IS 0.00021 TO EACH ONE DEGREE CELCIUS INCREASE!!
RAR
IT COULDN'T HAVE INCREASED THAT MUCH!!
RAR
THEN, BIG BROTHER, YOUR JUICE MUST HAVE EVAPORATED AND...
NUH-UH, IT'S...
NO WAY, IT'S...
SMART KIDS CAN BE SUCH A PAIN.

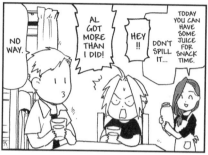

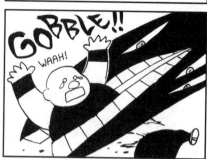

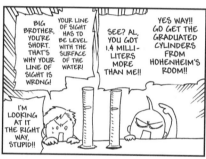

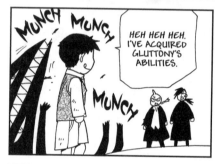

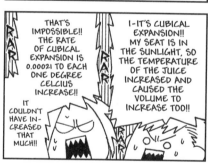

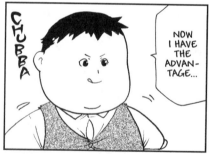

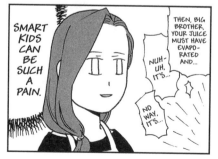

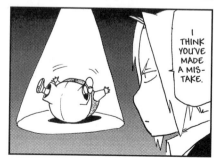

THE ROACH'S REVENGE

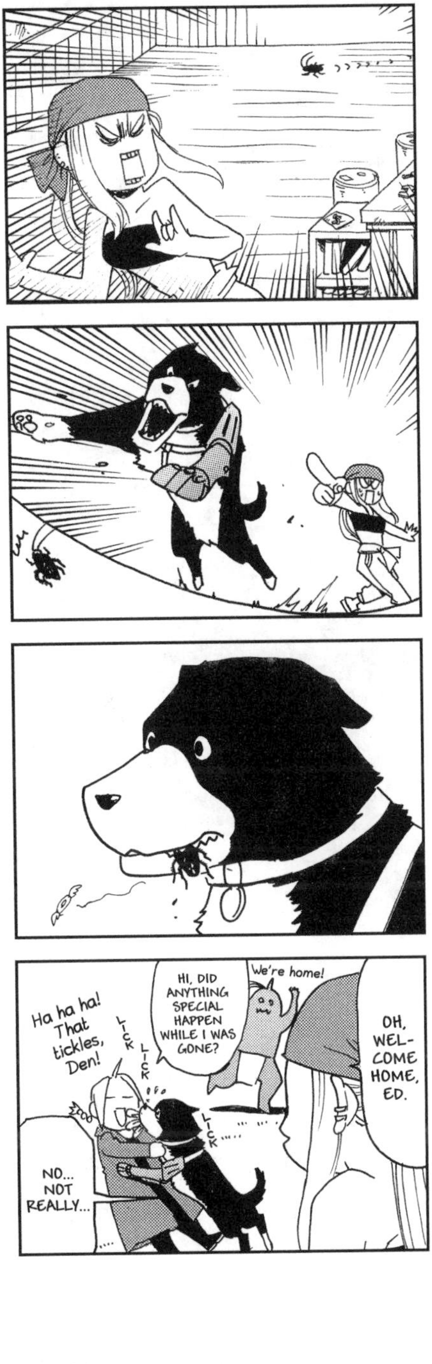

OH, WEL-COME HOME, ED.
We're home!
HI, DID ANYTHING SPECIAL HAPPEN WHILE I WAS GONE?
Ha ha ha! That tickles, Den!
LICK
LICK
LICK...
NO... NOT REALLY...

CAMPAIGN PROMISES

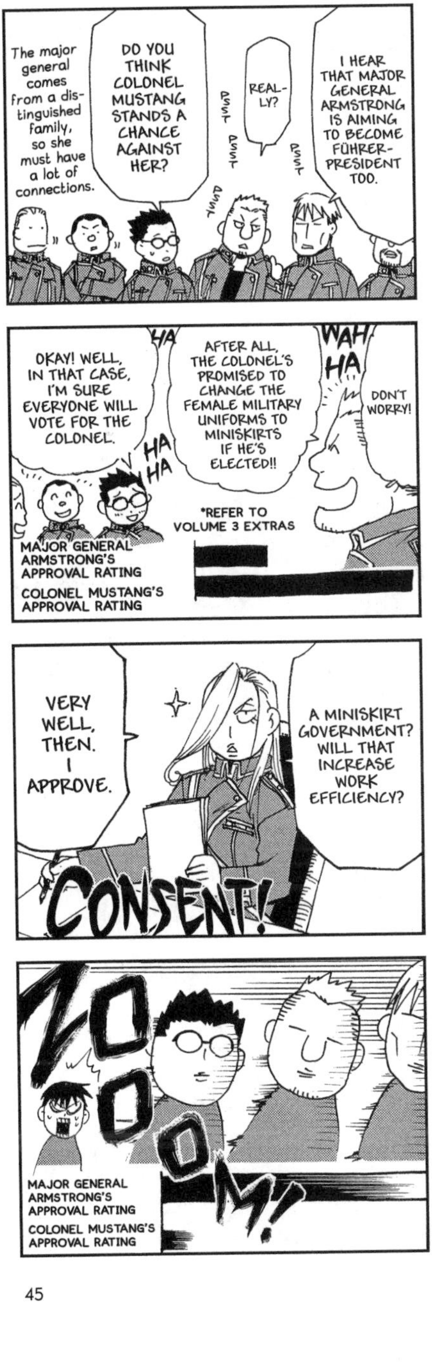

I HEAR THAT MAJOR GENERAL ARMSTRONG IS AIMING TO BECOME FÜHRER-PRESIDENT TOO.
PSST
REAL-LY?
PSST
PSST
PSST
DO YOU THINK COLONEL MUSTANG STANDS A CHANCE AGAINST HER?
The major general comes from a distinguished family, so she must have a lot of connections.
DON'T WORRY!
WAH HA
AFTER ALL, THE COLONEL'S PROMISED TO CHANGE THE FEMALE MILITARY UNIFORMS TO MINISKIRTS IF HE'S ELECTED!!
HA
OKAY! WELL, IN THAT CASE, I'M SURE EVERYONE WILL VOTE FOR THE COLONEL.
HA HA
*REFER TO VOLUME 3 EXTRAS
MAJOR GENERAL ARMSTRONG'S APPROVAL RATING
COLONEL MUSTANG'S APPROVAL RATING
A MINISKIRT GOVERNMENT? WILL THAT INCREASE WORK EFFICIENCY?
VERY WELL, THEN. I APPROVE.
CONSENT!
ZOOOOM!
MAJOR GENERAL ARMSTRONG'S APPROVAL RATING
COLONEL MUSTANG'S APPROVAL RATING

FULLMETAL IS COMING TO THE WII

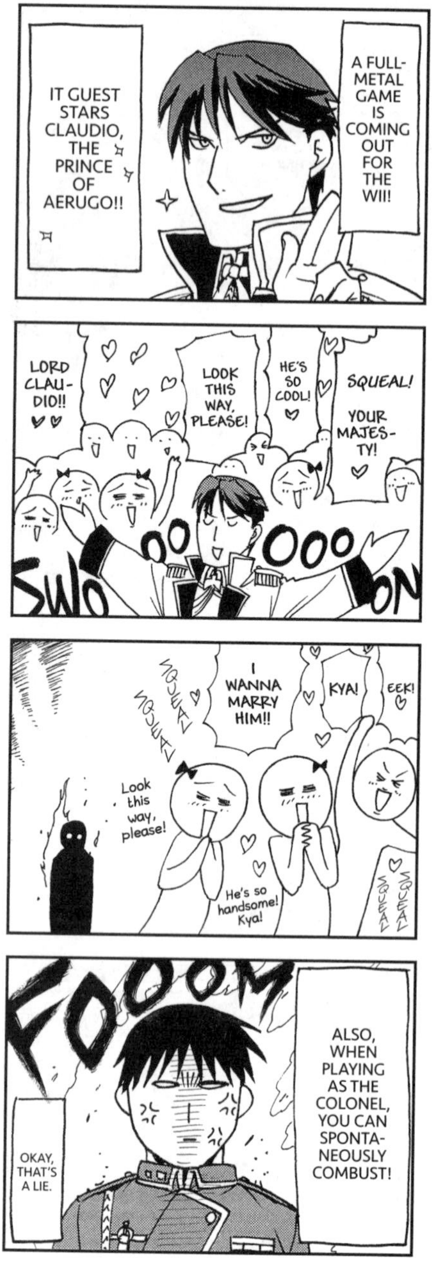
A FULL-METAL GAME IS COMING OUT FOR THE WII!
IT GUEST STARS CLAUDIO, THE PRINCE OF AERUGO!!
SQUEAL!
YOUR MAJES-TY!
HE'S SO COOL!
LOOK THIS WAY, PLEASE!
LORD CLAU-DIO!!
SWOOOOOOON
EEK!
KYA!
I WANNA MARRY HIM!!
SQUEAL SQUEAL
SQUEAL SQUEAL
Look this way, please!
He's so handsome! Kya!
ALSO, WHEN PLAYING AS THE COLONEL, YOU CAN SPONTA-NEOUSLY COMBUST!
FOOOOM
OKAY, THAT'S A LIE.

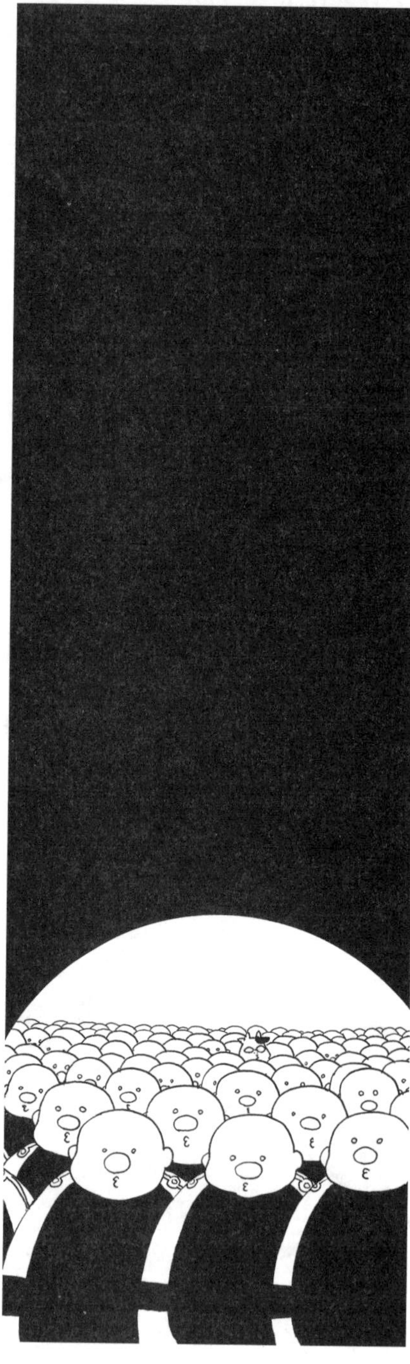

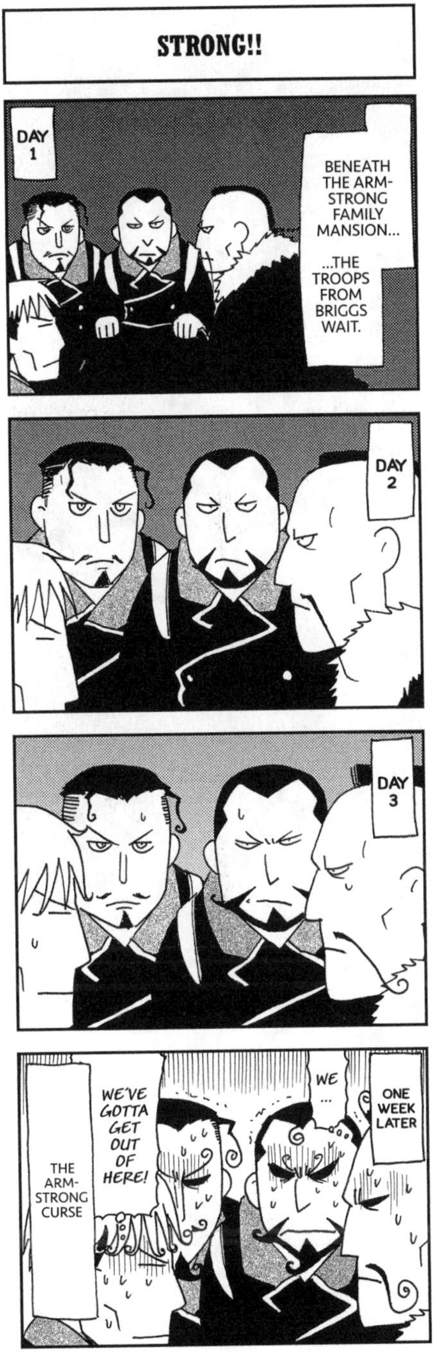
STRONG!!
DAY 1
BENEATH THE ARM-STRONG FAMILY MANSION...
...THE TROOPS FROM BRIGGS WAIT.
DAY 2
DAY 3
ONE WEEK LATER
WE ...
WE'VE GOTTA GET OUT OF HERE!
THE ARM-STRONG CURSE

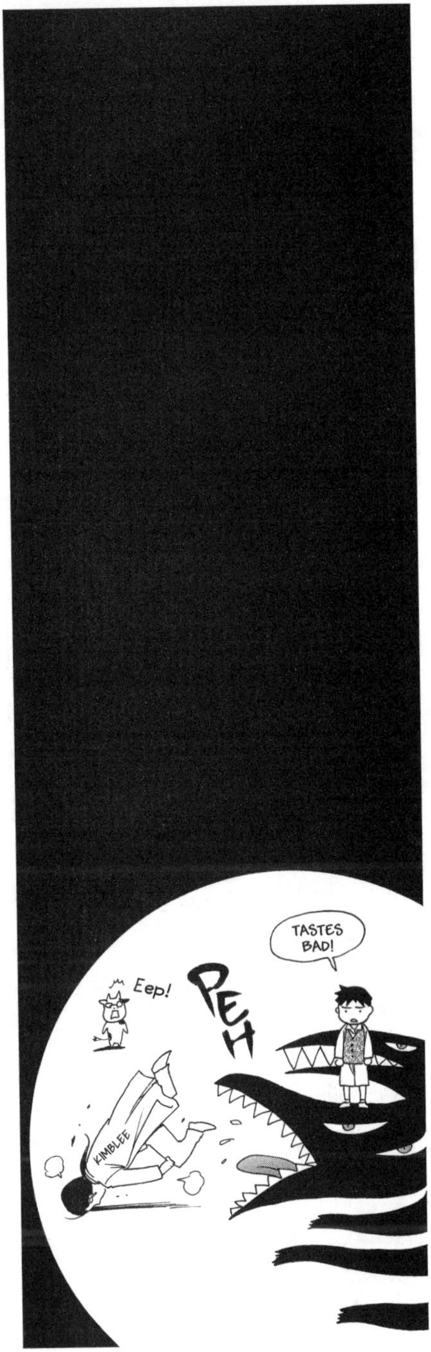
TASTES BAD!
PEH
Eep!
KIMBLEE

FROM CHAPTER 97

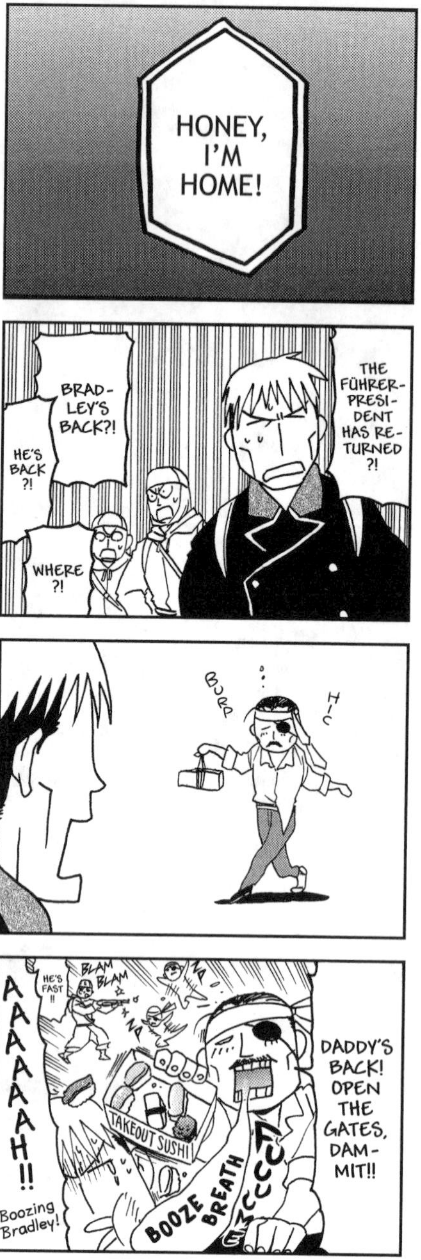
HONEY, I'M HOME!
THE FÜHRER-PRESIDENT HAS RETURNED?!
BRADLEY'S BACK?!
HE'S BACK?!
WHERE?!
HIC
BURP
DADDY'S BACK! OPEN THE GATES, DAMMIT!!
BLAM BLAM
HE'S FAST!!
TAKEOUT SUSHI
BOOZE BREATH
AAAAAAH!!
Boozing Bradley!

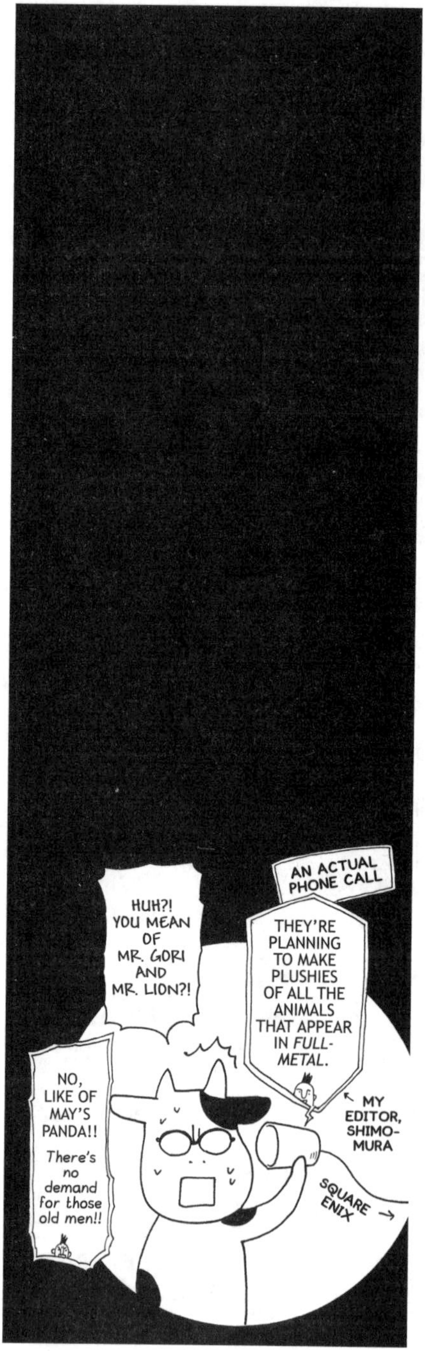
AN ACTUAL PHONE CALL
THEY'RE PLANNING TO MAKE PLUSHIES OF ALL THE ANIMALS THAT APPEAR IN *FULLMETAL*.
HUH?! YOU MEAN OF MR. GORI AND MR. LION?!
MY EDITOR, SHIMOMURA
SQUARE ENIX
NO, LIKE OF MAY'S PANDA!!
There's no demand for those old men!!

LOTS OF WEAKNESSES

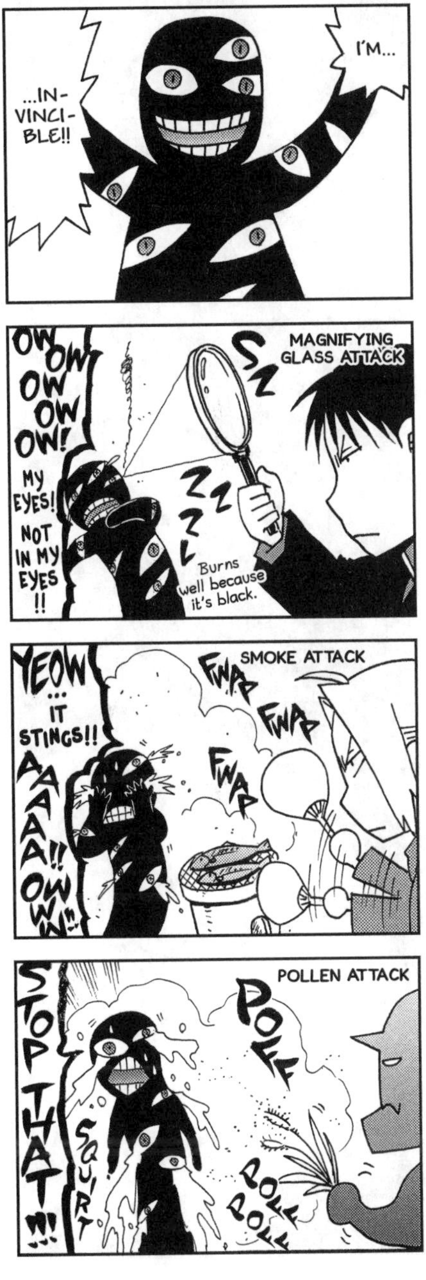
I'M...
...IN-VINCIBLE!!
MAGNIFYING GLASS ATTACK
Burns well because it's black.
OW OW OW OW OW!
MY EYES! NOT IN MY EYES!!
SMOKE ATTACK
FWAP
FWAP
FWAP
YEOW... IT STINGS!!
AAAAAAA!! OWWW!!
POLLEN ATTACK
POFF
POFF POFF POFF
SQUIRT
STOP THAT!!!

PSYCHOLOGICAL WARFARE

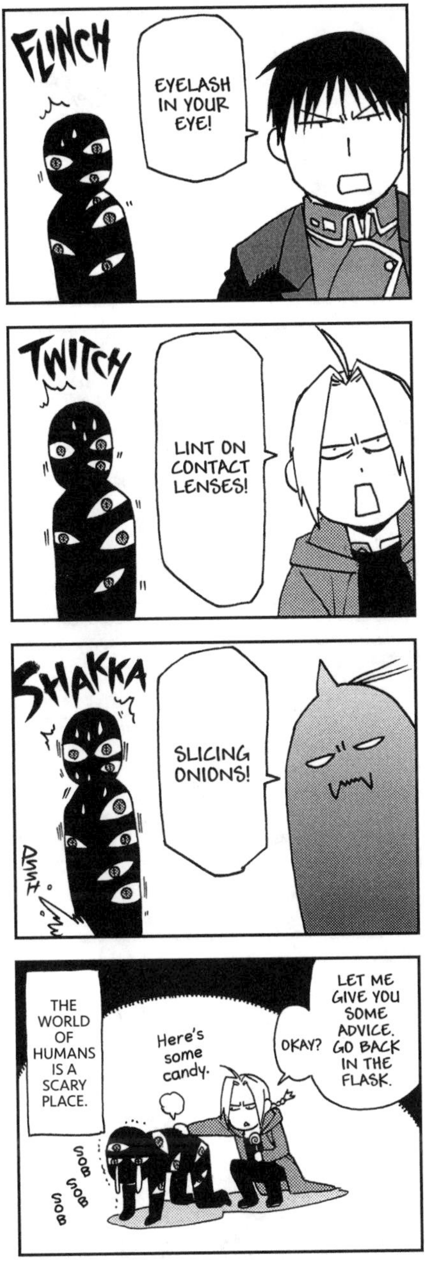
EYELASH IN YOUR EYE!
FLINCH
LINT ON CONTACT LENSES!
TWITCH
SLICING ONIONS!
SHAKKA
LET ME GIVE YOU SOME ADVICE. GO BACK IN THE FLASK.
OKAY?
Here's some candy.
THE WORLD OF HUMANS IS A SCARY PLACE.
SOB SOB SOB

AN RPG IS COMING OUT FOR THE PSP!

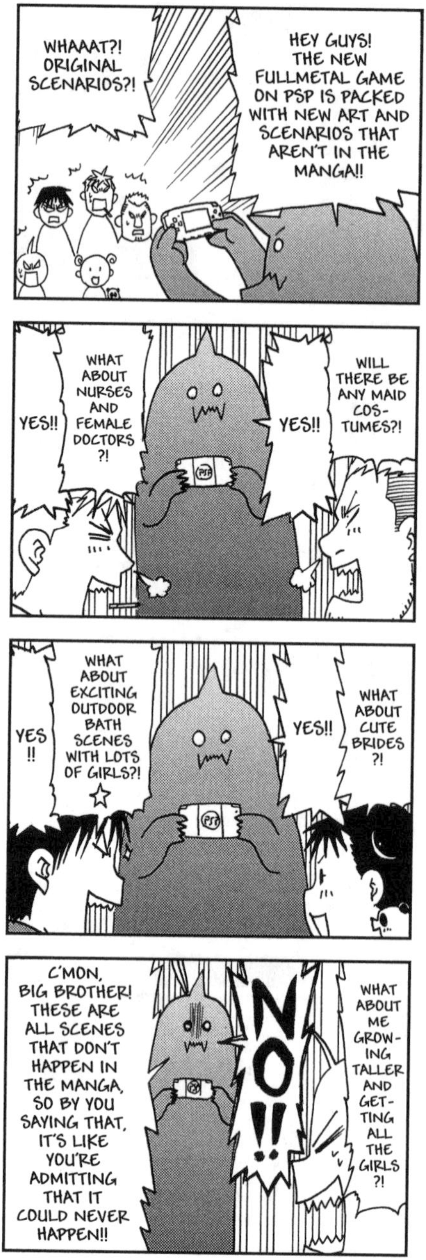
HEY GUYS! THE NEW FULLMETAL GAME ON PSP IS PACKED WITH NEW ART AND SCENARIOS THAT AREN'T IN THE MANGA!!
WHAAAT?! ORIGINAL SCENARIOS?!
WILL THERE BE ANY MAID COS-TUMES?!
YES!!
WHAT ABOUT NURSES AND FEMALE DOCTORS ?!
YES!!
WHAT ABOUT CUTE BRIDES ?!
YES!!
WHAT ABOUT EXCITING OUTDOOR BATH SCENES WITH LOTS OF GIRLS?!
YES !!
WHAT ABOUT ME GROW-ING TALLER AND GET-TING ALL THE GIRLS ?!
NO!!
C'MON, BIG BROTHER! THESE ARE ALL SCENES THAT DON'T HAPPEN IN THE MANGA, SO BY YOU SAYING THAT, IT'S LIKE YOU'RE ADMITTING THAT IT COULD NEVER HAPPEN!!

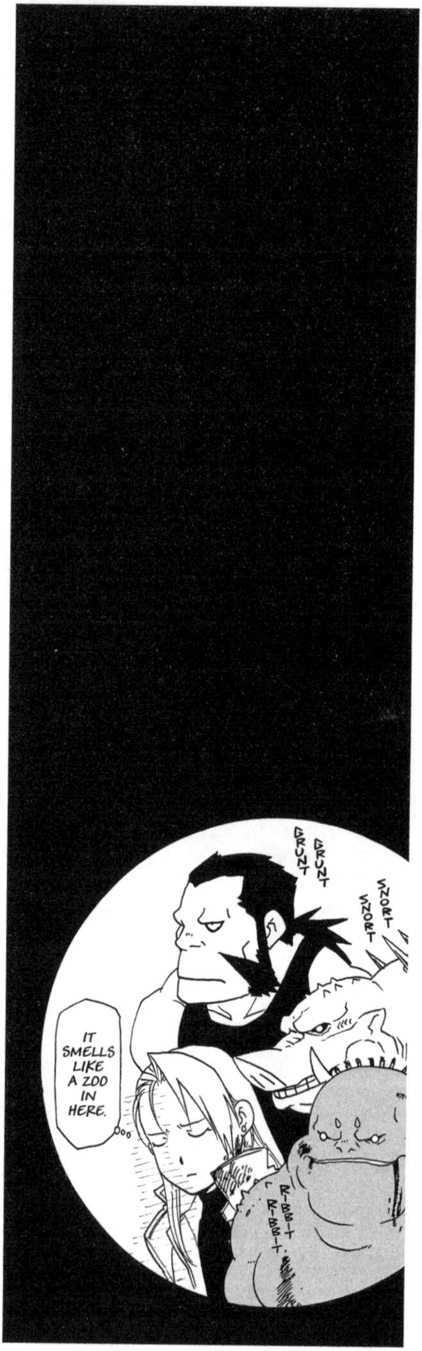
GRUNT GRUNT
SNORT SNORT
IT SMELLS LIKE A ZOO IN HERE.
RIBBIT RIBBIT

YOU BRUTE!!

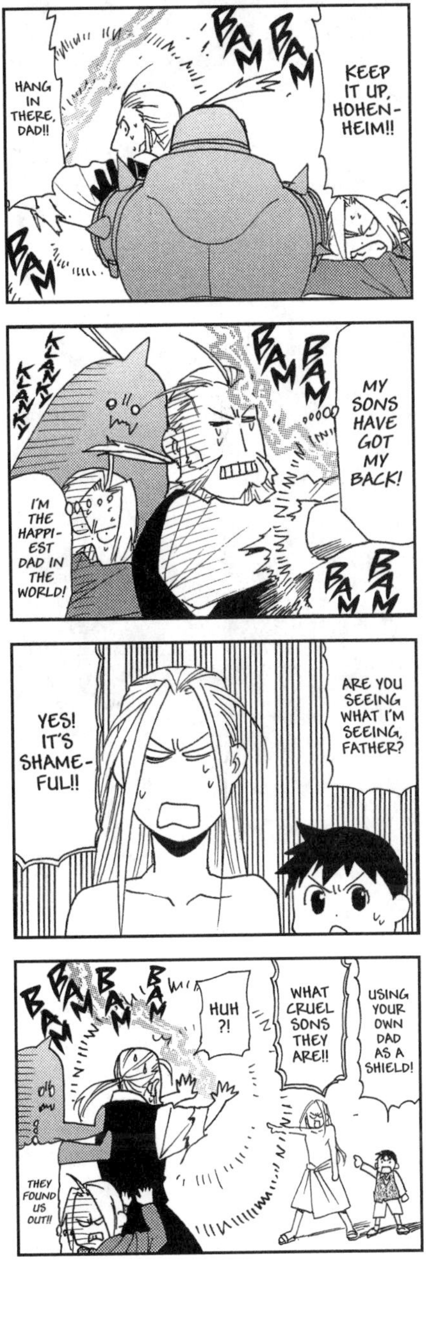
BAM BAM
KEEP IT UP, HOHENHEIM!!
HANG IN THERE, DAD!!
BAM
MY SONS HAVE GOT MY BACK!
BAM BAM
KLANK KLANK
I'M THE HAPPIEST DAD IN THE WORLD!
BAM BAM
ARE YOU SEEING WHAT I'M SEEING, FATHER?
YES! IT'S SHAMEFUL!!
USING YOUR OWN DAD AS A SHIELD!
WHAT CRUEL SONS THEY ARE!!
HUH?!
BAM BAM BAM BAM BAM
THEY FOUND US OUT!!

I WANT TO SEE

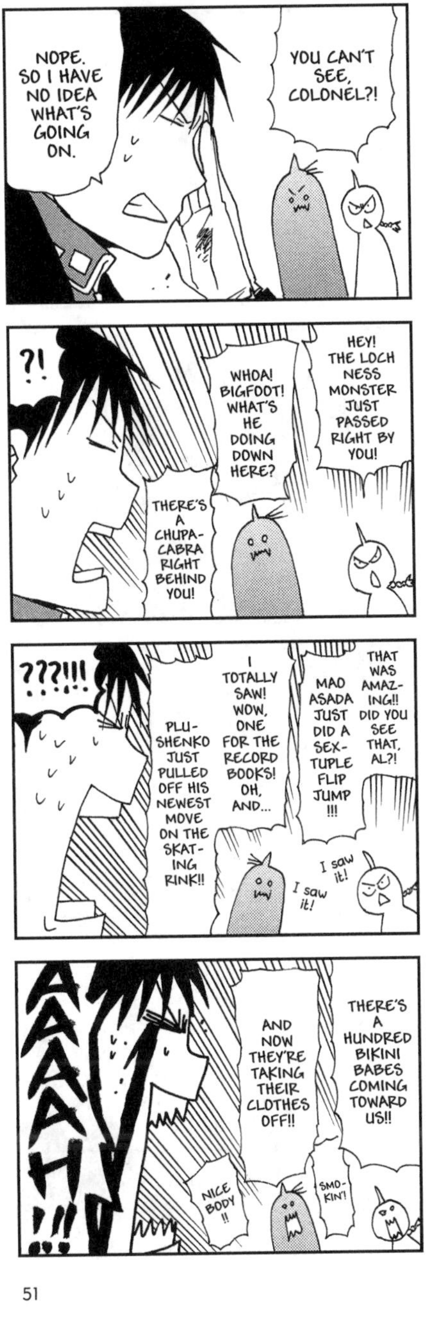
YOU CAN'T SEE, COLONEL?!
NOPE. SO I HAVE NO IDEA WHAT'S GOING ON.
HEY! THE LOCH NESS MONSTER JUST PASSED RIGHT BY YOU!
WHOA! BIGFOOT! WHAT'S HE DOING DOWN HERE?
?!
THERE'S A CHUPACABRA RIGHT BEHIND YOU!
THAT WAS AMAZING!! DID YOU SEE THAT, AL?!
MAO ASADA JUST DID A SEXTUPLE FLIP JUMP!!!
I TOTALLY SAW! WOW, ONE FOR THE RECORD BOOKS! OH, AND...
???!!!
PLUSHENKO JUST PULLED OFF HIS NEWEST MOVE ON THE SKATING RINK!!
I saw it!
I saw it!
THERE'S A HUNDRED BIKINI BABES COMING TOWARD US!!
AND NOW THEY'RE TAKING THEIR CLOTHES OFF!!
AAAAH!!!
SMOKIN'!
NICE BODY!!

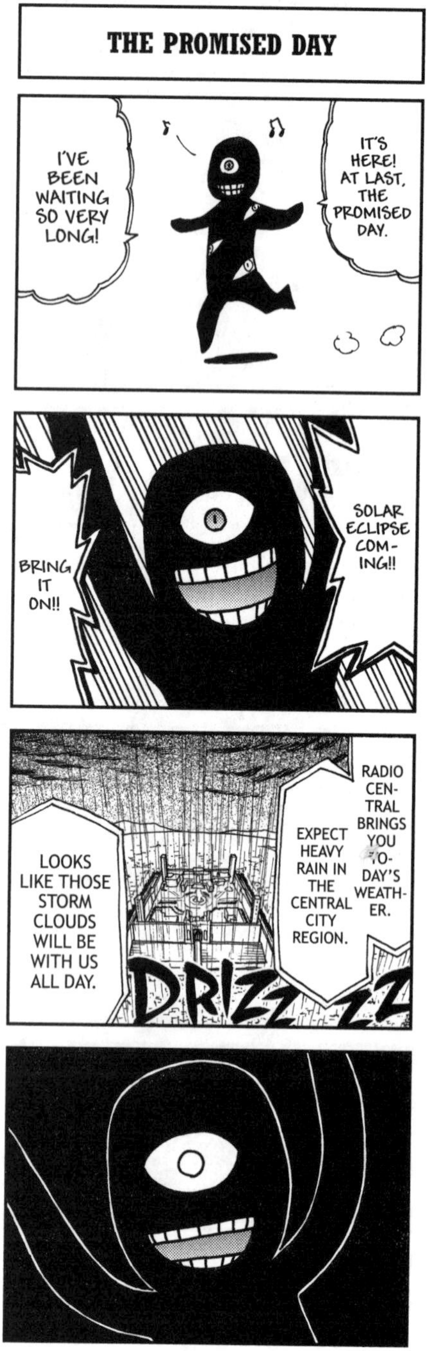
THE PROMISED DAY
IT'S HERE! AT LAST, THE PROMISED DAY.
I'VE BEEN WAITING SO VERY LONG!
SOLAR ECLIPSE COMING!!
BRING IT ON!!
RADIO CENTRAL BRINGS YOU TODAY'S WEATHER.
EXPECT HEAVY RAIN IN THE CENTRAL CITY REGION.
LOOKS LIKE THOSE STORM CLOUDS WILL BE WITH US ALL DAY.
DRIZZZZ

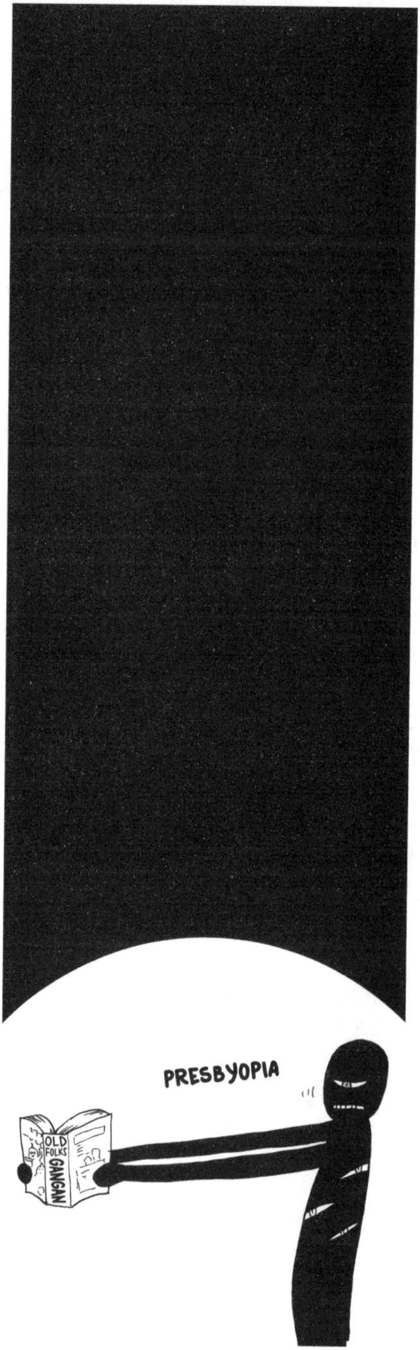
PRESBYOPIA
OLD FOLKS GANGAN

FROM SCRATCH

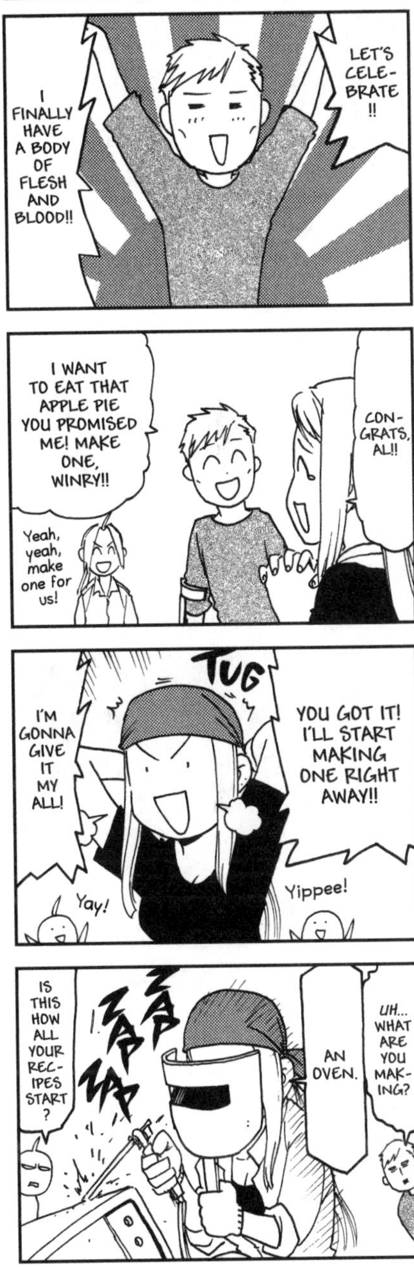
LET'S CELEBRATE!!
I FINALLY HAVE A BODY OF FLESH AND BLOOD!!
CONGRATS, AL!!
I WANT TO EAT THAT APPLE PIE YOU PROMISED ME! MAKE ONE, WINRY!!
Yeah, yeah, make one for us!
TUG
YOU GOT IT! I'LL START MAKING ONE RIGHT AWAY!!
I'M GONNA GIVE IT MY ALL!
Yippee!
Yay!
UH... WHAT ARE YOU MAKING?
AN OVEN.
ZAP
ZAP
ZAP
ZAP
IS THIS HOW ALL YOUR RECIPES START?

THE LAW

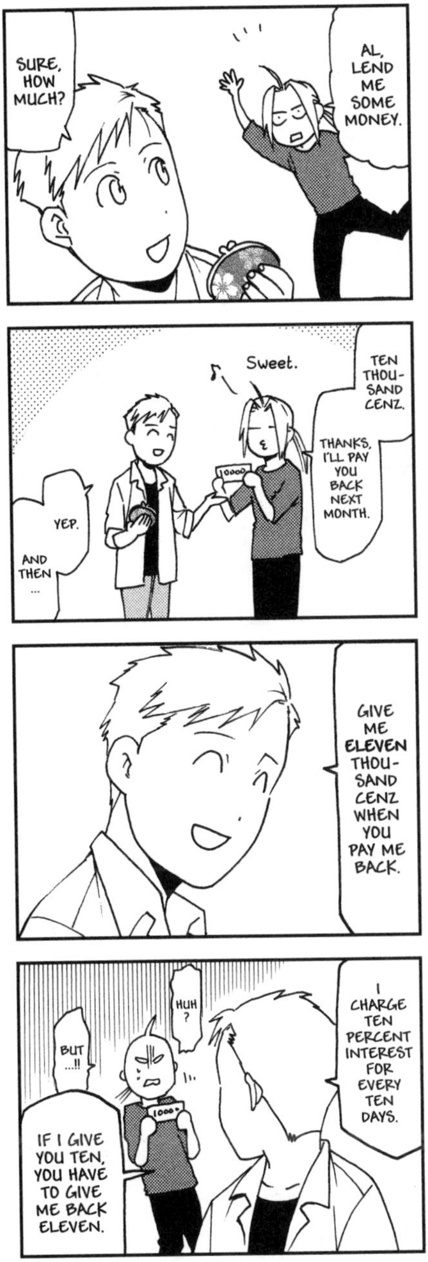
AL, LEND ME SOME MONEY.
SURE, HOW MUCH?
TEN THOUSAND CENZ.
Sweet.
THANKS, I'LL PAY YOU BACK NEXT MONTH.
YEP.
AND THEN ...
GIVE ME ELEVEN THOUSAND CENZ WHEN YOU PAY ME BACK.
I CHARGE TEN PERCENT INTEREST FOR EVERY TEN DAYS.
HUH?
BUT ...!!
IF I GIVE YOU TEN, YOU HAVE TO GIVE ME BACK ELEVEN.

♀

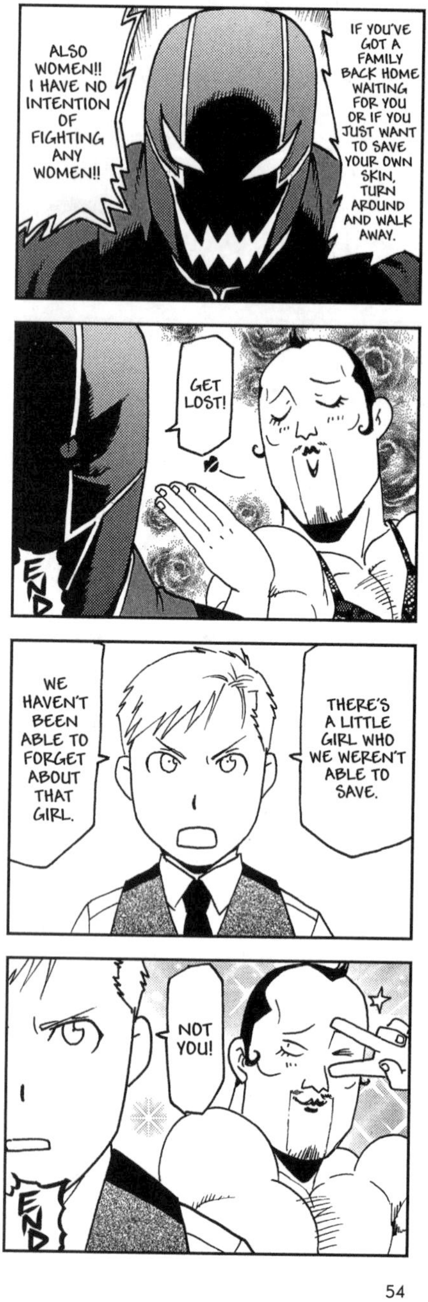
IF YOU'VE GOT A FAMILY BACK HOME WAITING FOR YOU OR IF YOU JUST WANT TO SAVE YOUR OWN SKIN, TURN AROUND AND WALK AWAY.
ALSO WOMEN!! I HAVE NO INTENTION OF FIGHTING ANY WOMEN!!
GET LOST!
END
THERE'S A LITTLE GIRL WHO WE WEREN'T ABLE TO SAVE.
WE HAVEN'T BEEN ABLE TO FORGET ABOUT THAT GIRL.
NOT YOU!
END

THE PYTHAGORAS SWITCH

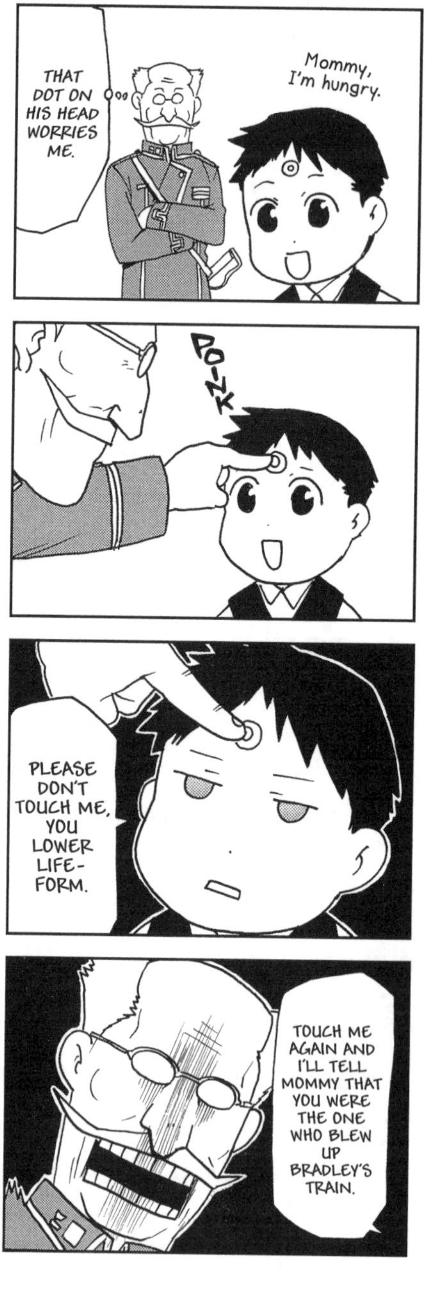
Mommy, I'm hungry.
THAT DOT ON HIS HEAD WORRIES ME.
POINK
PLEASE DON'T TOUCH ME, YOU LOWER LIFE-FORM.
TOUCH ME AGAIN AND I'LL TELL MOMMY THAT YOU WERE THE ONE WHO BLEW UP BRADLEY'S TRAIN.

UNEXPECTED RESULTS

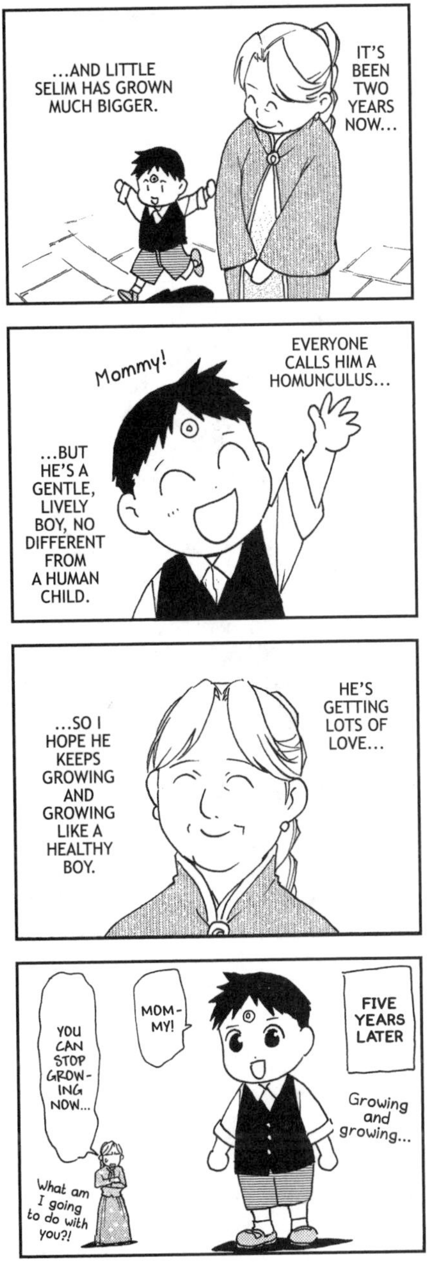
IT'S BEEN TWO YEARS NOW...
...AND LITTLE SELIM HAS GROWN MUCH BIGGER.
EVERYONE CALLS HIM A HOMUNCULUS...
Mommy!
...BUT HE'S A GENTLE, LIVELY BOY, NO DIFFERENT FROM A HUMAN CHILD.
HE'S GETTING LOTS OF LOVE...
...SO I HOPE HE KEEPS GROWING AND GROWING LIKE A HEALTHY BOY.
FIVE YEARS LATER
Growing and growing...
MOM-MY!
YOU CAN STOP GROW-ING NOW...
What am I going to do with you?!

THE EMBARRASSING PROTAGONIST

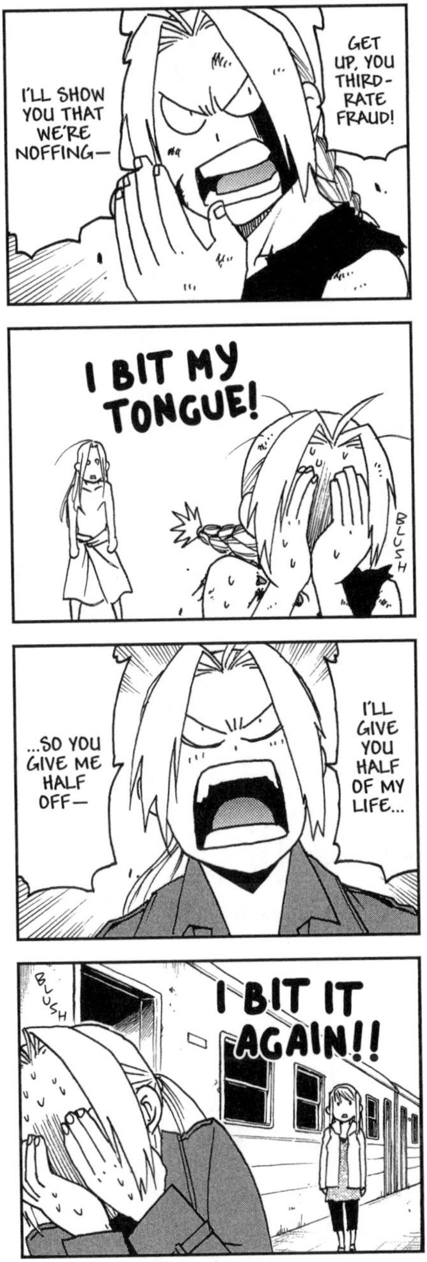
GET UP, YOU THIRD-RATE FRAUD!
I'LL SHOW YOU THAT WE'RE NOFFING—
I BIT MY TONGUE!
BLUSH
I'LL GIVE YOU HALF OF MY LIFE...
...SO YOU GIVE ME HALF OFF—
I BIT IT AGAIN!!
BLUSH

DVDs

DVDs
Volume 1, December 2003

PREACHING THE GOSPEL OF LETO: MANGA

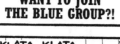

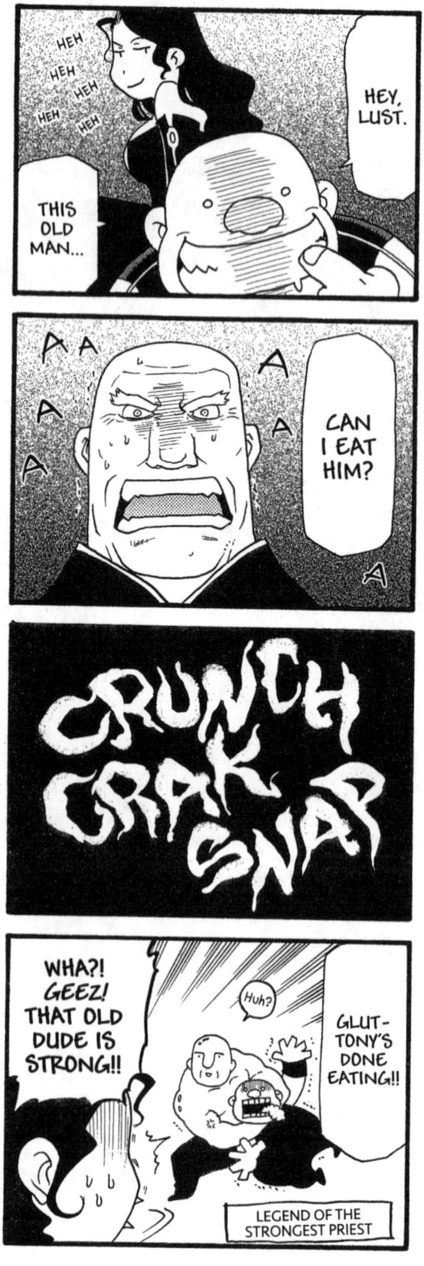
HEY, LUST.
HEH HEH HEH HEH HEH HEH
THIS OLD MAN...
A A A A A A A
CAN I EAT HIM?
CRUNCH CRAK SNAP
GLUT-TONY'S DONE EATING!!
Huh?
WHA?! GEEZ! THAT OLD DUDE IS STRONG!!
LEGEND OF THE STRONGEST PRIEST

DVDs
Volume 2, January 2004

WANT TO JOIN THE BLUE GROUP?!

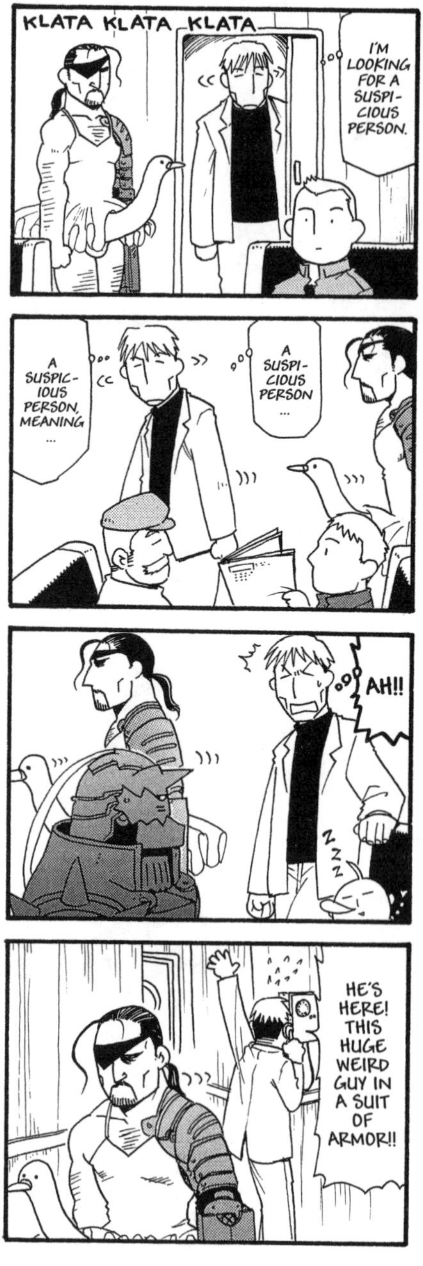
I'M LOOKING FOR A SUSPI-CIOUS PERSON.
KLATA KLATA KLATA
A SUSPI-CIOUS PERSON ...
A SUSPIC-IOUS PERSON, MEANING ...
AH!!
Z Z Z
HE'S HERE! THIS HUGE WEIRD GUY IN A SUIT OF ARMOR!!

IS THAT REALLY OKAY, HERO?

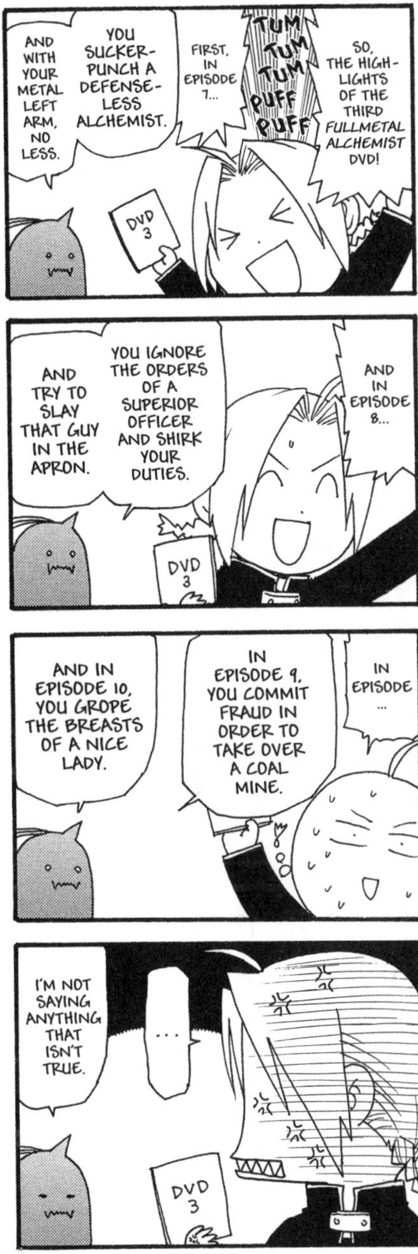
SO, THE HIGH-LIGHTS OF THE THIRD FULLMETAL ALCHEMIST DVD!
TUM TUM TUM PUFF PUFF
FIRST, IN EPISODE 7...
YOU SUCKER-PUNCH A DEFENSE-LESS ALCHEMIST.
AND WITH YOUR METAL LEFT ARM, NO LESS.
DVD 3
AND IN EPISODE 8...
YOU IGNORE THE ORDERS OF A SUPERIOR OFFICER AND SHIRK YOUR DUTIES.
AND TRY TO SLAY THAT GUY IN THE APRON.
DVD 3
IN EPISODE ...
IN EPISODE 9, YOU COMMIT FRAUD IN ORDER TO TAKE OVER A COAL MINE.
AND IN EPISODE 10, YOU GROPE THE BREASTS OF A NICE LADY.
...
I'M NOT SAYING ANYTHING THAT ISN'T TRUE.
DVD 3

YESTERDAY'S FRIEND IS TODAY'S ENEMY

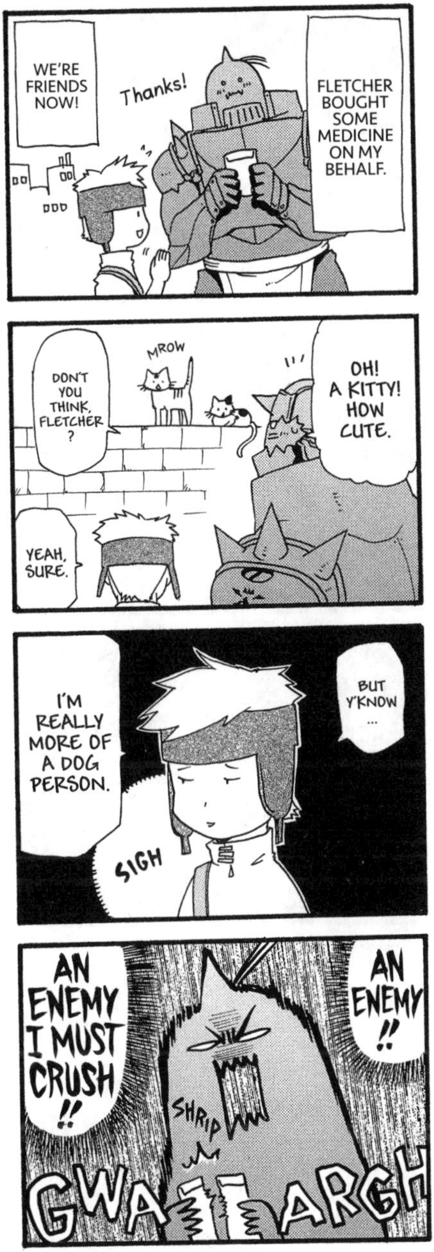
FLETCHER BOUGHT SOME MEDICINE ON MY BEHALF.
Thanks!
WE'RE FRIENDS NOW!
OH! A KITTY! HOW CUTE.
MROW
DON'T YOU THINK, FLETCHER?
YEAH, SURE.
BUT Y'KNOW ...
I'M REALLY MORE OF A DOG PERSON.
SIGH
AN ENEMY!!
AN ENEMY I MUST CRUSH!!
SHRIP
GWA ARGH

DVDs
Volume 5, May 2004

NIGHTS IN RESEMBOOL

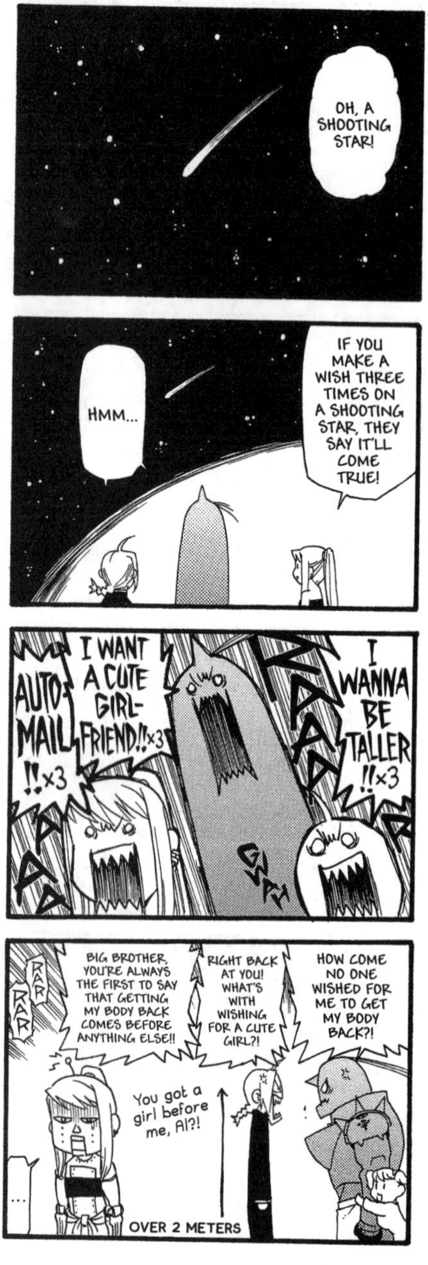
OH, A SHOOTING STAR!
IF YOU MAKE A WISH THREE TIMES ON A SHOOTING STAR, THEY SAY IT'LL COME TRUE!
HMM...
I WANNA BE TALLER!!×3
I WANT A CUTE GIRLFRIEND!!×3
AUTOMAIL!!×3
HOW COME NO ONE WISHED FOR ME TO GET MY BODY BACK?
RIGHT BACK AT YOU! WHAT'S WITH WISHING FOR A CUTE GIRL?!
BIG BROTHER, YOU'RE ALWAYS THE FIRST TO SAY THAT GETTING MY BODY BACK COMES BEFORE ANYTHING ELSE!!
RAR
RAR
RAR
You got a girl before me, Al?!
...
OVER 2 METERS

DVDs
Volume 6, June 2004

THE CHIMERA'S CRYING...NOT

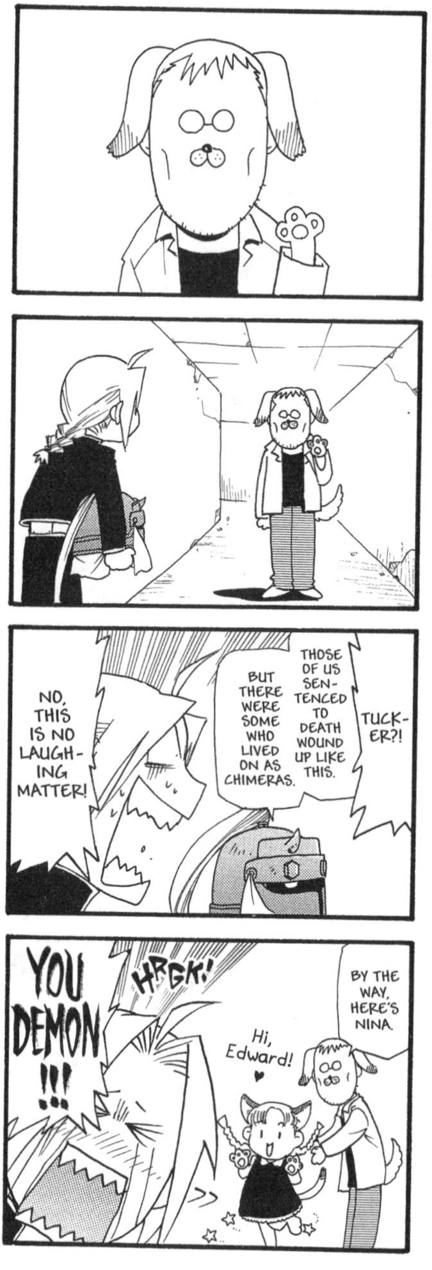
TUCKER?!
THOSE OF US SENTENCED TO DEATH WOUND UP LIKE THIS.
BUT THERE WERE SOME WHO LIVED ON AS CHIMERAS.
NO, THIS IS NO LAUGHING MATTER!
BY THE WAY, HERE'S NINA.
HRGK!
Hi, Edward! ♥
YOU DEMON!!!

MUSCLE FEST

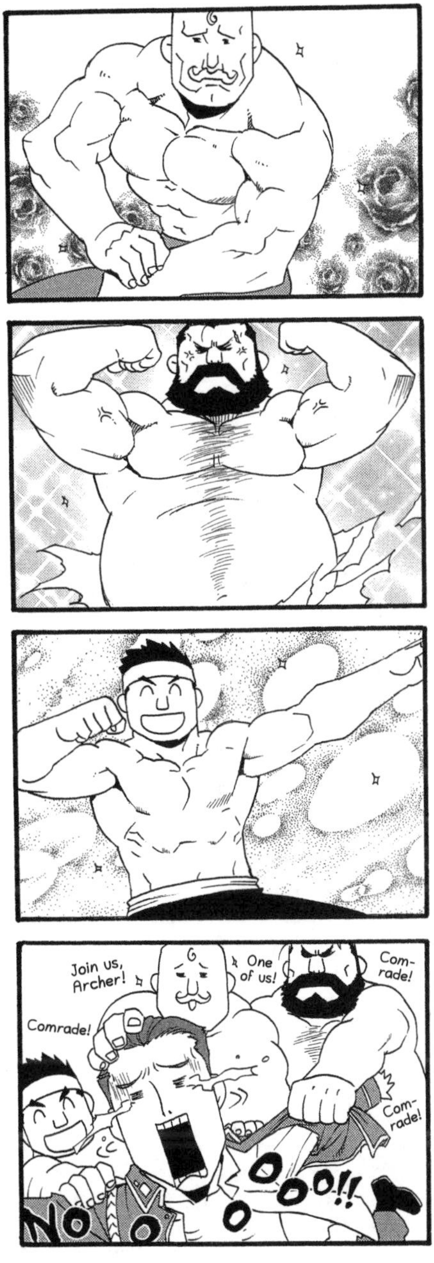
Com-rade!
One of us!
Join us, Archer!
Comrade!
Com-rade!
NOOOOOO!!

LEADER OF A DEN OF THIEVES

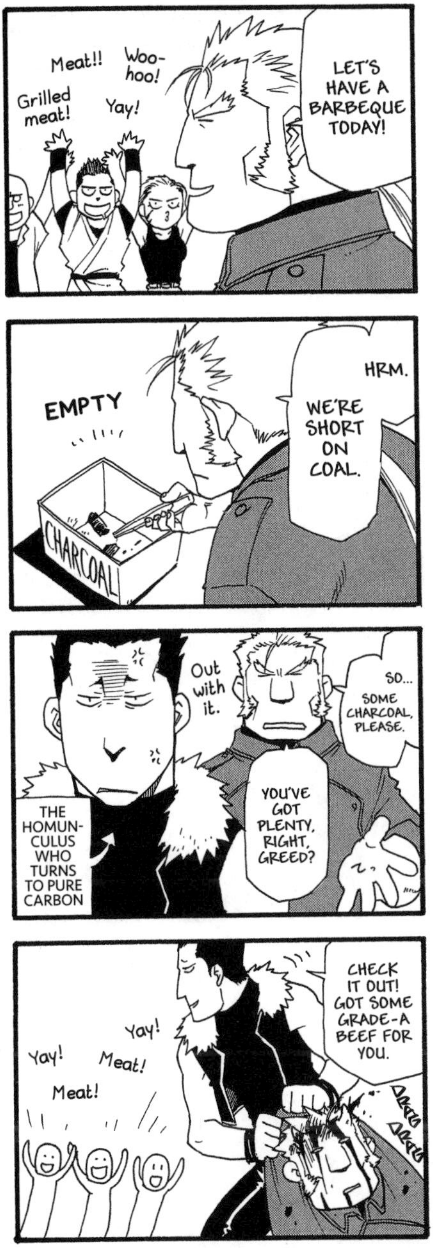
LET'S HAVE A BARBEQUE TODAY!
Woo-hoo!
Meat!!
Yay!
Grilled meat!
HRM.
WE'RE SHORT ON COAL.
EMPTY
CHARCOAL
SO... SOME CHARCOAL, PLEASE.
Out with it.
YOU'VE GOT PLENTY, RIGHT, GREED?
THE HOMUNCULUS WHO TURNS TO PURE CARBON
CHECK IT OUT! GOT SOME GRADE-A BEEF FOR YOU.
Yay!
Meat.
Yay!
Meat!

DVDs
Volume 9, September 2004

ENVY'S TOTALLY GOING TO CRY

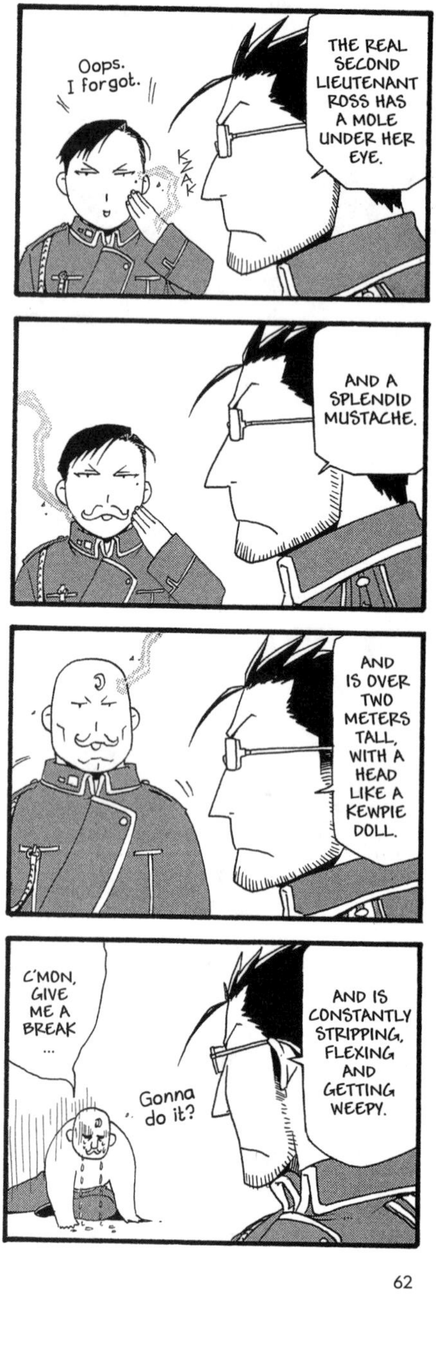
THE REAL SECOND LIEUTENANT ROSS HAS A MOLE UNDER HER EYE.
KZAK
Oops. I forgot.
AND A SPLENDID MUSTACHE.
AND IS OVER TWO METERS TALL, WITH A HEAD LIKE A KEWPIE DOLL.
AND IS CONSTANTLY STRIPPING, FLEXING AND GETTING WEEPY.
Gonna do it?
C'MON, GIVE ME A BREAK ...

DVDs
Volume 10, October 2004

LITERALLY

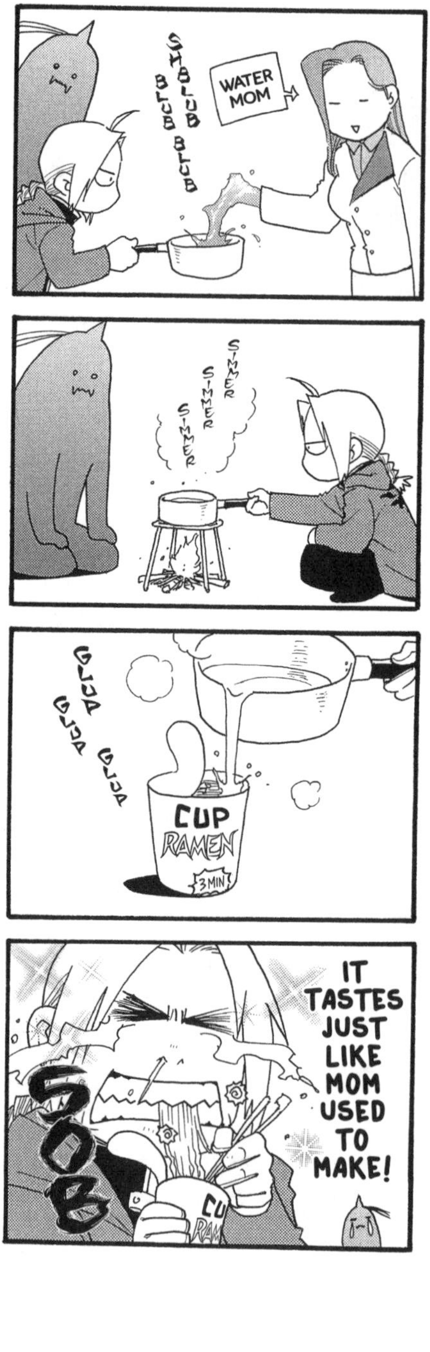
WATER MOM
SHBLUB
BLUB BLUB BLUB
SIMMER
SIMMER
SIMMER
GLUP GLUP GLUP GLUP
CUP RAMEN
3 MIN
IT TASTES JUST LIKE MOM USED TO MAKE!
SOB

DVDs
Volume 11, November 2004

AWESOME EYE

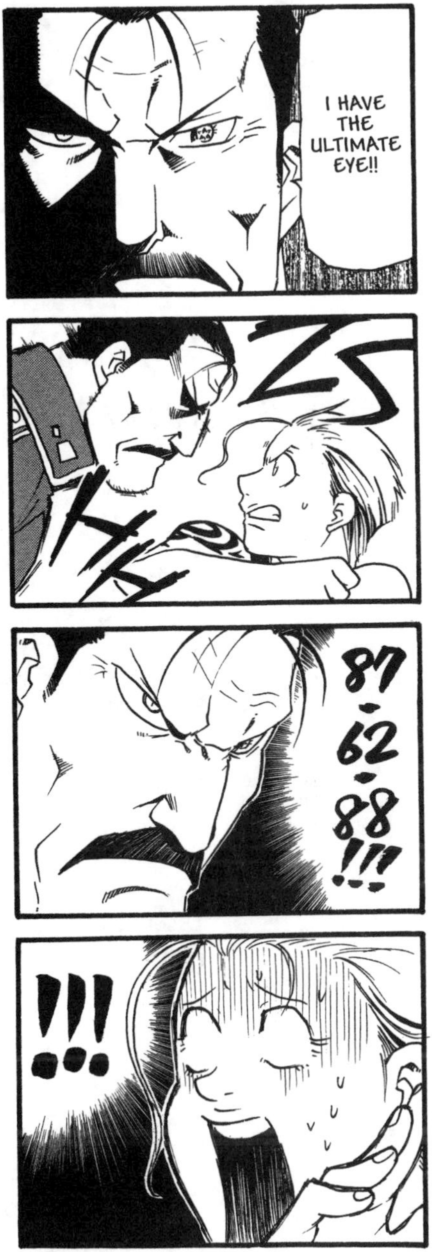
I HAVE THE ULTIMATE EYE!!
87-62-88!!!
!!!

DVDs
Volume 12, December 2004

DINNER BUDDIES

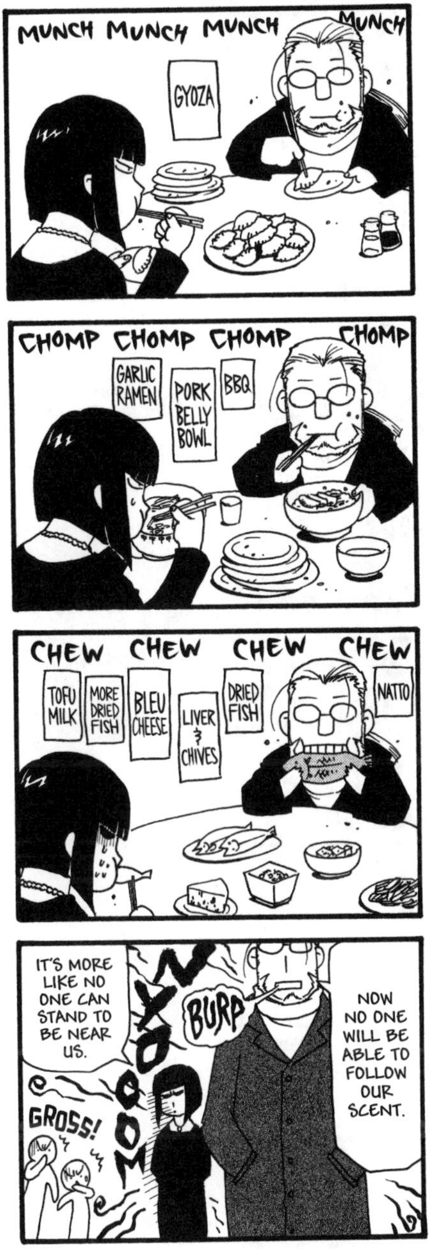
MUNCH MUNCH MUNCH MUNCH
GYOZA
CHOMP CHOMP CHOMP CHOMP
BBQ
PORK BELLY BOWL
GARLIC RAMEN
CHEW CHEW CHEW CHEW
NATTO
DRIED FISH
LIVER & CHIVES
BLEU CHEESE
MORE DRIED FISH
TOFU MILK
NOW NO ONE WILL BE ABLE TO FOLLOW OUR SCENT.
BURP
IT'S MORE LIKE NO ONE CAN STAND TO BE NEAR US.
WOOOOM
GROSS!

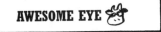

IMPOSSIBLE

TA-DA!
I'M GONNA DEFEAT ...
... SLOTH!
SLAM
SHUT UP, YOU LITTLE BEAN-SIZED SHRIMPY DWARF! YOU LOOK LIKE YOU NEED TO GET YOUR DIAPER CHANGED!
WHIP
BOX LUNCH
IF YOU'RE GONNA TALK IN YOUR SLEEP, YOU MIGHT AS WELL GET UP AND GET TO SCHOOL!
AND YOU, AL! WHAT'S UP WITH THAT DUMB LOIN-CLOTH?!
YOU'LL MAKE PEOPLE THINK WE CAN'T AFFORD CLOTHING IN THIS HOUSE!
IF ALL THOSE NEIGHBOR-HOOD GOSSIPS GET AHOLD OF THAT, IT'LL BE NO END OF TROUBLE FOR ME! SHAPE UP!
AND YOU, DARLING, YOU SCAMPER OFF WITH SOME WOMAN, LEAVING US WITH NO MONEY?!
I'm so sorry, Mother!
OUR HOUSEHOLD BUDGET IS IN DIRE STRAIGHTS! GET A JOB, YOU DEADBEAT!
THE STRONGEST MOM

DVDs
Fullmetal Alchemist Anime
Festival Event Bonus, December 2004

HAPPY END...?

MY BROTHER WITH HIS HAIR-TRIGGER TEMPER ISN'T HERE...
Good afternoon!
'Sup?
...SO I NO LONGER WIND UP GETTING INTO FIGHTS WITH THE LOCAL THUGS.
WHEN I'M IN RESEMBOOL I DON'T NEED TO FEAR FOR MY LIFE...
THE FRESH AIR IS INVIGORATING AND THE WHOLESOME FOOD IS DELICIOUS.
MY LIFE IS FULL OF WOMEN.
THEY ARE ALL KIND AND DOTE ON ME IN THIS BODY.
I NEVER KNEW THAT I'D BE SO HAPPY WITHOUT MY BROTHER!
AH HA HA!
I HOPE I CAN STAY THIS WAY FOREVER!
HEE HEE HEE!
HEH HEH HEH!
JUST YOU WAIT FOR THE MOVIE!!

ONE OF THOSE BLU-THINGIES

I AM THE RESULT OF GENETICS PASSED DOWN THROUGH GENERATIONS OF THE ARMSTRONG FAMILY...
ARTISTIC ALCHEMY!
BREDA
THE ONE WAITING FOR THE COLONEL ISN'T THE LIEUTENANT.
OH MY. IF YOU DO ANY MORE THAN THAT, I, YOKI, WON'T BE ABLE TO KEEP QUIET ABOUT IT.
YOKI
BLACK HAYATE
WOOF WOOF WO-WOOF WOOF
THESE BLU-RAYS ARE SO AMAZING!!
THE PICTURE IS SO BEAUTIFUL!
I'll go myself!
SHAMBALL
THAT'S ENOUGH!!

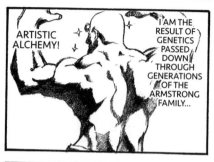

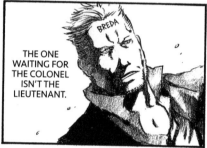

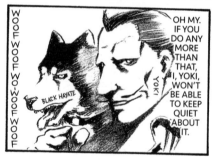

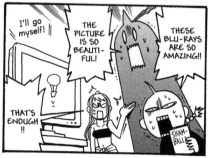

DVDs

Blu-ray Disc Box Bonus, October 2014

HOW MUSTANG'S DOING

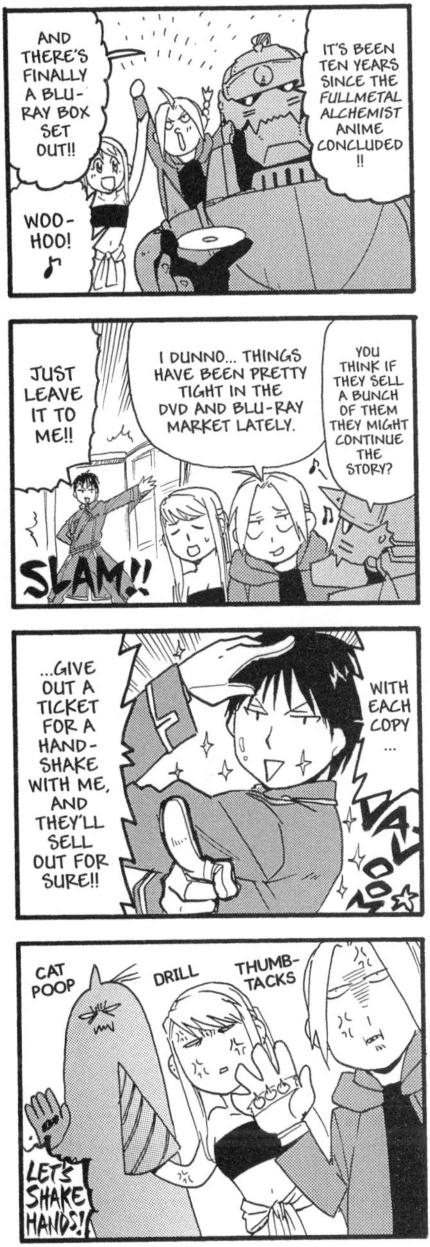
IT'S BEEN TEN YEARS SINCE THE FULLMETAL ALCHEMIST ANIME CONCLUDED!!
AND THERE'S FINALLY A BLU-RAY BOX SET OUT!!
WOO-HOO!
YOU THINK IF THEY SELL A BUNCH OF THEM THEY MIGHT CONTINUE THE STORY?
I DUNNO... THINGS HAVE BEEN PRETTY TIGHT IN THE DVD AND BLU-RAY MARKET LATELY.
JUST LEAVE IT TO ME!!
SLAM!!
WITH EACH COPY ...
...GIVE OUT A TICKET FOR A HAND-SHAKE WITH ME, AND THEY'LL SELL OUT FOR SURE!!
VA-VOOM☆
THUMB-TACKS
DRILL
CAT POOP
LET'S SHAKE HANDS!

HOW THE HOMUNCULI ARE DOING

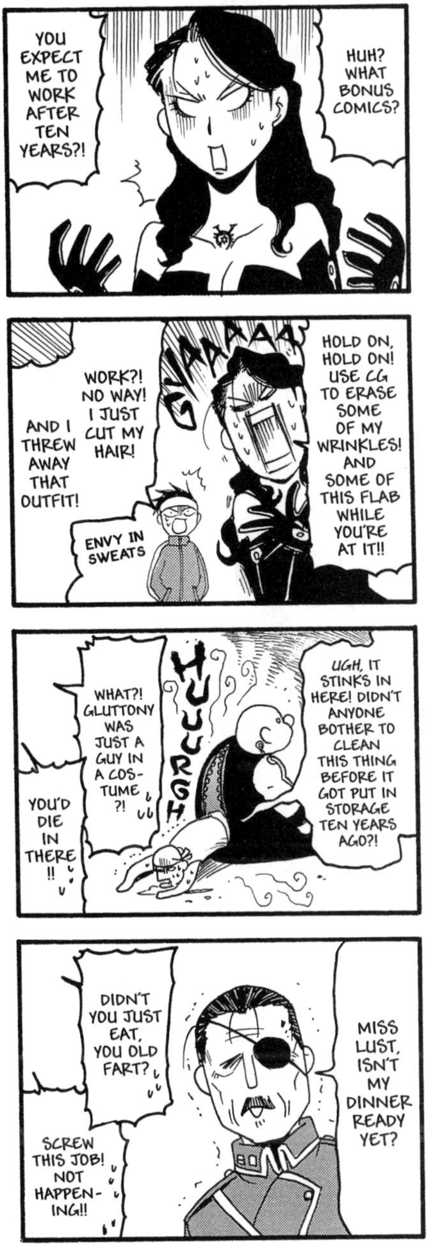
HUH? WHAT BONUS COMICS?
YOU EXPECT ME TO WORK AFTER TEN YEARS?!
HOLD ON, HOLD ON! USE CG TO ERASE SOME OF MY WRINKLES! AND SOME OF THIS FLAB WHILE YOU'RE AT IT!!
WORK?! NO WAY! I JUST CUT MY HAIR!
AND I THREW AWAY THAT OUTFIT!
ENVY IN SWEATS
UGH, IT STINKS IN HERE! DIDN'T ANYONE BOTHER TO CLEAN THIS THING BEFORE IT GOT PUT IN STORAGE TEN YEARS AGO?!
HUUURGH
WHAT?! GLUTTONY WAS JUST A GUY IN A COSTUME?!
YOU'D DIE IN THERE!!
MISS LUST, ISN'T MY DINNER READY YET?
DIDN'T YOU JUST EAT, YOU OLD FART?
SCREW THIS JOB! NOT HAPPENING!!

DVDs
Fullmetal Alchemist: The Conqueror of Shamballa
Absolute Cinema Guide Bonus, September 2005

GLOMP
ED!!!
WHOA!!
UH...
ER...
UM...
WINR...
...EE!!
KRAK
LET'S GO HOME, AL.
DRAG
CONGRATS TO THE HAPPY COUPLE!
DRAG
DRAG
BUB BUB

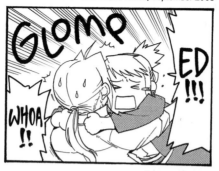

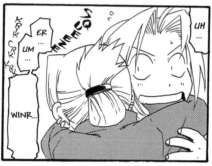

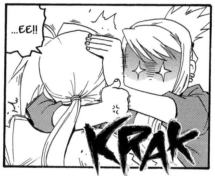

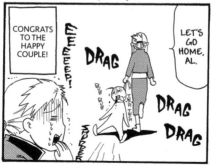

IT'S BEEN TEN YEARS

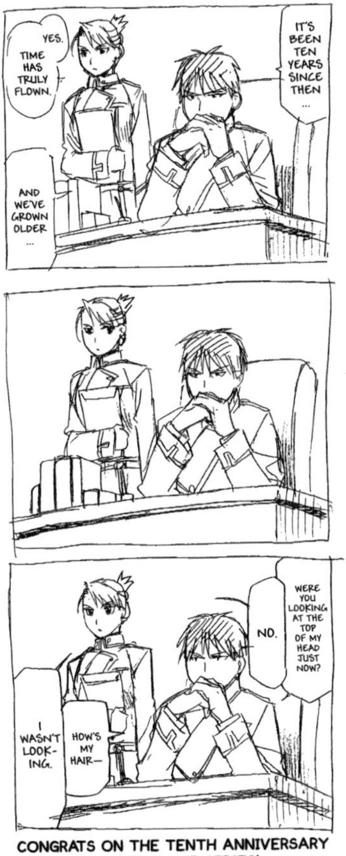
IT'S BEEN TEN YEARS SINCE THEN ...
YES. TIME HAS TRULY FLOWN.
AND WE'VE GROWN OLDER ...
WERE YOU LOOKING AT THE TOP OF MY HEAD JUST NOW?
NO.
HOW'S MY HAIR—
I WASN'T LOOK-ING.

CONGRATS ON THE TENTH ANNIVERSARY OF THE ANIME SERIES!

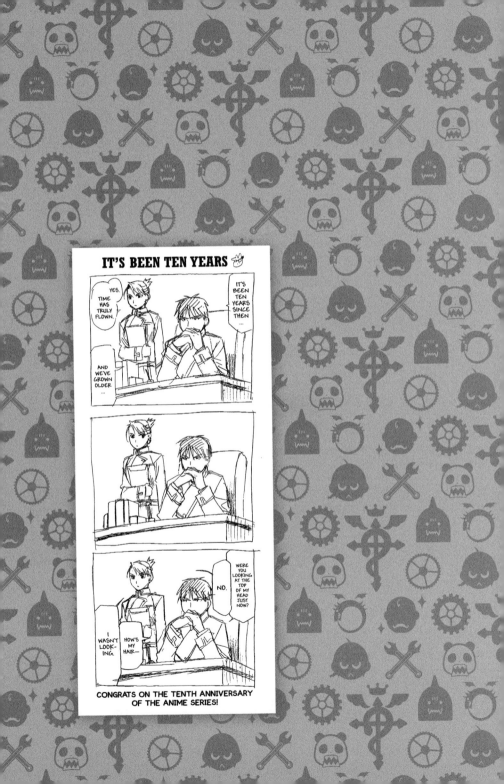

BROTHERHOOD DVDs

STATE ALCHEMY EXAM

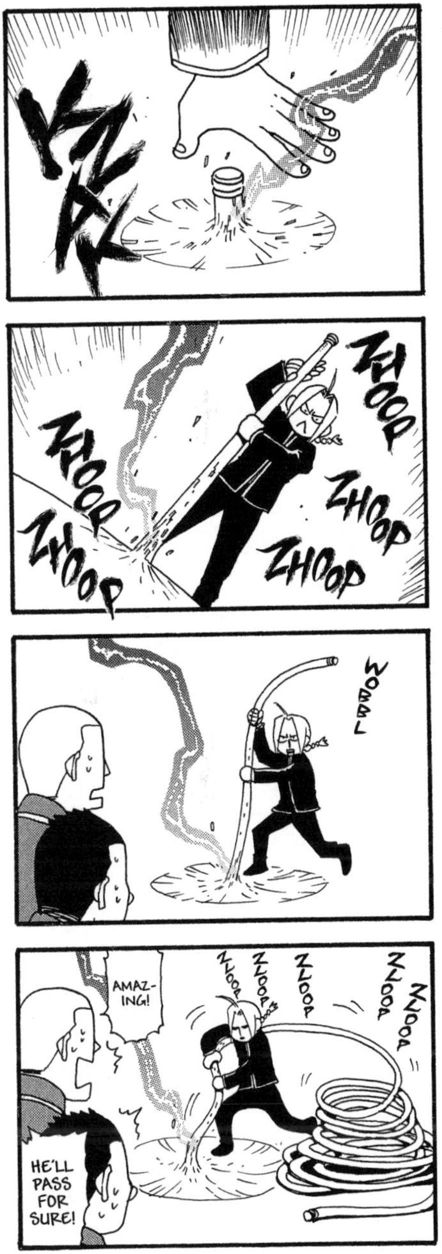
ZHOOP
ZHOOP
ZHOOP
ZHOOP
ZHOOP
ZHOOP
WOBBL
ZLOOP
ZLOOP
ZLOOP
ZLOOP
ZLOOP
AMAZING!
HE'LL PASS FOR SURE!

MR. FREEZE

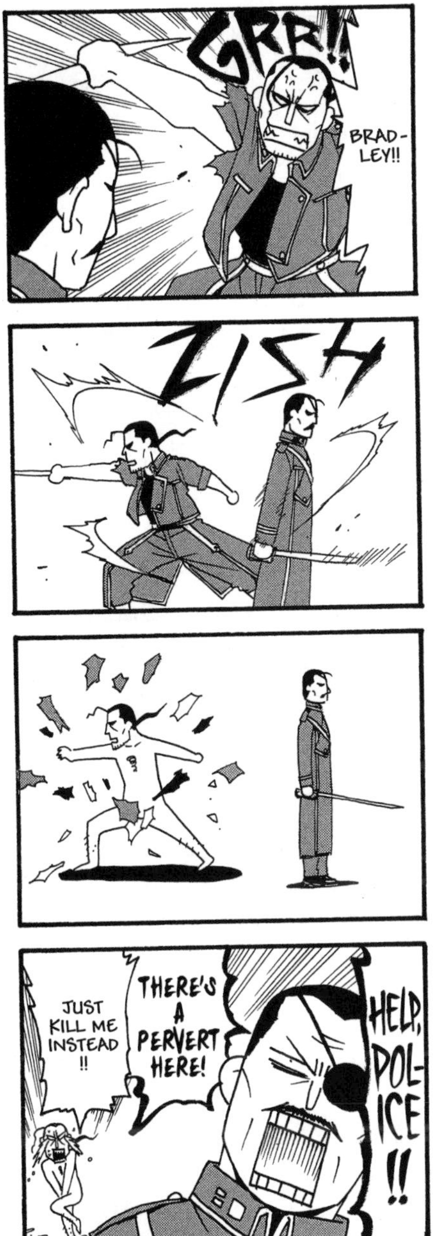
GRR!!
BRADLEY!!
ZISH
HELP, POLICE!!
THERE'S A PERVERT HERE!
JUST KILL ME INSTEAD!!

Brotherhood DVDs
Volume 2, September 2009

HAUNTED HOUSE

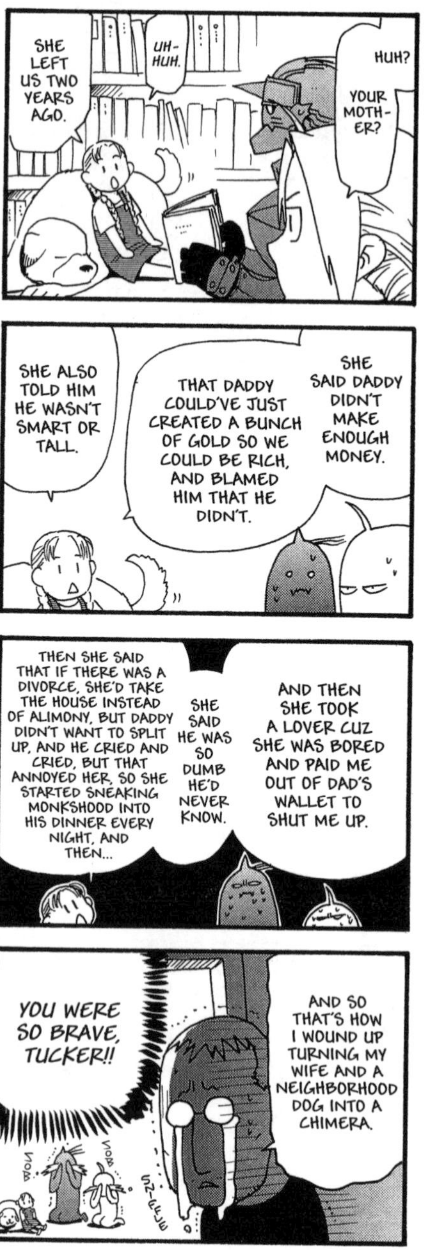
HUH?
YOUR MOTHER?
UH-HUH.
SHE LEFT US TWO YEARS AGO.
SHE SAID DADDY DIDN'T MAKE ENOUGH MONEY.
THAT DADDY COULD'VE JUST CREATED A BUNCH OF GOLD SO WE COULD BE RICH, AND BLAMED HIM THAT HE DIDN'T.
SHE ALSO TOLD HIM HE WASN'T SMART OR TALL.
AND THEN SHE TOOK A LOVER CUZ SHE WAS BORED AND PAID ME OUT OF DAD'S WALLET TO SHUT ME UP.
SHE SAID HE WAS SO DUMB HE'D NEVER KNOW.
THEN SHE SAID THAT IF THERE WAS A DIVORCE, SHE'D TAKE THE HOUSE INSTEAD OF ALIMONY, BUT DADDY DIDN'T WANT TO SPLIT UP, AND HE CRIED AND CRIED, BUT THAT ANNOYED HER, SO SHE STARTED SNEAKING MONKSHOOD INTO HIS DINNER EVERY NIGHT, AND THEN...
AND SO THAT'S HOW I WOUND UP TURNING MY WIFE AND A NEIGHBORHOOD DOG INTO A CHIMERA.
YOU WERE SO BRAVE, TUCKER!!
SOB
SOB

OVERDOING IT

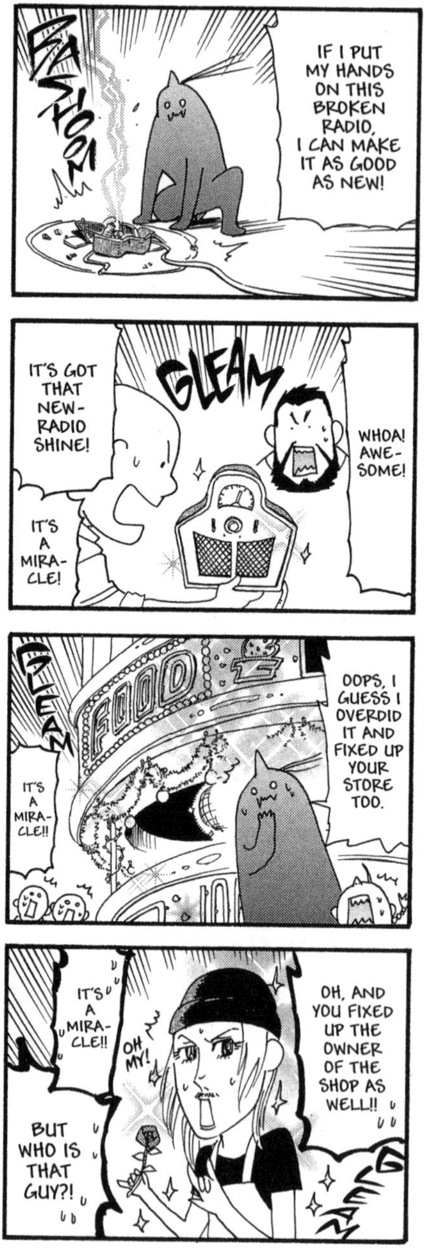
IF I PUT MY HANDS ON THIS BROKEN RADIO, I CAN MAKE IT AS GOOD AS NEW!
BASHOOM
WHOA! AWESOME!
GLEAM
IT'S GOT THAT NEW-RADIO SHINE!
IT'S A MIRACLE!
OOPS, I GUESS I OVERDID IT AND FIXED UP YOUR STORE TOO.
FOOD
GLEAM
IT'S A MIRACLE!!
OH, AND YOU FIXED UP THE OWNER OF THE SHOP AS WELL!!
IT'S A MIRACLE!!
OH MY!
BUT WHO IS THAT GUY?!
GLEAM

THE PERFECT GIRL

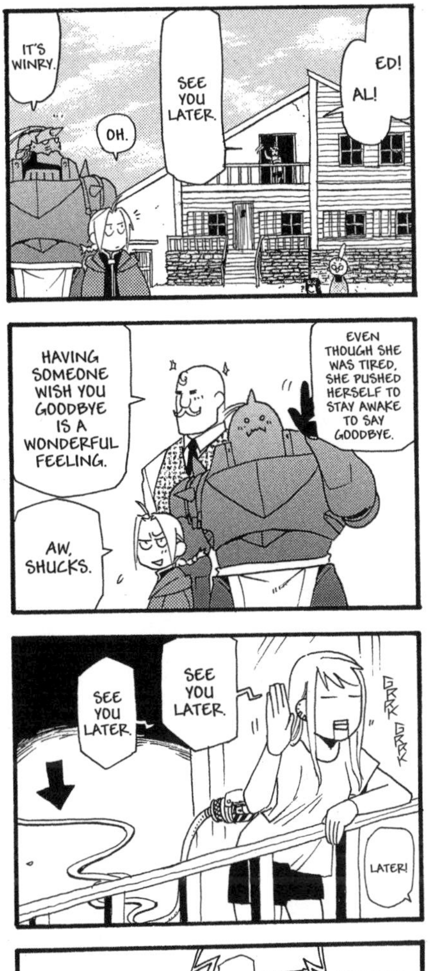
ED!
AL!
SEE YOU LATER.
IT'S WINRY.
OH.
EVEN THOUGH SHE WAS TIRED, SHE PUSHED HERSELF TO STAY AWAKE TO SAY GOODBYE.
HAVING SOMEONE WISH YOU GOODBYE IS A WONDERFUL FEELING.
AW, SHUCKS.
GRRK GRRK
SEE YOU LATER.
SEE YOU LATER.
LATER!
ROCKBELL ENGINEERING'S BYE-BYE-O-MATIC COMES WITH TIMER INCLUDED!
SEE YOU LATER.
GRRK
CATCH SOME Z'S AND ALL THE BOYS' HEARTS WITH THIS MUST-HAVE MECH!
SPECIAL PRICE: 250,000 CENZ!!

FIRST IMPRESSION

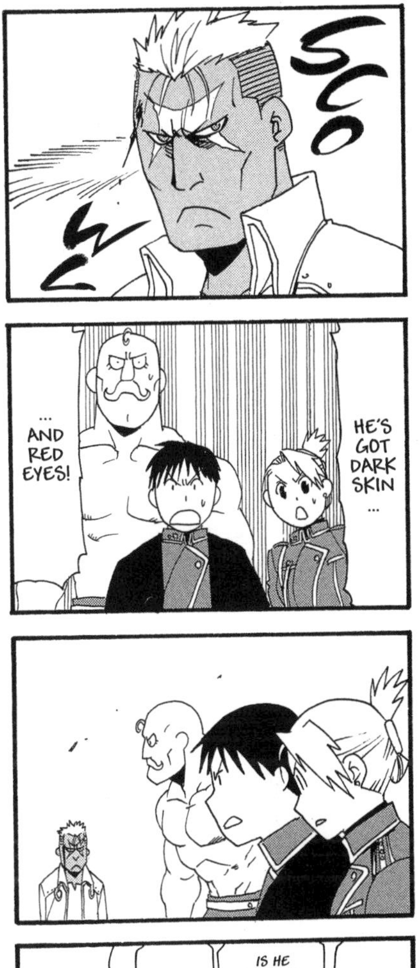
SCOWL
HE'S GOT DARK SKIN ...
... AND RED EYES!
IS HE A TIRED SHIGERU MATSU-ZAKI?*
IS HE A GRADE-SCHOOLER WHO SPENT ALL SUMMER AT THE POOL?
IS HE A SNOW-BLINDED SKIER?
I'M FROM ISHVAL!!
And don't you forget it!

*POPULAR SINGER

NO ENTHUSIASM

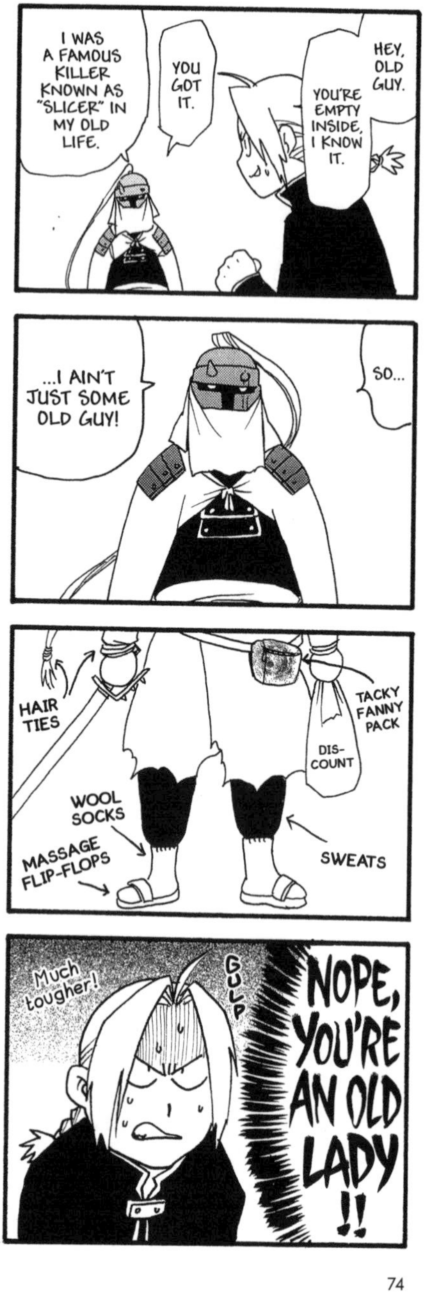
HEY, OLD GUY.
YOU'RE EMPTY INSIDE, I KNOW IT.
YOU GOT IT.
I WAS A FAMOUS KILLER KNOWN AS "SLICER" IN MY OLD LIFE.
SO...
...I AIN'T JUST SOME OLD GUY!
TACKY FANNY PACK
DIS-COUNT
HAIR TIES
SWEATS
WOOL SOCKS
MASSAGE FLIP-FLOPS
NOPE, YOU'RE AN OLD LADY!!
GULP
Much tougher!

GOD!!

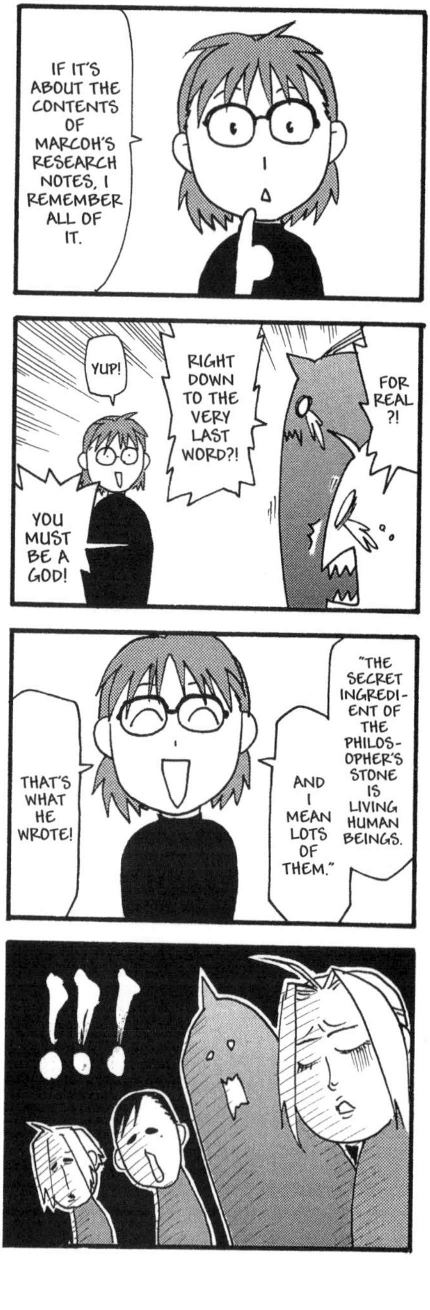
IF IT'S ABOUT THE CONTENTS OF MARCOH'S RESEARCH NOTES, I REMEMBER ALL OF IT.
FOR REAL?!
RIGHT DOWN TO THE VERY LAST WORD?!
YUP!
YOU MUST BE A GOD!
"THE SECRET INGREDIENT OF THE PHILOSOPHER'S STONE IS LIVING HUMAN BEINGS.
AND I MEAN LOTS OF THEM."
THAT'S WHAT HE WROTE!
!!!

YOU COULD HAVE SAID SO!

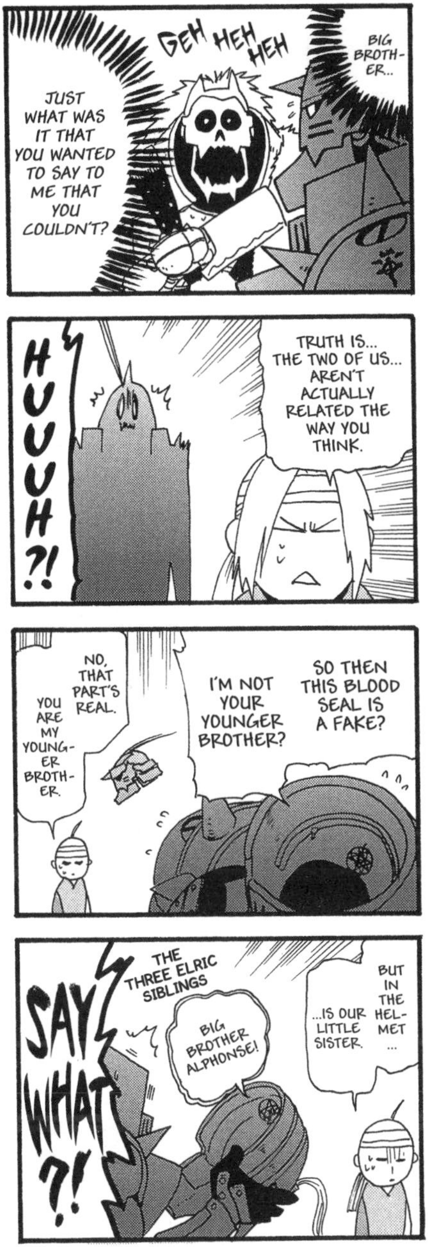
BIG BROTHER-ER...
GEH HEH HEH
JUST WHAT WAS IT THAT YOU WANTED TO SAY TO ME THAT YOU COULDN'T?
TRUTH IS... THE TWO OF US... AREN'T ACTUALLY RELATED THE WAY YOU THINK.
HUUUUH?!
SO THEN THIS BLOOD SEAL IS A FAKE?
I'M NOT YOUR YOUNGER BROTHER?
NO, THAT PART'S REAL.
YOU ARE MY YOUNGER BROTHER.
BUT IN THE HELMET...
...IS OUR LITTLE SISTER.
THE THREE ELRIC SIBLINGS
BIG BROTHER ALPHONSE!
SAY WHAT?!

MUSTANG'S IN TROUBLE

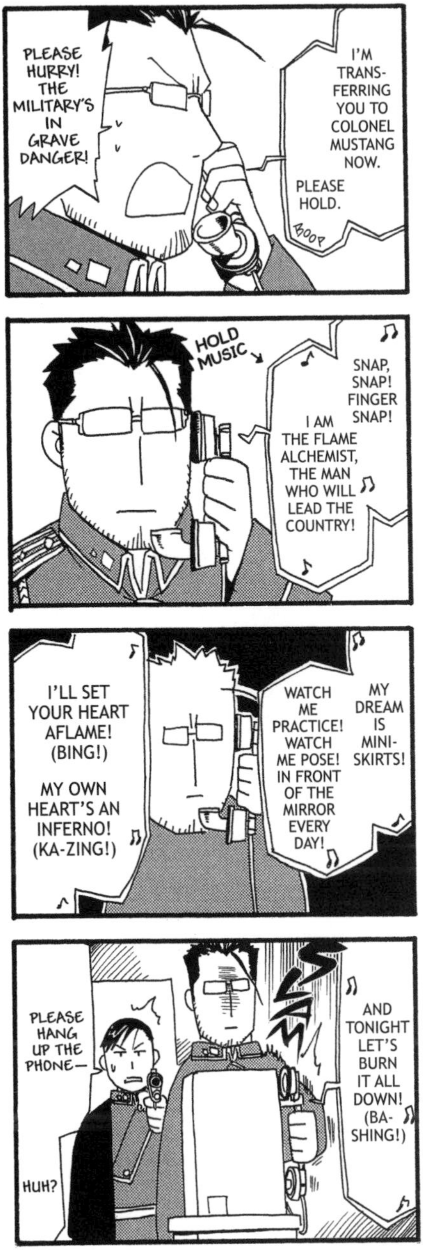
I'M TRANSFERRING YOU TO COLONEL MUSTANG NOW.
PLEASE HOLD.
BOOP
PLEASE HURRY! THE MILITARY'S IN GRAVE DANGER!
SNAP, SNAP! FINGER SNAP!
I AM THE FLAME ALCHEMIST, THE MAN WHO WILL LEAD THE COUNTRY!
HOLD MUSIC
MY DREAM IS MINI-SKIRTS!
WATCH ME PRACTICE! WATCH ME POSE! IN FRONT OF THE MIRROR EVERY DAY!
I'LL SET YOUR HEART AFLAME! (BING!)
MY OWN HEART'S AN INFERNO! (KA-ZING!)
AND TONIGHT LET'S BURN IT ALL DOWN! (BA-SHING!)
PLEASE HANG UP THE PHONE—
HUH?

Brotherhood DVDs
Volume 4, November 2009

I FEEL BETTER NOW

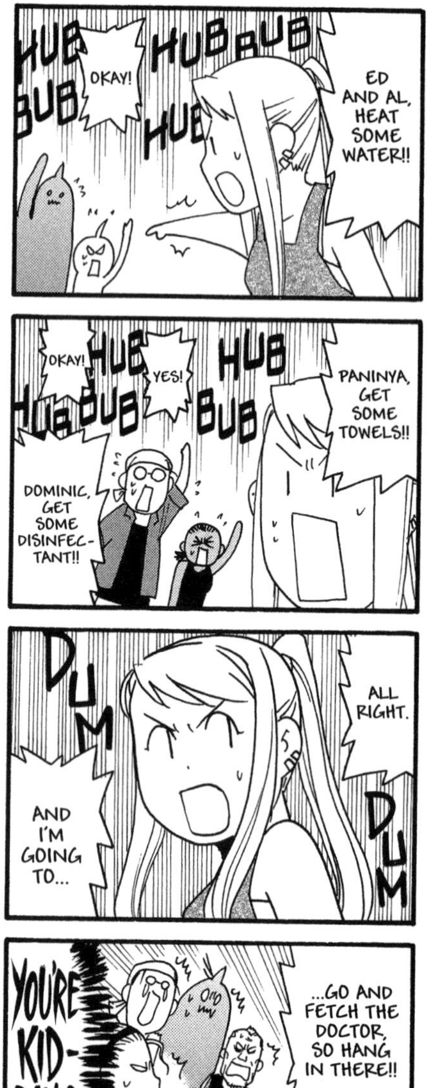

ED AND AL, HEAT SOME WATER!!
HUB BUB
HUB BUB
OKAY!
HUB BUB
PANINYA, GET SOME TOWELS!!
HUB BUB
YES!
HUB BUB
OKAY!
DOMINIC, GET SOME DISINFECTANT!!
ALL RIGHT.
DUM DUM
AND I'M GOING TO...
...GO AND FETCH THE DOCTOR, SO HANG IN THERE!!
YOU'RE KIDDING ME!!

NOTHING'S MORE EXPENSIVE THAN FREE

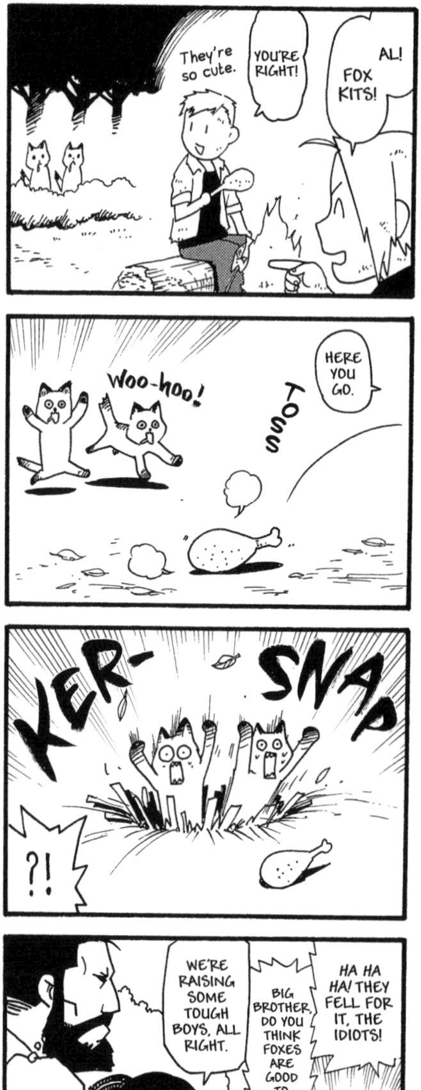

AL! FOX KITS!
YOU'RE RIGHT!
They're so cute.
HERE YOU GO.
TOSS
Woo-hoo!
KER-SNAP
?!
HA HA HA! THEY FELL FOR IT, THE IDIOTS!
BIG BROTHER, DO YOU THINK FOXES ARE GOOD TO EAT?
Yay! Yes!
WE'RE RAISING SOME TOUGH BOYS, ALL RIGHT.
Heh heh...
THEY'RE... DYNAMIC.

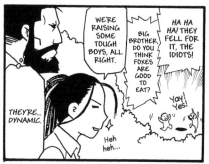

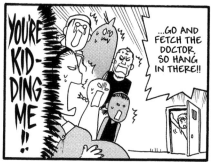

TRUE NATURE

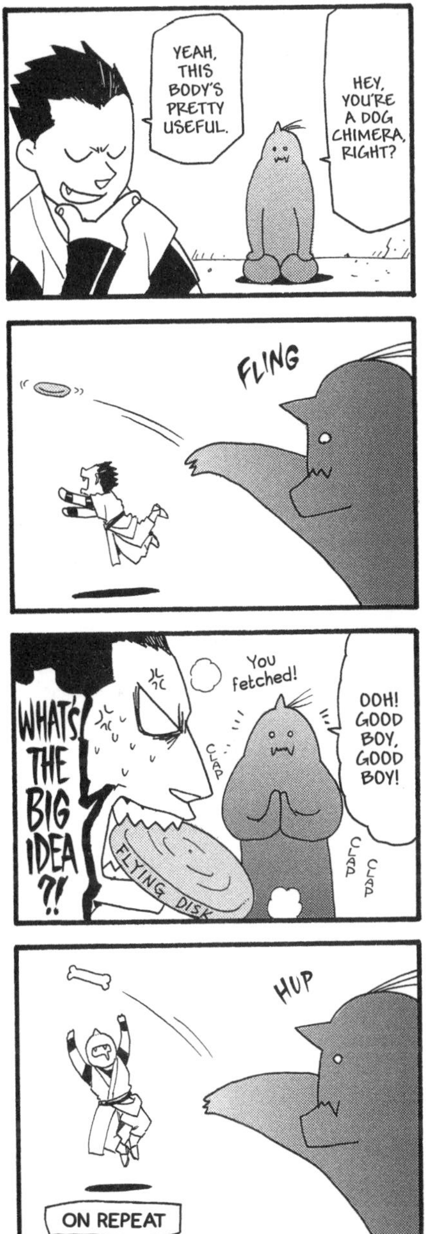
HEY, YOU'RE A DOG CHIMERA, RIGHT?
YEAH, THIS BODY'S PRETTY USEFUL.
FLING
OOH! GOOD BOY, GOOD BOY!
You fetched!
CLAP
CLAP
CLAP
WHAT'S THE BIG IDEA?!
FLYING DISK
HUP
ON REPEAT

MEETING THE NATIVES

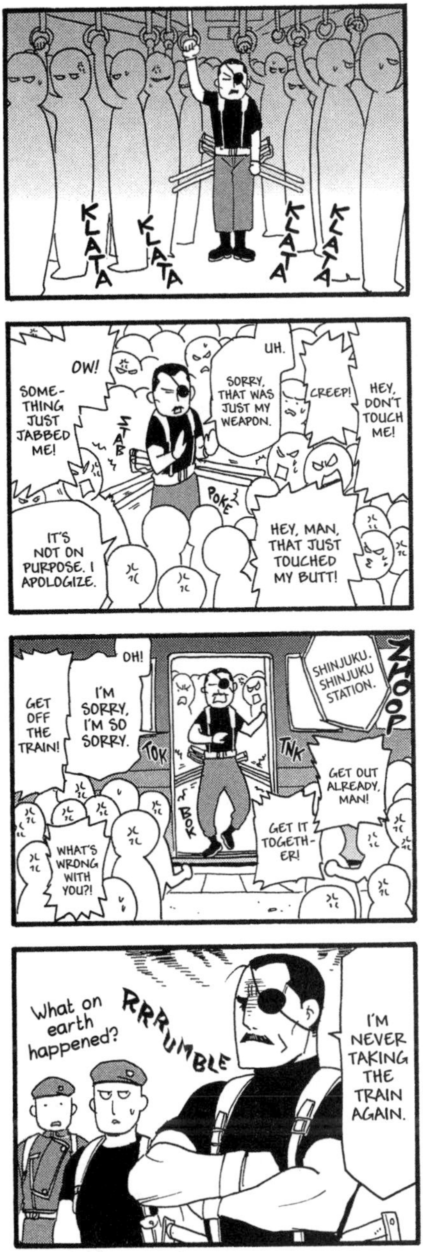
KLATA
KLATA
KLATA
KLATA
HEY, DON'T TOUCH ME!
CREEP!
UH.
SORRY, THAT WAS JUST MY WEAPON.
OW!
SOME-THING JUST JABBED ME!
STAB
POKE
HEY, MAN, THAT JUST TOUCHED MY BUTT!
IT'S NOT ON PURPOSE. I APOLOGIZE.
ZHOOP
SHINJUKU, SHINJUKU STATION.
OH!
I'M SORRY, I'M SO SORRY.
GET OFF THE TRAIN!
TNK
TOK
GET OUT ALREADY, MAN!
GET IT TOGETH-ER!
BOK
WHAT'S WRONG WITH YOU?!
I'M NEVER TAKING THE TRAIN AGAIN.
RRRUMBLE
What on earth happened?

Brotherhood DVDs
Volume 5, December 2009

IDENTITY

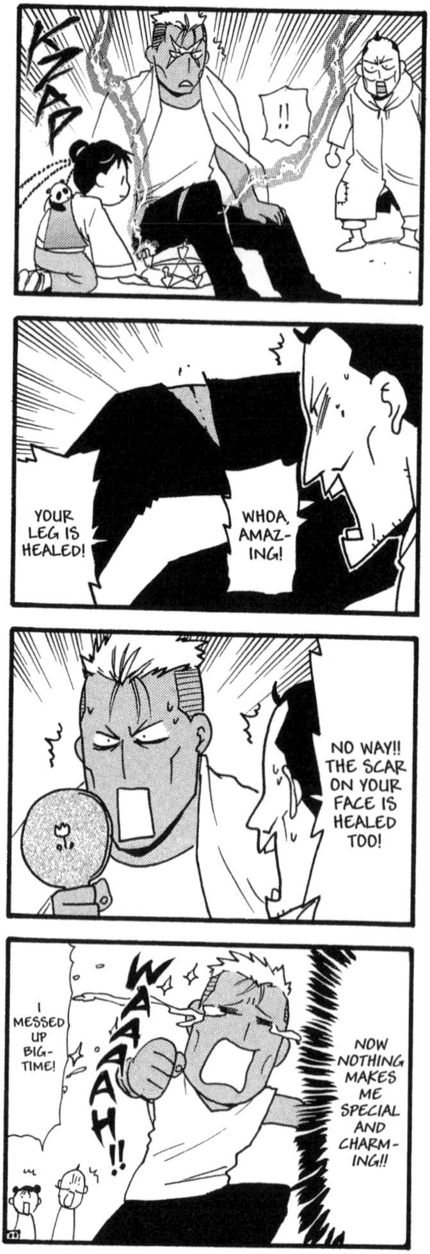
KZAP
!!
WHOA, AMAZ-ING!
YOUR LEG IS HEALED!
NO WAY!! THE SCAR ON YOUR FACE IS HEALED TOO!
NOW NOTHING MAKES ME SPECIAL AND CHARM-ING!!
WAAAAH!!
I MESSED UP BIG-TIME!

LOVE IS BLIND

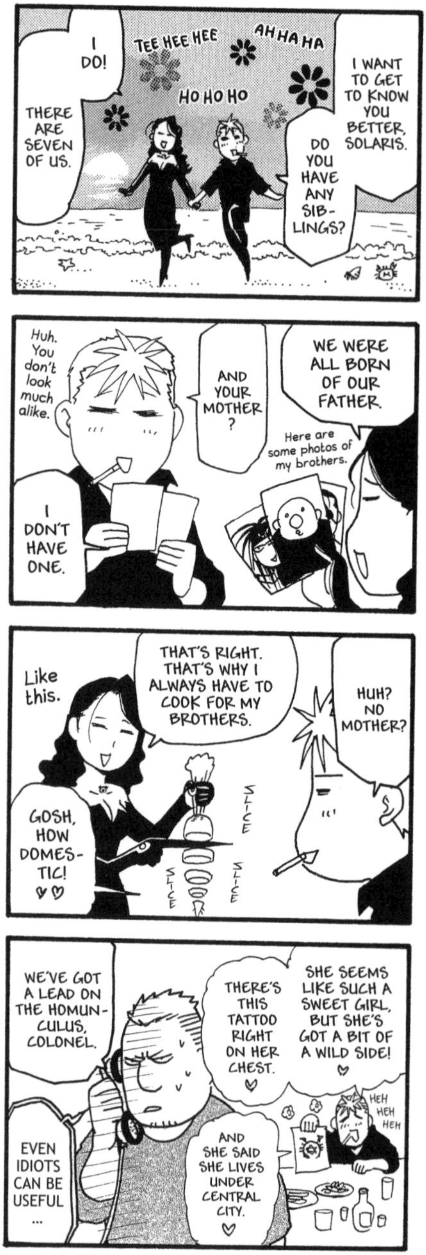
I WANT TO GET TO KNOW YOU BETTER, SOLARIS.
AH HA HA
DO YOU HAVE ANY SIB-LINGS?
TEE HEE HEE
HO HO HO
I DO!
THERE ARE SEVEN OF US.
WE WERE ALL BORN OF OUR FATHER.
Here are some photos of my brothers.
AND YOUR MOTHER?
Huh. You don't look much alike.
I DON'T HAVE ONE.
HUH? NO MOTHER?
THAT'S RIGHT. THAT'S WHY I ALWAYS HAVE TO COOK FOR MY BROTHERS.
Like this.
SLICE
SLICE
SLICE
GOSH, HOW DOMES-TIC!
SHE SEEMS LIKE SUCH A SWEET GIRL, BUT SHE'S GOT A BIT OF A WILD SIDE!
THERE'S THIS TATTOO RIGHT ON HER CHEST.
WE'VE GOT A LEAD ON THE HOMUN-CULUS, COLONEL.
HEH HEH HEH
AND SHE SAID SHE LIVES UNDER CENTRAL CITY.
EVEN IDIOTS CAN BE USEFUL ...

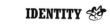

MY TYPE

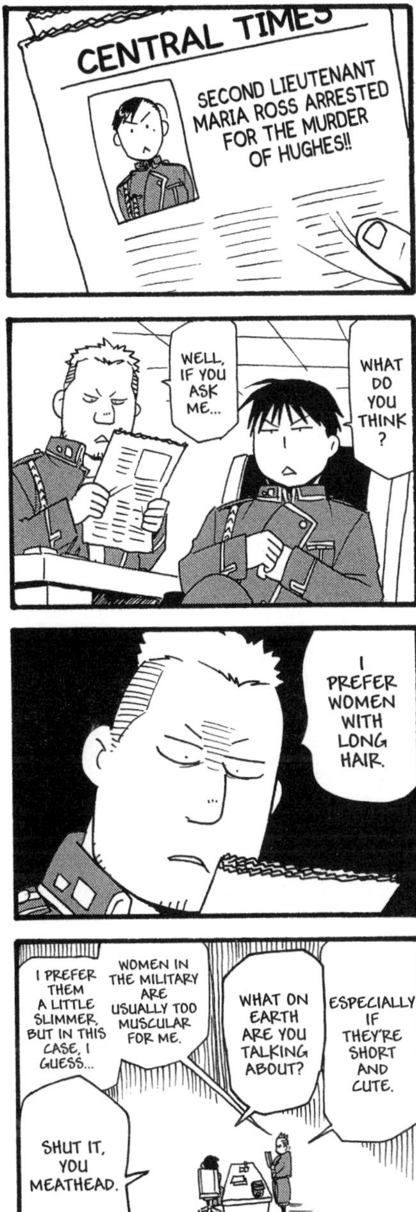

CENTRAL TIMES
SECOND LIEUTENANT MARIA ROSS ARRESTED FOR THE MURDER OF HUGHES!!
WHAT DO YOU THINK?
WELL, IF YOU ASK ME...
I PREFER WOMEN WITH LONG HAIR.
ESPECIALLY IF THEY'RE SHORT AND CUTE.
WHAT ON EARTH ARE YOU TALKING ABOUT?
WOMEN IN THE MILITARY ARE USUALLY TOO MUSCULAR FOR ME.
I PREFER THEM A LITTLE SLIMMER, BUT IN THIS CASE, I GUESS...
SHUT IT, YOU MEATHEAD.

BURNABLE TRASH

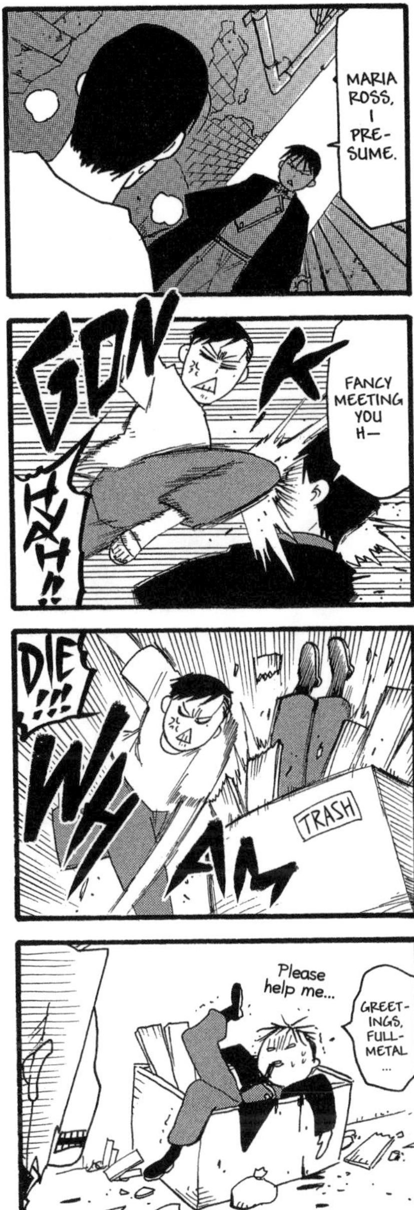

MARIA ROSS, I PRESUME.
FANCY MEETING YOU H—
GONK
HYAH!!
DIE!!!
WHAM
TRASH
GREETINGS, FULLMETAL...
Please help me...

Brotherhood DVDs
Volume 6, January 2010

THE FRIZZ

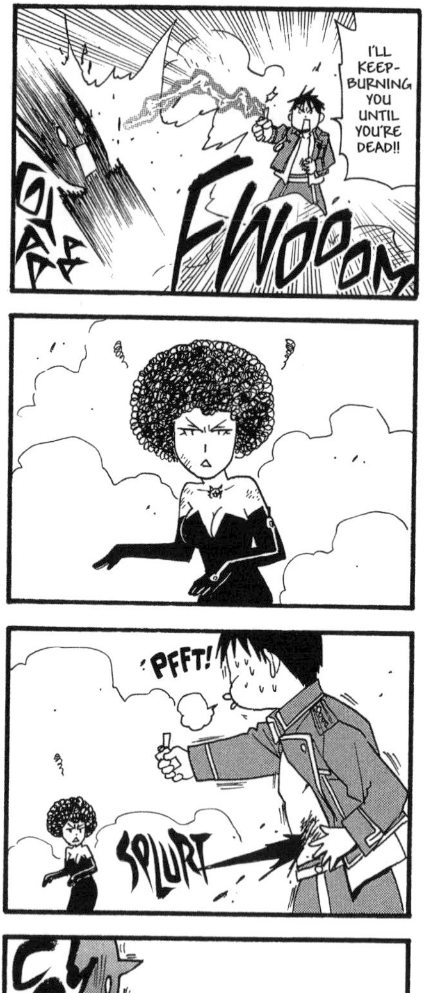
I'LL KEEP-BURNING YOU UNTIL YOU'RE DEAD!!
FWOOOM
PFFT!
SPLURT
COLONEL!!
His wound opened up.

IRON LAD

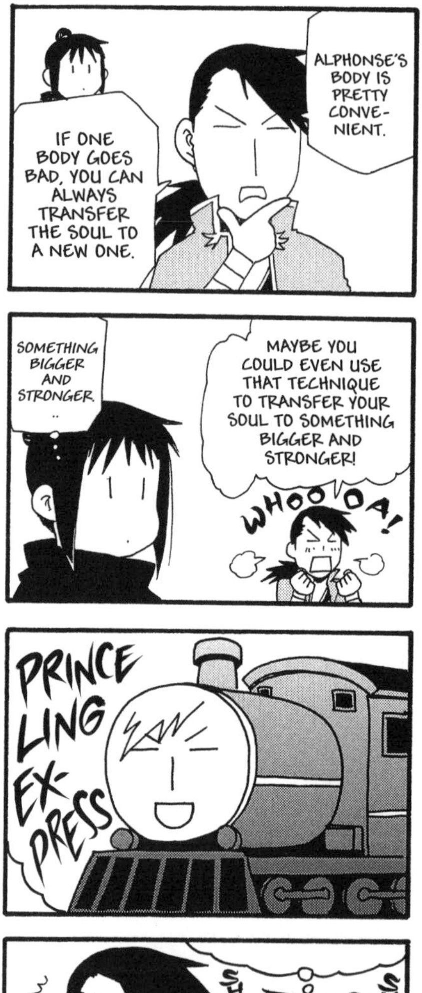
ALPHONSE'S BODY IS PRETTY CONVENIENT.
IF ONE BODY GOES BAD, YOU CAN ALWAYS TRANSFER THE SOUL TO A NEW ONE.
MAYBE YOU COULD EVEN USE THAT TECHNIQUE TO TRANSFER YOUR SOUL TO SOMETHING BIGGER AND STRONGER!
WHOOOA!
SOMETHING BIGGER AND STRONGER...
PRINCE LING EX-PRESS
SHAKE
SHAKE
HUH? WHAT? WHAT'S WRONG?

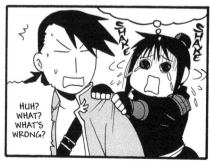

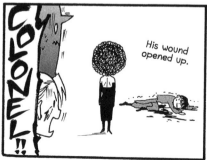

MACH SPEED!!

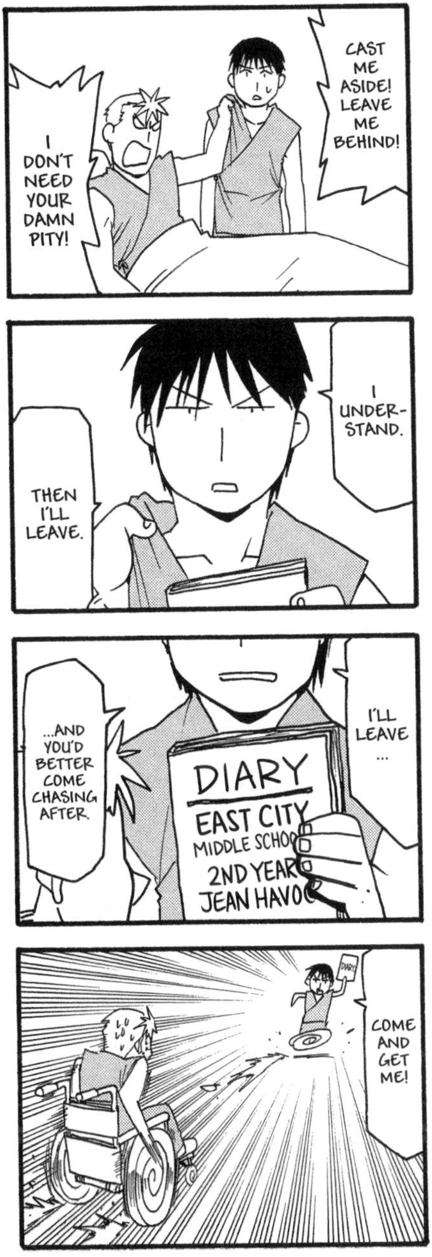

CAST ME ASIDE! LEAVE ME BEHIND!
I DON'T NEED YOUR DAMN PITY!
I UNDERSTAND.
THEN I'LL LEAVE.
I'LL LEAVE ...
...AND YOU'D BETTER COME CHASING AFTER.
DIARY
EAST CITY
MIDDLE SCHOO
2ND YEAR
JEAN HAVO
DIARY
COME AND GET ME!

EYELID FATHER

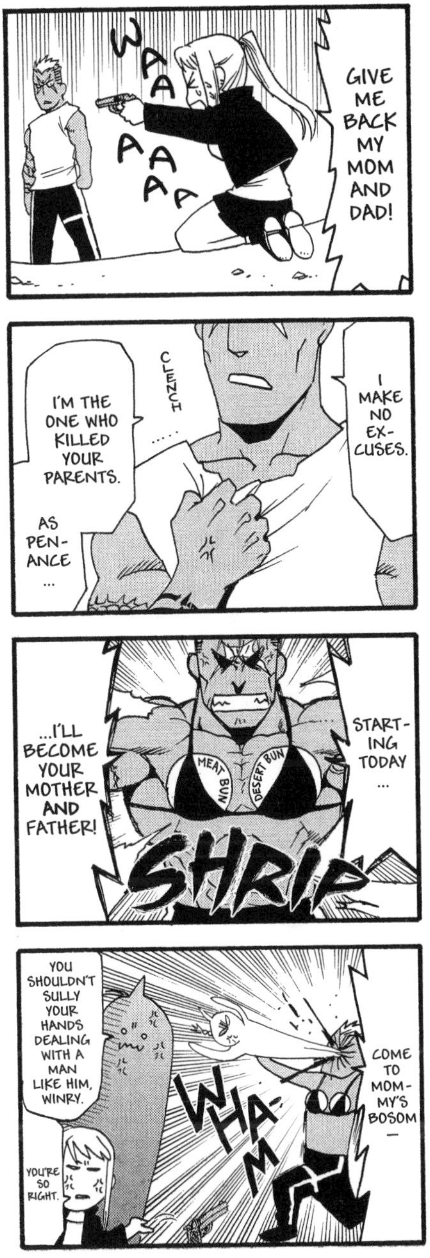

GIVE ME BACK MY MOM AND DAD!
WAAAAAAA
I MAKE NO EXCUSES.
CLENCH
.....
I'M THE ONE WHO KILLED YOUR PARENTS.
AS PENANCE ...
STARTING TODAY ...
...I'LL BECOME YOUR MOTHER AND FATHER!
MEAT BUN
DESERT BUN
SHRIP
COME TO MOMMY'S BOSOM —
WHAM
YOU SHOULDN'T SULLY YOUR HANDS DEALING WITH A MAN LIKE HIM, WINRY.
YOU'RE SO RIGHT.

AGAR NOODLES

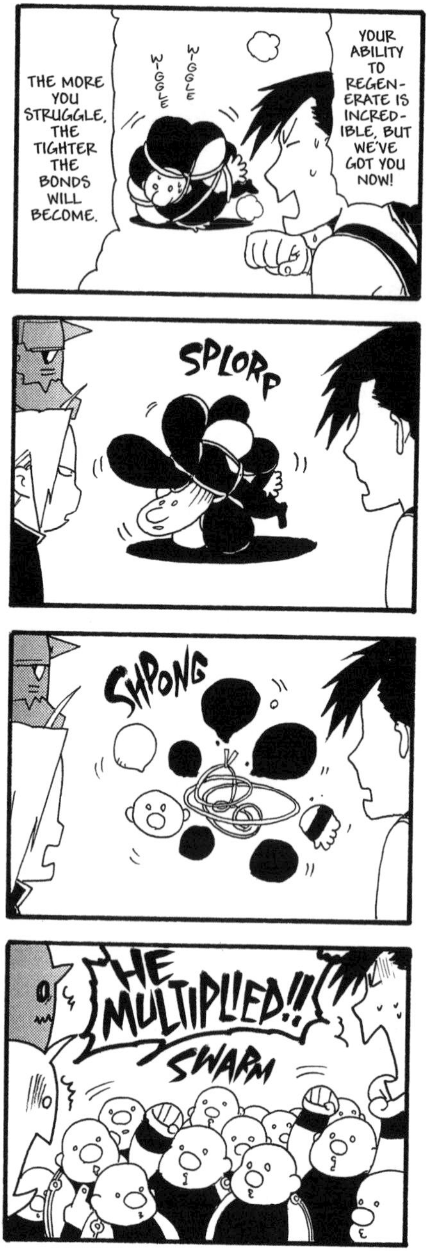
YOUR ABILITY TO REGEN-ERATE IS INCRED-IBLE, BUT WE'VE GOT YOU NOW!
WIGGLE
WIGGLE
THE MORE YOU STRUGGLE, THE TIGHTER THE BONDS WILL BECOME.
SPLORP
SHPONG
HE MULTIPLIED!!
SWARM

BELOVED FATHER

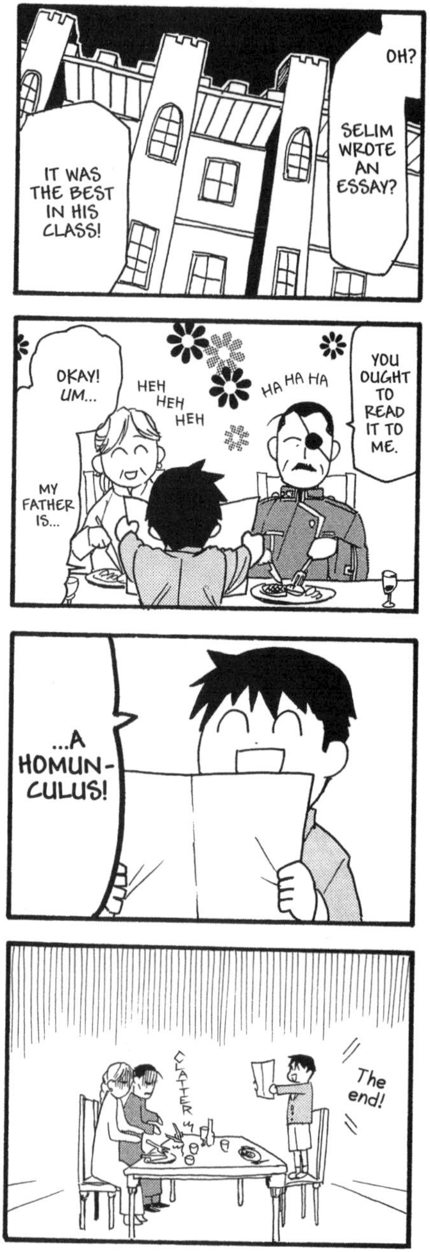
OH?
SELIM WROTE AN ESSAY?
IT WAS THE BEST IN HIS CLASS!
YOU OUGHT TO READ IT TO ME.
HA HA HA
HEH HEH HEH
OKAY! UM...
MY FATHER IS...
...A HOMUNCULUS!
The end!
CLATTER

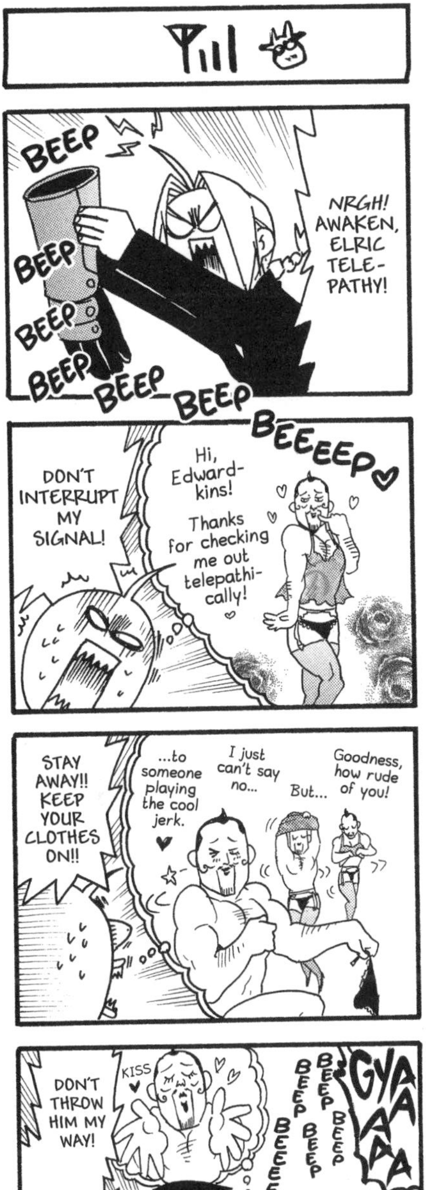
BEEP
NRGH! AWAKEN, ELRIC TELEPATHY!
BEEP
BEEP
BEEP
BEEP
BEEP
BEEEEEP
Hi, Edward-kins! Thanks for checking me out telepathically!
DON'T INTERRUPT MY SIGNAL!
Goodness, how rude of you!
But...
I just can't say no...
...to someone playing the cool jerk.
STAY AWAY!! KEEP YOUR CLOTHES ON!!
GYAAAAA
BEEP BEEP BEEP
BEEP BEEP
BEEEEEP
KISS
DON'T THROW HIM MY WAY!
BUT SERIOUSLY, THIS ELRIC TELEPATHY IS INTENSE!

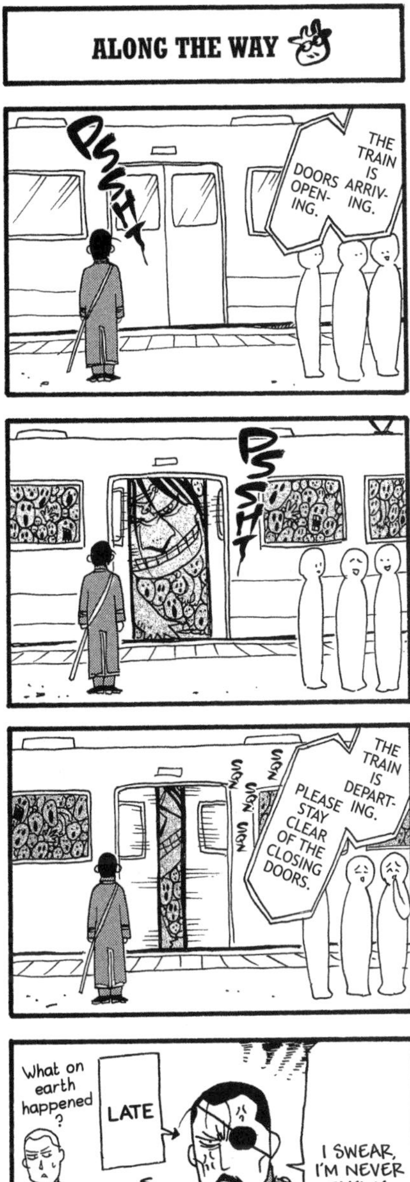
ALONG THE WAY
PSSHT
THE TRAIN IS ARRIVING. DOORS OPENING.
PSSHT
THE TRAIN IS DEPARTING. PLEASE STAY CLEAR OF THE CLOSING DOORS.
I SWEAR, I'M NEVER TAKING THE TRAIN AGAIN.
LATE
What on earth happened?
SNAP

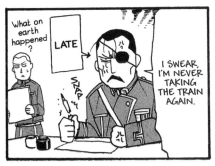

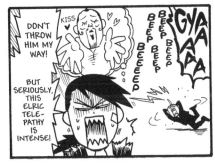

GOOD CHILDREN MIND THEIR MANNERS!

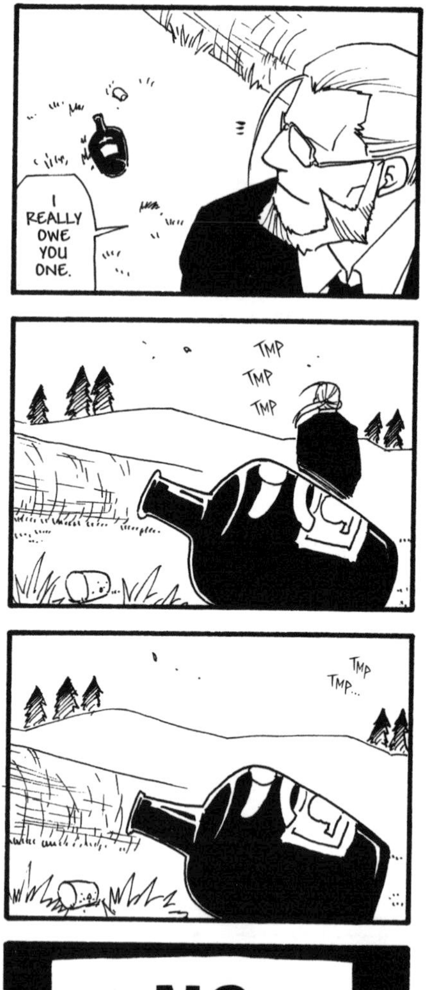
I REALLY OWE YOU ONE.
TMP
TMP
TMP
TMP
TMP...
NO LITTERING!
EVER!

APPETITE OF A GROWING BOY

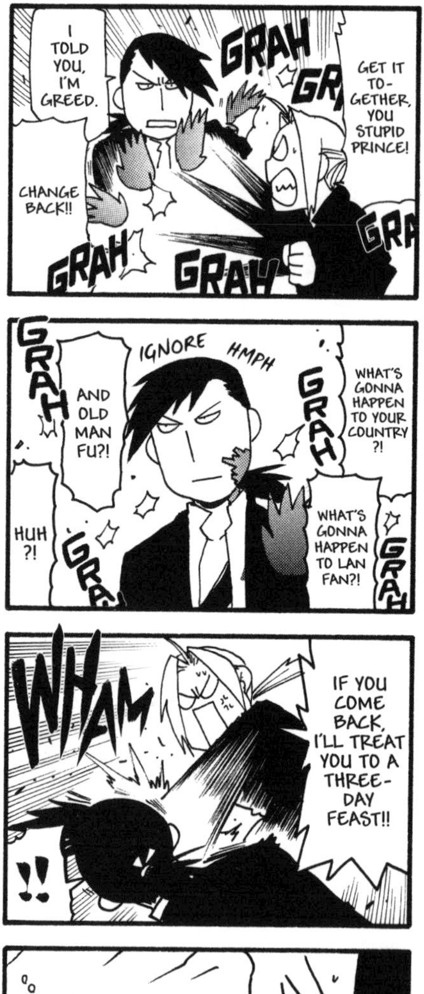
GET IT TO-GETHER, YOU STUPID PRINCE!
GRAH
GR
I TOLD YOU, I'M GREED.
CHANGE BACK!!
GRA
GRAH
GRAH
WHAT'S GONNA HAPPEN TO YOUR COUNTRY?!
HMPH
IGNORE
GRAH
AND OLD MAN FU?!
GRAH
WHAT'S GONNA HAPPEN TO LAN FAN?!
GRAH
GRA
HUH?!
IF YOU COME BACK, I'LL TREAT YOU TO A THREE-DAY FEAST!!
WHAM
!!
HEH HEH
HE'S STILL IN THERE!
DROOL

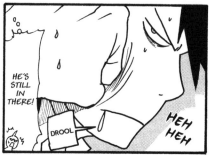

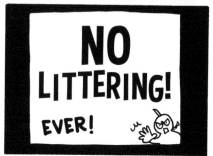

BEAUTIFUL MEMORIES

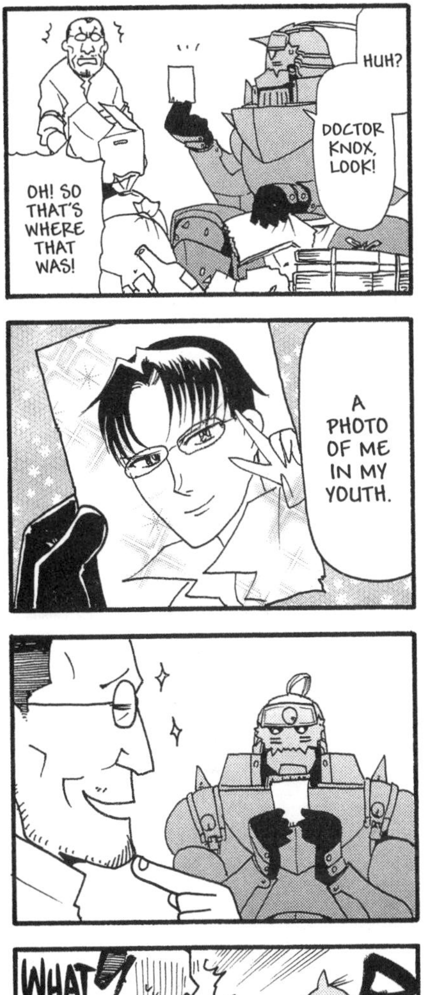
HUH?
DOCTOR KNOX, LOOK!
OH! SO THAT'S WHERE THAT WAS!
A PHOTO OF ME IN MY YOUTH.
RIP
TOSS
WHAT ARE YOU DOING?!
TRASH

BURNABLE GARBAGE

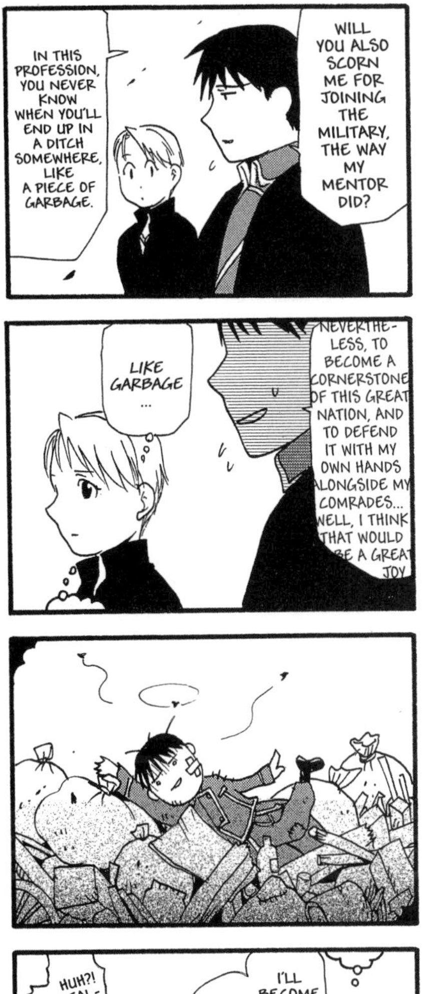
WILL YOU ALSO SCORN ME FOR JOINING THE MILITARY, THE WAY MY MENTOR DID?
IN THIS PROFESSION, YOU NEVER KNOW WHEN YOU'LL END UP IN A DITCH SOMEWHERE, LIKE A PIECE OF GARBAGE.
NEVERTHELESS, TO BECOME A CORNERSTONE OF THIS GREAT NATION, AND TO DEFEND IT WITH MY OWN HANDS ALONGSIDE MY COMRADES... WELL, I THINK THAT WOULD BE A GREAT JOY
LIKE GARBAGE...
NOW THAT I'D LIKE TO SEE.
I'LL BECOME A SOLDIER AS WELL.
I'D LIKE TO STAY BY YOUR SIDE, MUSTANG.
HUH?! REALLY?
I MEAN, I WOULDN'T MIND AT ALL, BUT...
ARE YOU SURE?

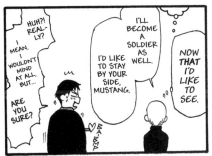

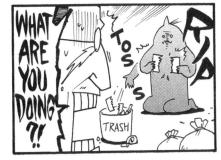

Brotherhood DVDs
Volume 9, April 2010

I'M A BIG BOY NOW

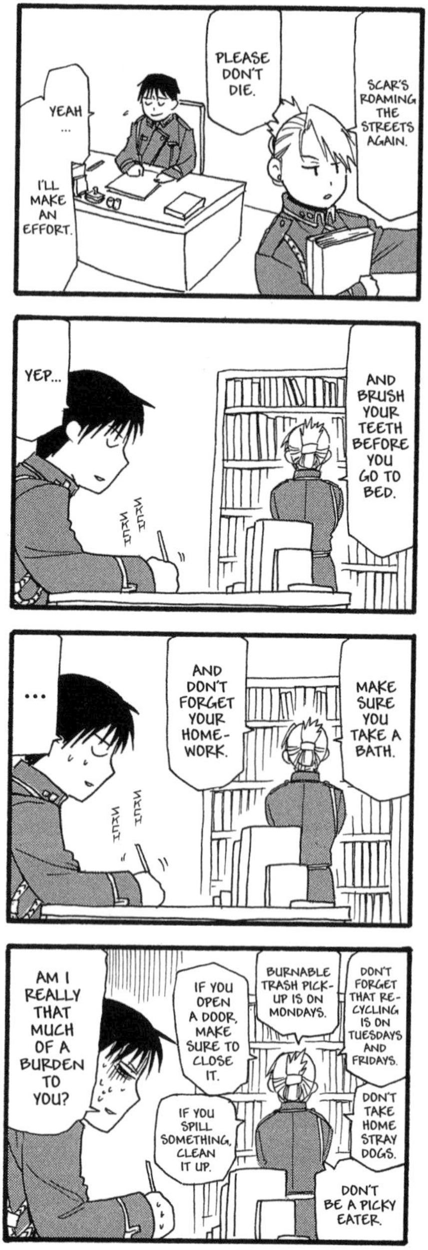
SCAR'S ROAMING THE STREETS AGAIN.
PLEASE DON'T DIE.
YEAH ...
I'LL MAKE AN EFFORT.
AND BRUSH YOUR TEETH BEFORE YOU GO TO BED.
YEP...
MAKE SURE YOU TAKE A BATH.
AND DON'T FORGET YOUR HOMEWORK.
...
DON'T FORGET THAT RECYCLING IS ON TUESDAYS AND FRIDAYS.
BURNABLE TRASH PICKUP IS ON MONDAYS.
IF YOU OPEN A DOOR, MAKE SURE TO CLOSE IT.
AM I REALLY THAT MUCH OF A BURDEN TO YOU?
DON'T TAKE HOME STRAY DOGS.
IF YOU SPILL SOMETHING, CLEAN IT UP.
DON'T BE A PICKY EATER.

A TERRIFYING CHILD

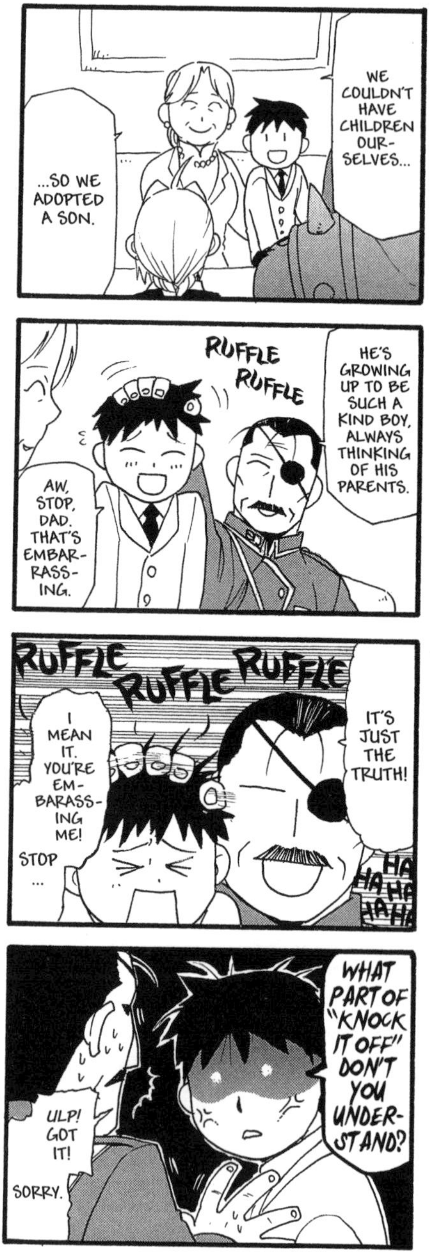
WE COULDN'T HAVE CHILDREN OURSELVES...
...SO WE ADOPTED A SON.
HE'S GROWING UP TO BE SUCH A KIND BOY, ALWAYS THINKING OF HIS PARENTS.
RUFFLE RUFFLE
AW, STOP, DAD. THAT'S EMBARRASSING.
RUFFLE RUFFLE RUFFLE
IT'S JUST THE TRUTH!
HA HA HA HA
I MEAN IT. YOU'RE EMBARASSING ME!
STOP ...
WHAT PART OF "KNOCK IT OFF" DON'T YOU UNDERSTAND?
ULP! GOT IT!
SORRY.

RUN AWAY!!

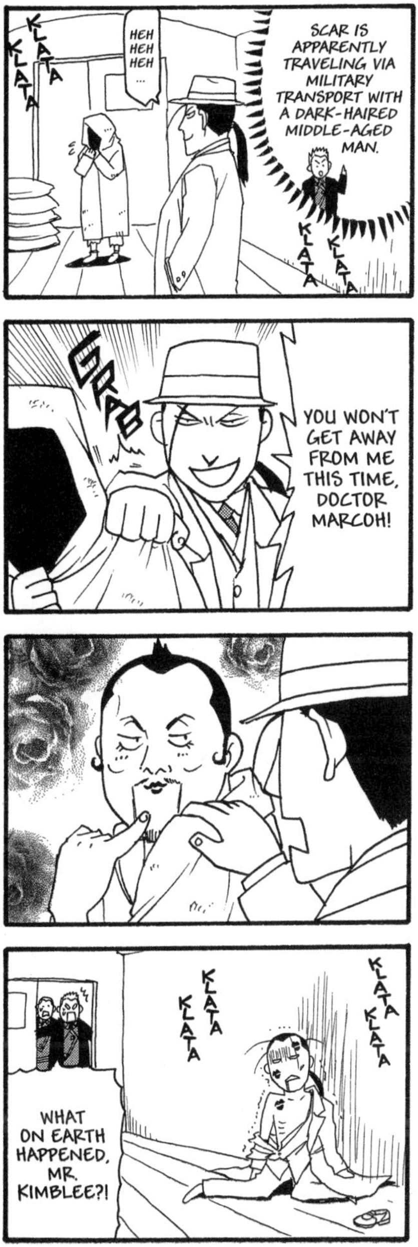
SCAR IS APPARENTLY TRAVELING VIA MILITARY TRANSPORT WITH A DARK-HAIRED MIDDLE-AGED MAN.
KLATA KLATA
HEH HEH HEH ...
KLATA KLATA
YOU WON'T GET AWAY FROM ME THIS TIME, DOCTOR MARCOH!
GRAB
KLATA KLATA
KLATA KLATA
WHAT ON EARTH HAPPENED, MR. KIMBLEE?!

MATURE INTERACTIONS

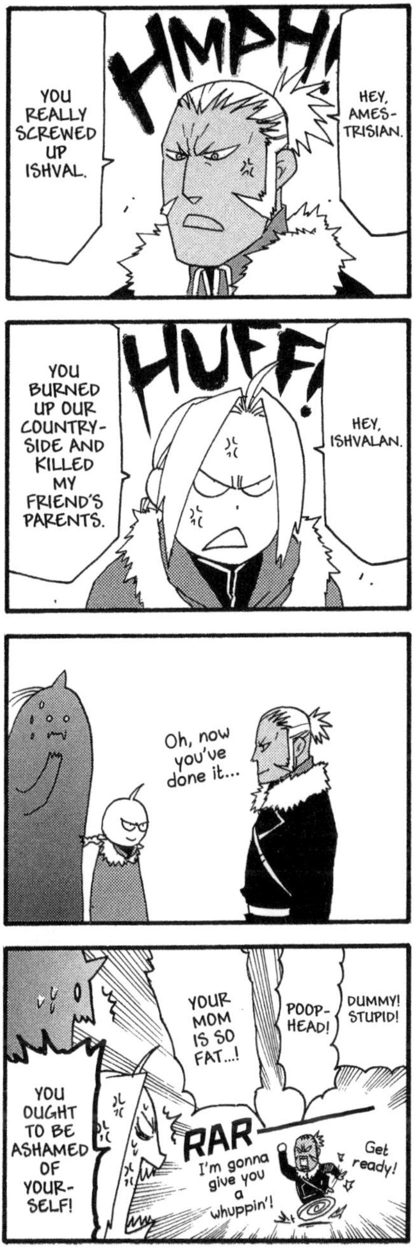
HEY, AMES-TRISIAN.
HMPH!
YOU REALLY SCREWED UP ISHVAL.
HEY, ISHVALAN.
HUFF!
YOU BURNED UP OUR COUNTRY-SIDE AND KILLED MY FRIEND'S PARENTS.
Oh, now you've done it...
DUMMY! STUPID!
POOP-HEAD!
YOUR MOM IS SO FAT...!
Get ready!
I'm gonna give you a whuppin'!
RAR
YOU OUGHT TO BE ASHAMED OF YOUR-SELF!

SO WARM

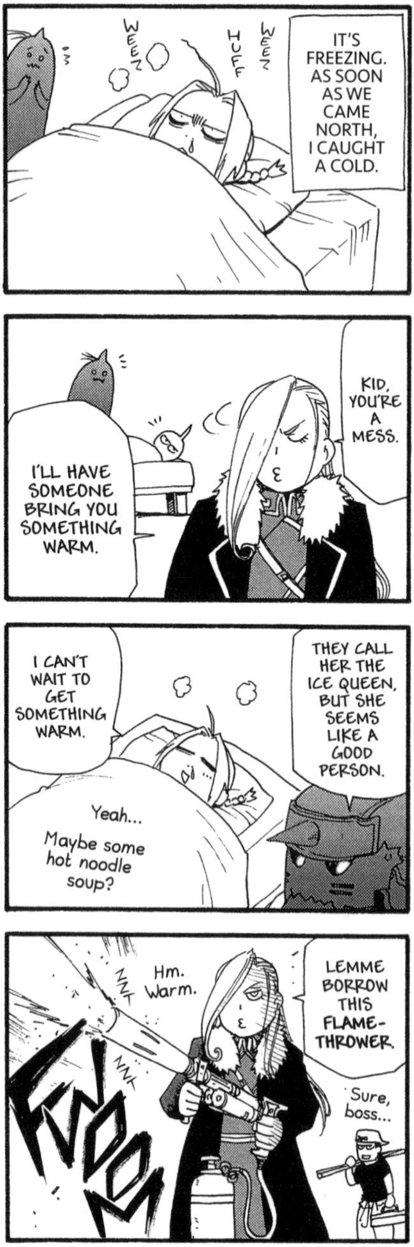
IT'S FREEZING. AS SOON AS WE CAME NORTH, I CAUGHT A COLD.
WEEZ
HUFF
WEEZ
KID, YOU'RE A MESS.
I'LL HAVE SOMEONE BRING YOU SOMETHING WARM.
THEY CALL HER THE ICE QUEEN, BUT SHE SEEMS LIKE A GOOD PERSON.
I CAN'T WAIT TO GET SOMETHING WARM.
Yeah...
Maybe some hot noodle soup?
LEMME BORROW THIS **FLAME-THROWER**.
Hm. Warm.
Sure, boss...
FWOOM

BEHIND YOU, KIMBLEE!!

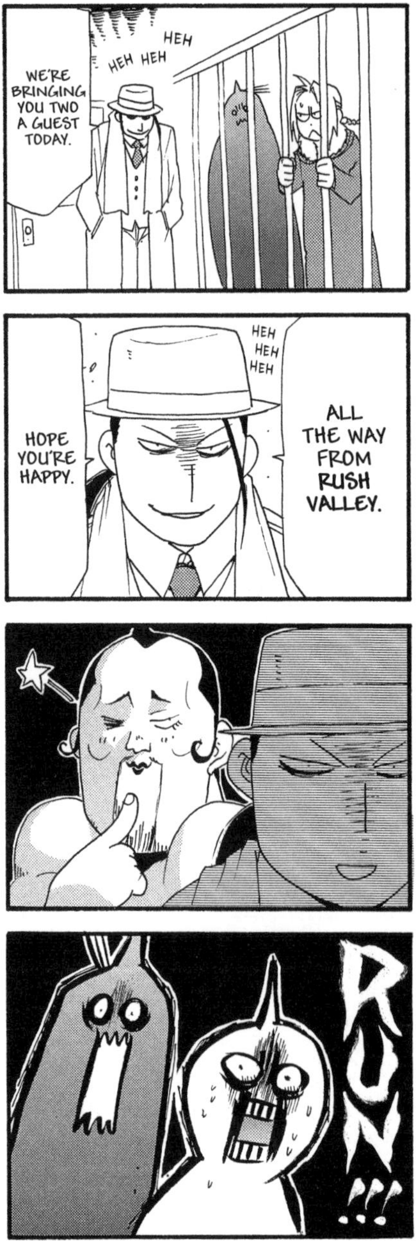
HEH
HEH HEH
WE'RE BRINGING YOU TWO A GUEST TODAY.
HEH HEH HEH
ALL THE WAY FROM **RUSH VALLEY**.
HOPE YOU'RE HAPPY.
RUN!!!

GIVE UP!!

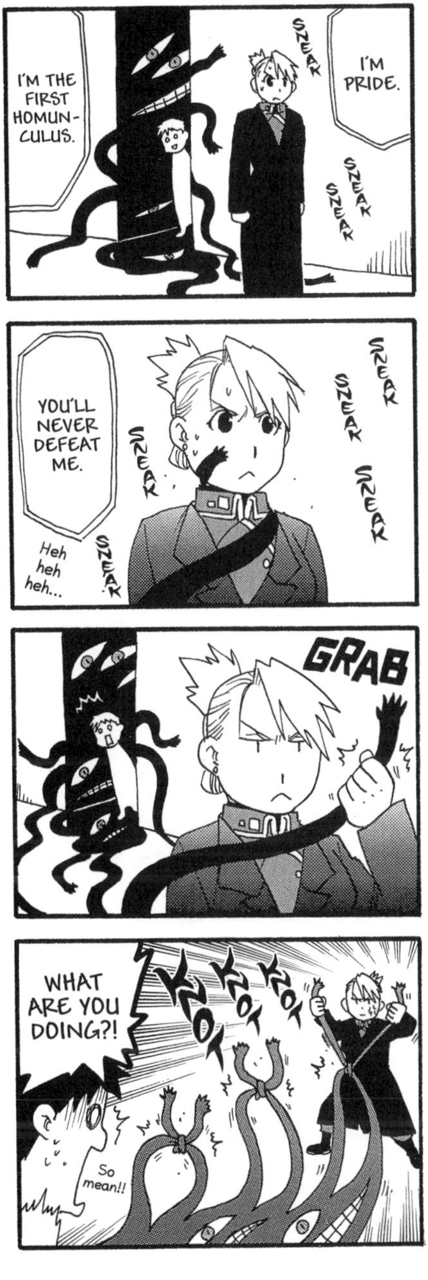
I'M PRIDE.
SNEAK
SNEAK SNEAK
I'M THE FIRST HOMUN-CULUS.
SNEAK
SNEAK
SNEAK
YOU'LL NEVER DEFEAT ME.
SNEAK
SNEAK
Heh heh heh...
GRAB
KNOT KNOT KNOT
WHAT ARE YOU DOING?!
So mean!!

WEATHERMAN

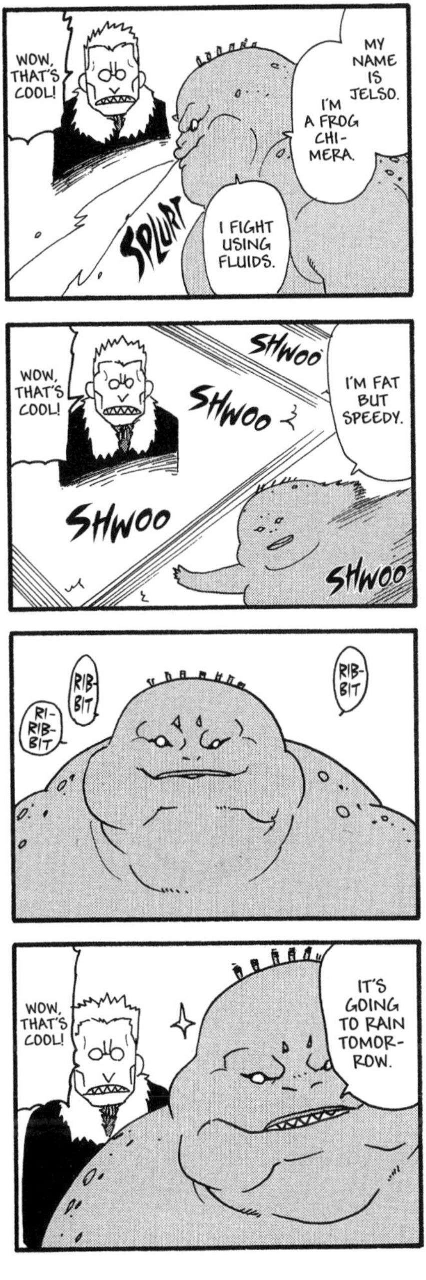
MY NAME IS JELSO.
I'M A FROG CHI-MERA.
I FIGHT USING FLUIDS.
SPLURT
WOW, THAT'S COOL!
I'M FAT BUT SPEEDY.
SHWOO
SHWOO
WOW, THAT'S COOL!
SHWOO
SHWOO
RIB-BIT
RIB-BIT
RI-RIB-BIT
IT'S GOING TO RAIN TOMOR-ROW.
WOW, THAT'S COOL!

Brotherhood DVDs
Volume 11, June 2010

TAKE BACK WHAT'S OURS!!

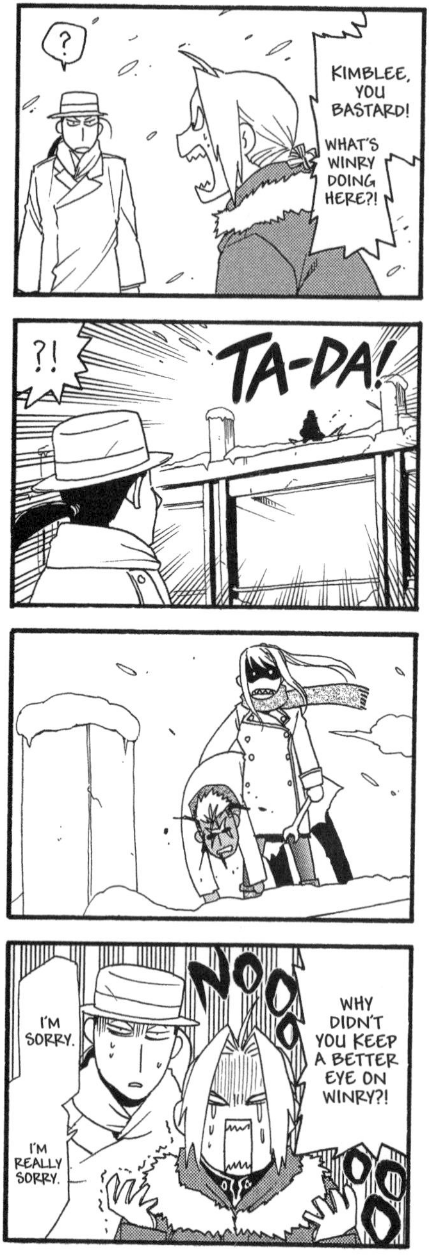
KIMBLEE, YOU BASTARD!
WHAT'S WINRY DOING HERE?!
?
TA-DA!
?!
NOOOOOO
WHY DIDN'T YOU KEEP A BETTER EYE ON WINRY?!
I'M SORRY.
I'M REALLY SORRY.

POTTY TIME

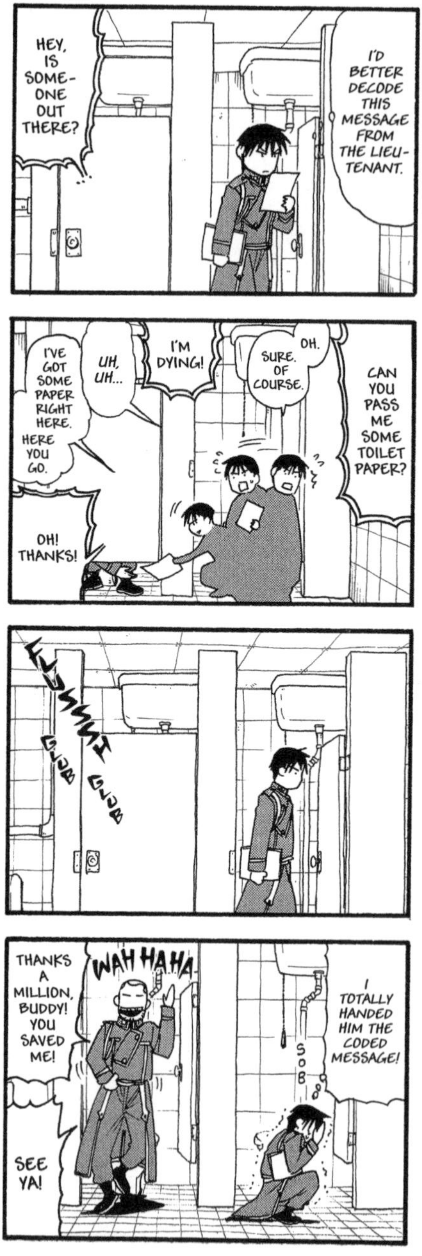
I'D BETTER DECODE THIS MESSAGE FROM THE LIEUTENANT.
HEY, IS SOMEONE OUT THERE?
CAN YOU PASS ME SOME TOILET PAPER?
OH.
SURE. OF COURSE.
I'M DYING!
UH, UH...
I'VE GOT SOME PAPER RIGHT HERE. HERE YOU GO.
OH! THANKS!
FLUSSSH
GLUB
GLUB
I TOTALLY HANDED HIM THE CODED MESSAGE!
SOB
WAH HAHA
THANKS A MILLION, BUDDY! YOU SAVED ME!
SEE YA!

START OF A LOVE STORY

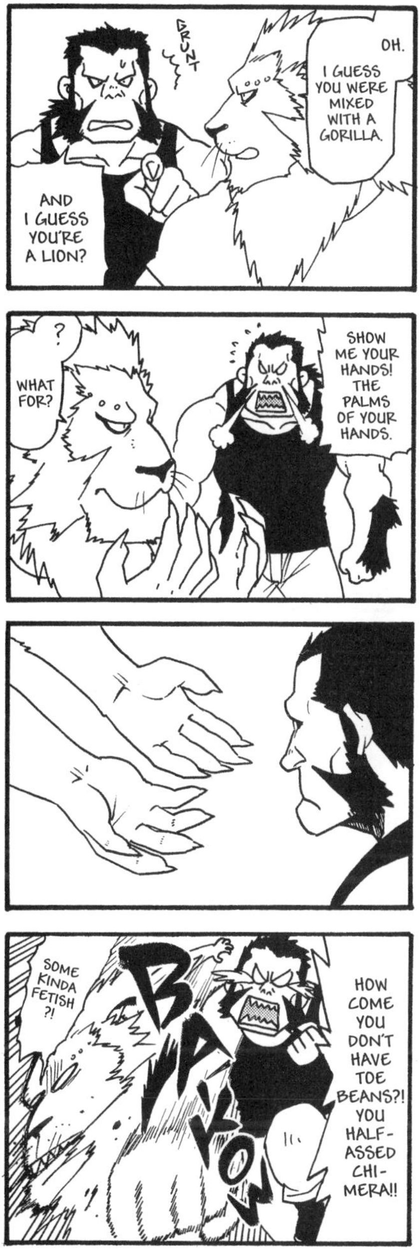
OH. I GUESS YOU WERE MIXED WITH A GORILLA.
GRUNT
AND I GUESS YOU'RE A LION?
SHOW ME YOUR HANDS! THE PALMS OF YOUR HANDS.
?
WHAT FOR?
HOW COME YOU DON'T HAVE TOE BEANS?! YOU HALF-ASSED CHI-MERA!!
BA-KOW
SOME KINDA FETISH ?!

LEGS ARE A BONUS

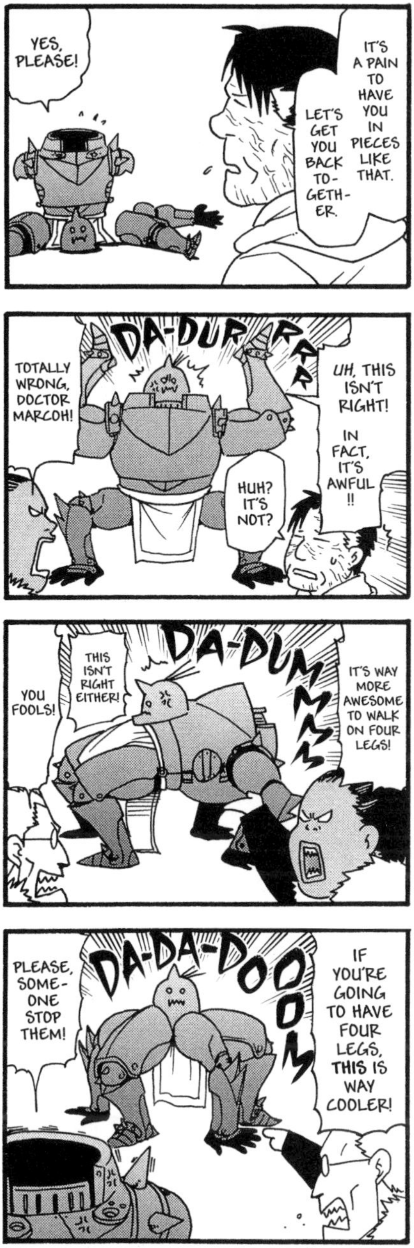
IT'S A PAIN TO HAVE YOU IN PIECES LIKE THAT.
LET'S GET YOU BACK TO-GETH-ER.
YES, PLEASE!
DA-DUR RRR
UH, THIS ISN'T RIGHT!
IN FACT, IT'S AWFUL !!
HUH? IT'S NOT?
TOTALLY WRONG, DOCTOR MARCOH!
DA-DUMMMM
IT'S WAY MORE AWESOME TO WALK ON FOUR LEGS!
THIS ISN'T RIGHT EITHER!
YOU FOOLS!
IF YOU'RE GOING TO HAVE FOUR LEGS, **THIS** IS WAY COOLER!
DA-DA-DOOOOM
PLEASE, SOME-ONE STOP THEM!

KISS OF DEATH

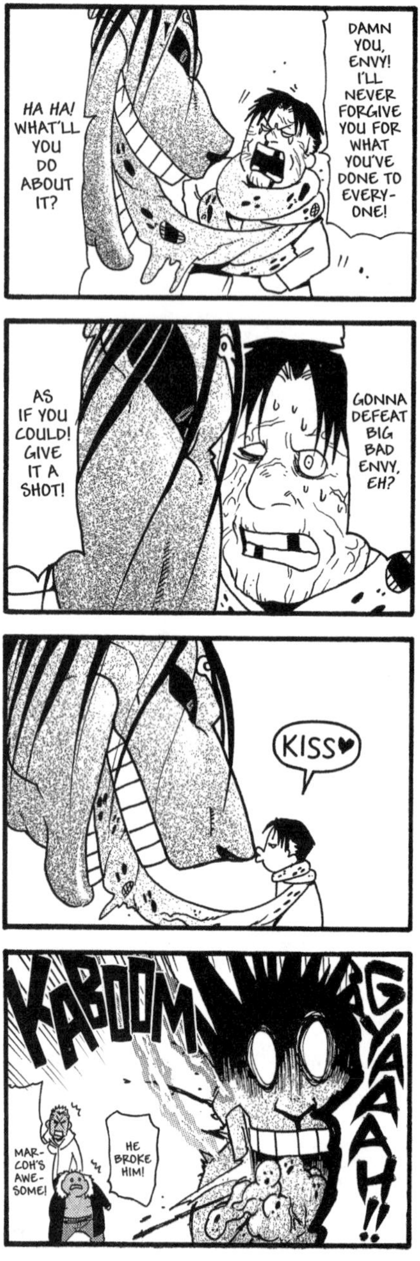
DAMN YOU, ENVY! I'LL NEVER FORGIVE YOU FOR WHAT YOU'VE DONE TO EVERY-ONE!
HA HA! WHAT'LL YOU DO ABOUT IT?
GONNA DEFEAT BIG BAD ENVY, EH?
AS IF YOU COULD! GIVE IT A SHOT!
KISS♥
RGYAAH!!
KABOOM
HE BROKE HIM!
MAR-COH'S AWE-SOME!

THE ROAD TO REUNION

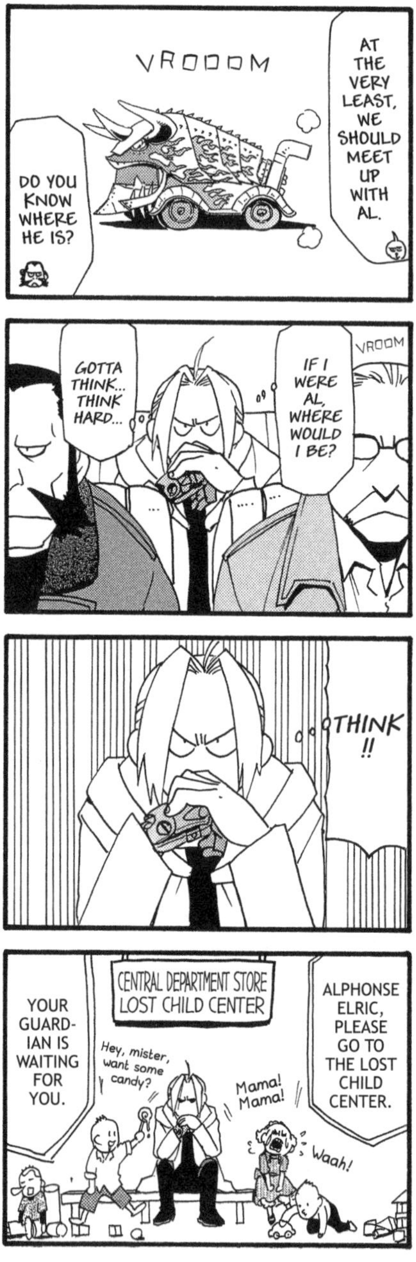
AT THE VERY LEAST, WE SHOULD MEET UP WITH AL.
VROOOM
DO YOU KNOW WHERE HE IS?
VROOM
IF I WERE AL, WHERE WOULD I BE?
GOTTA THINK... THINK HARD...
THINK !!
ALPHONSE ELRIC, PLEASE GO TO THE LOST CHILD CENTER.
CENTRAL DEPARTMENT STORE LOST CHILD CENTER
YOUR GUARD-IAN IS WAITING FOR YOU.
Mama! Mama!
Waah!
Hey, mister, want some candy?

THE FUN BRADLEY FAMILY

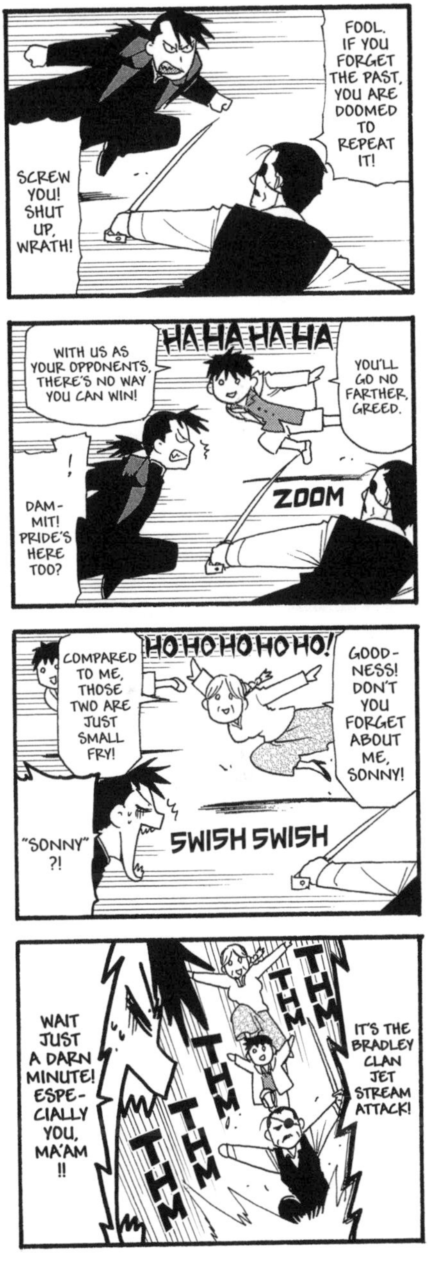
FOOL. IF YOU FORGET THE PAST, YOU ARE DOOMED TO REPEAT IT!
SCREW YOU! SHUT UP, WRATH!
HA HA HA HA
YOU'LL GO NO FARTHER, GREED.
WITH US AS YOUR OPPONENTS, THERE'S NO WAY YOU CAN WIN!
!
ZOOM
DAMMIT! PRIDE'S HERE TOO?
HO HO HO HO HO HO!
GOODNESS! DON'T YOU FORGET ABOUT ME, SONNY!
COMPARED TO ME, THOSE TWO ARE JUST SMALL FRY!
SWISH SWISH
"SONNY" ?!
THM THM
IT'S THE BRADLEY CLAN JET STREAM ATTACK!
THM THM THM
WAIT JUST A DARN MINUTE! ESPECIALLY YOU, MA'AM !!

THE WORLD'S SOFTEST TERRORISM

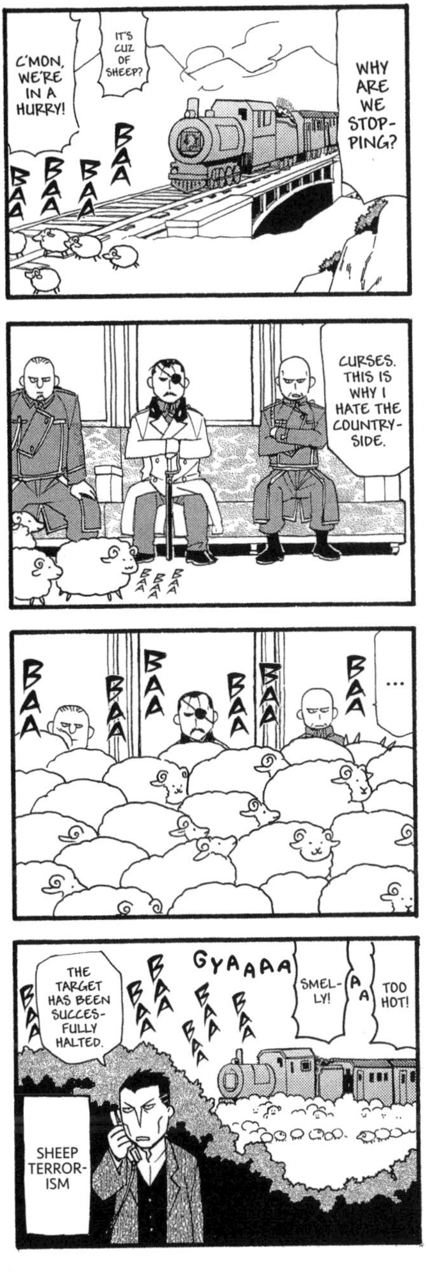
WHY ARE WE STOPPING?
IT'S CUZ OF SHEEP?
C'MON, WE'RE IN A HURRY!
BAA BAA BAA BAA
CURSES. THIS IS WHY I HATE THE COUNTRYSIDE.
BAA BAA BAA
...
BAA BAA BAA BAA BAA BAA
TOO HOT!
SMELLY!
GYAAAAA
BAA BAA BAA BAA BAA BAA
THE TARGET HAS BEEN SUCCESFULLY HALTED.
SHEEP TERRORISM

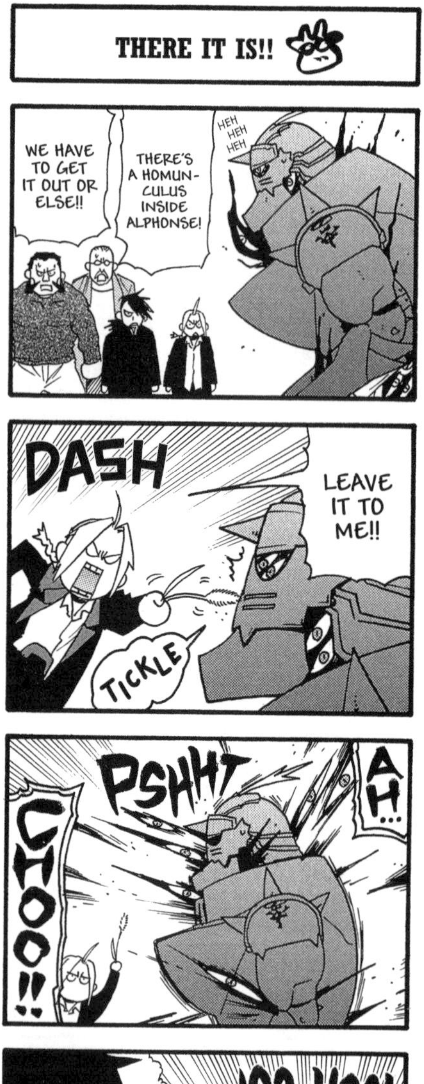
THERE IT IS!!
HEH HEH HEH
THERE'S A HOMUNCULUS INSIDE ALPHONSE!
WE HAVE TO GET IT OUT OR ELSE!!
LEAVE IT TO ME!!
DASH
TICKLE
AH...
PSHHT
CHOO!!
WOO-HOO!
GRIT

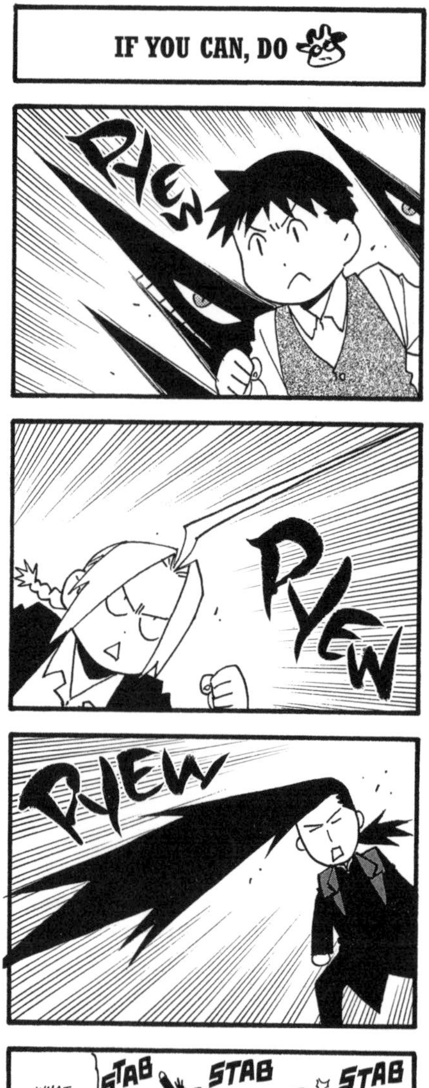
IF YOU CAN, DO
PYEW
PYEW
PYEW
STAB
STAB
STAB
STAB
WHAT MONSTERS ...
SHUNK
SHUNK

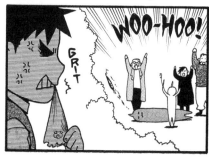

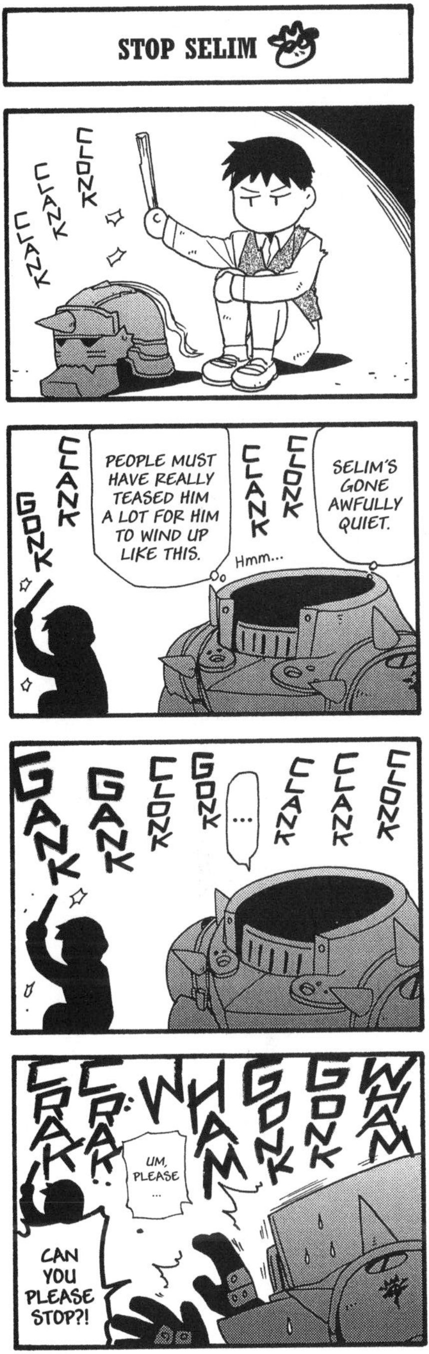
STOP SELIM
CLONK
CLANK
CLANK
SELIM'S GONE AWFULLY QUIET.
CLONK
CLANK
Hmm...
PEOPLE MUST HAVE REALLY TEASED HIM A LOT FOR HIM TO WIND UP LIKE THIS.
CLANK
GONK
CLONK
CLANK
CLANK
...
GONK
CLONK
GANK
GANK
WHAM
GONK
GONK
WHAM
CRAK!
CRAK
UM, PLEASE ...
CAN YOU PLEASE STOP?!

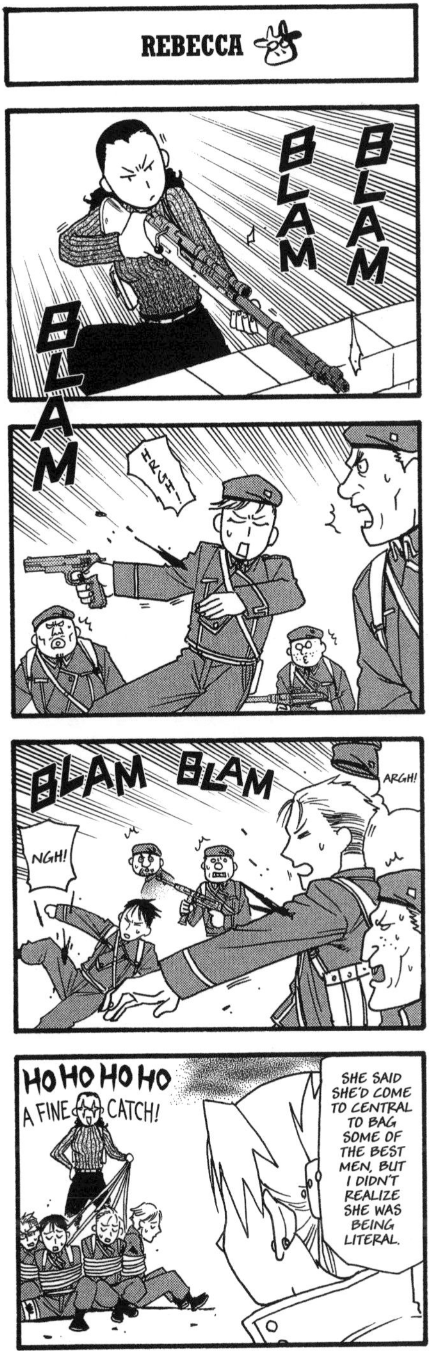
REBECCA
BLAM
BLAM
BLAM
HRGH!
ARGH!
BLAM
BLAM
NGH!
SHE SAID SHE'D COME TO CENTRAL TO BAG SOME OF THE BEST MEN, BUT I DIDN'T REALIZE SHE WAS BEING LITERAL.
HO HO HO HO
A FINE CATCH!

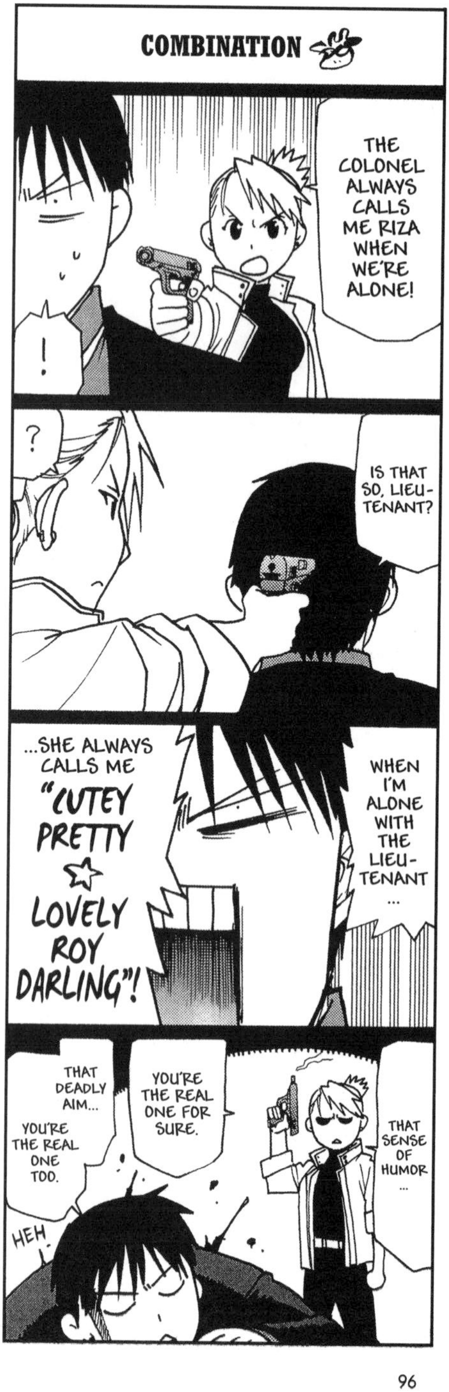
COMBINATION
THE COLONEL ALWAYS CALLS ME RIZA WHEN WE'RE ALONE!
!
IS THAT SO, LIEUTENANT?
?
WHEN I'M ALONE WITH THE LIEUTENANT...
...SHE ALWAYS CALLS ME "CUTEY PRETTY ☆ LOVELY ROY DARLING"!
THAT SENSE OF HUMOR...
YOU'RE THE REAL ONE FOR SURE.
THAT DEADLY AIM...
YOU'RE THE REAL ONE TOO.
HEH

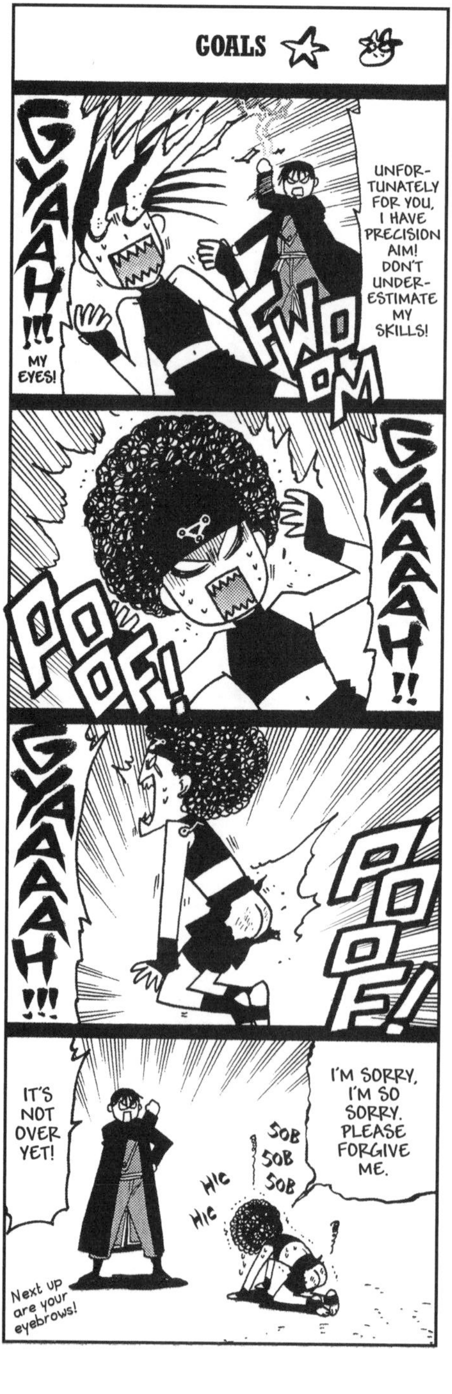
GOALS
UNFORTUNATELY FOR YOU, I HAVE PRECISION AIM! DON'T UNDERESTIMATE MY SKILLS!
FWOOM
GYAAH!!!
MY EYES!
GYAAAAH!!
POOF!
POOF!
GYAAAAH!!!
I'M SORRY, I'M SO SORRY. PLEASE FORGIVE ME.
SOB SOB SOB
HIC HIC
IT'S NOT OVER YET!
Next up are your eyebrows!

GETTING BACK IS A PAIN

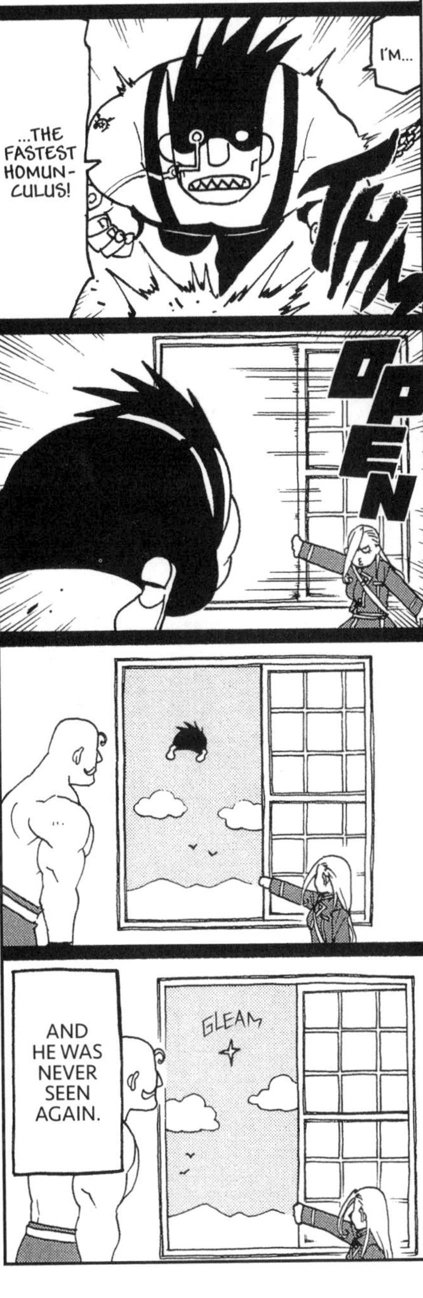
I'M...
...THE FASTEST HOMUNCULUS!
THM
OPEN
...
GLEAM
AND HE WAS NEVER SEEN AGAIN.

GET OUT!!

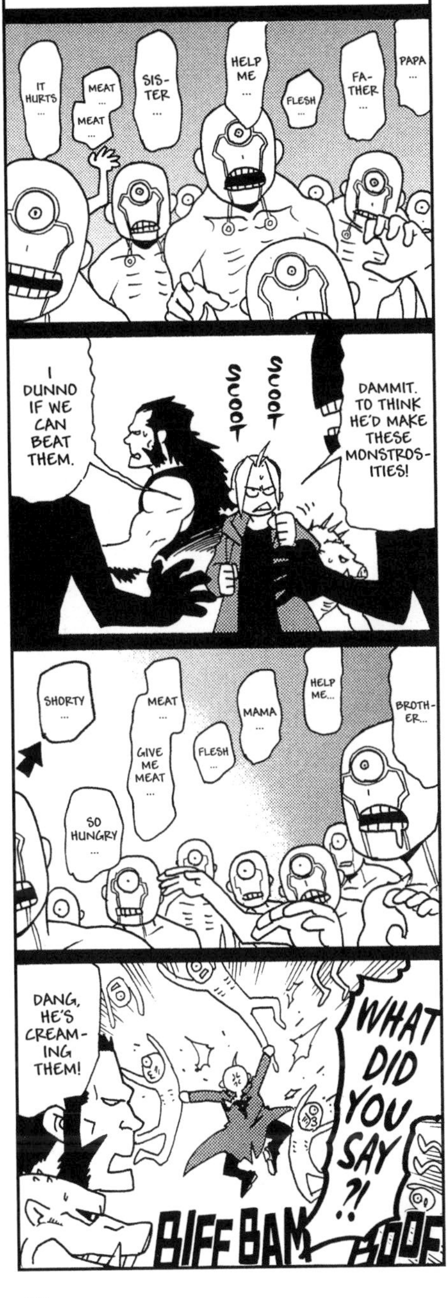
PAPA...
FATHER...
FLESH...
HELP ME...
SISTER...
MEAT... MEAT...
IT HURTS...
DAMMIT. TO THINK HE'D MAKE THESE MONSTROSITIES!
SCOOT
SCOOT
I DUNNO IF WE CAN BEAT THEM.
BROTHER...
HELP ME...
MAMA...
FLESH...
MEAT...
GIVE ME MEAT...
SHORTY...
SO HUNGRY...
WHAT DID YOU SAY?!
DANG, HE'S CREAMING THEM!
BIFF BAM

SPARKLE

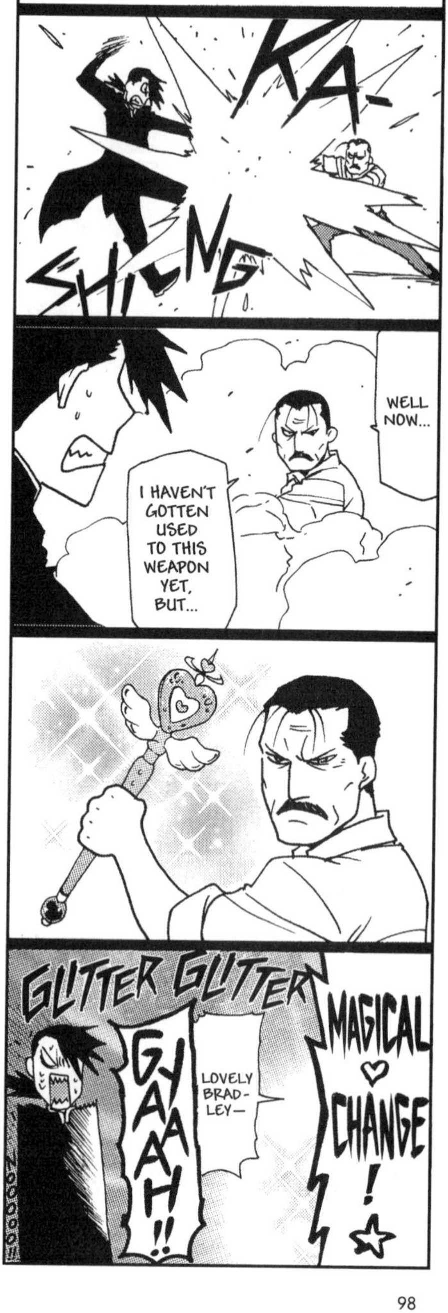
KA-
SHING
WELL NOW...
I HAVEN'T GOTTEN USED TO THIS WEAPON YET, BUT...
GLITTER GLITTER
MAGICAL ♡ CHANGE!
LOVELY BRAD-LEY—
GYAAAH!!

HEADING HOME

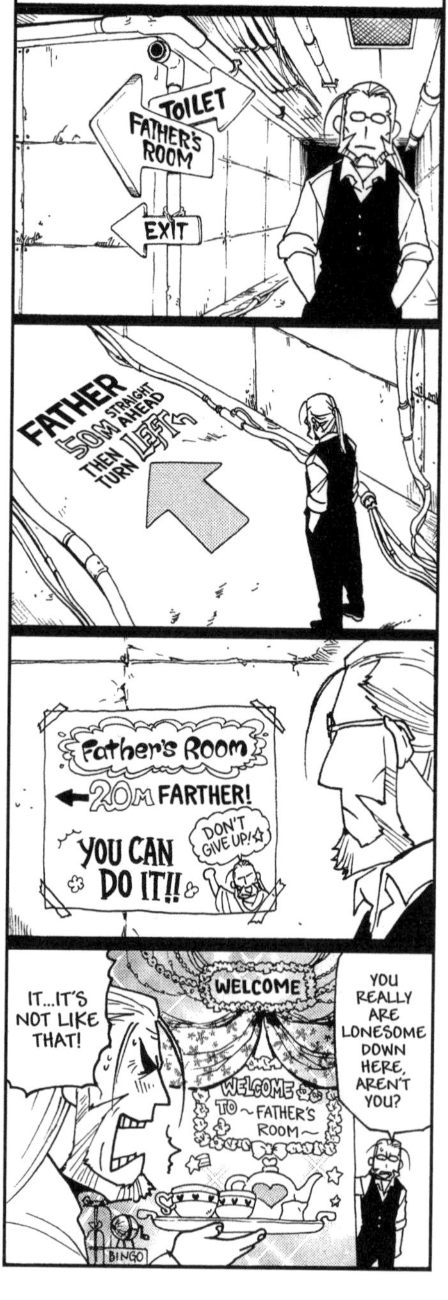
TOILET
FATHER'S ROOM
EXIT
FATHER 50M STRAIGHT AHEAD THEN TURN LEFT
Father's Room
← 20M FARTHER!
YOU CAN DO IT!!
DON'T GIVE UP!☆
YOU REALLY ARE LONESOME DOWN HERE, AREN'T YOU?
IT...IT'S NOT LIKE THAT!
WELCOME
WELCOME TO ~FATHER'S ROOM~
BINGO

BUCCANEER'S DEATH!!

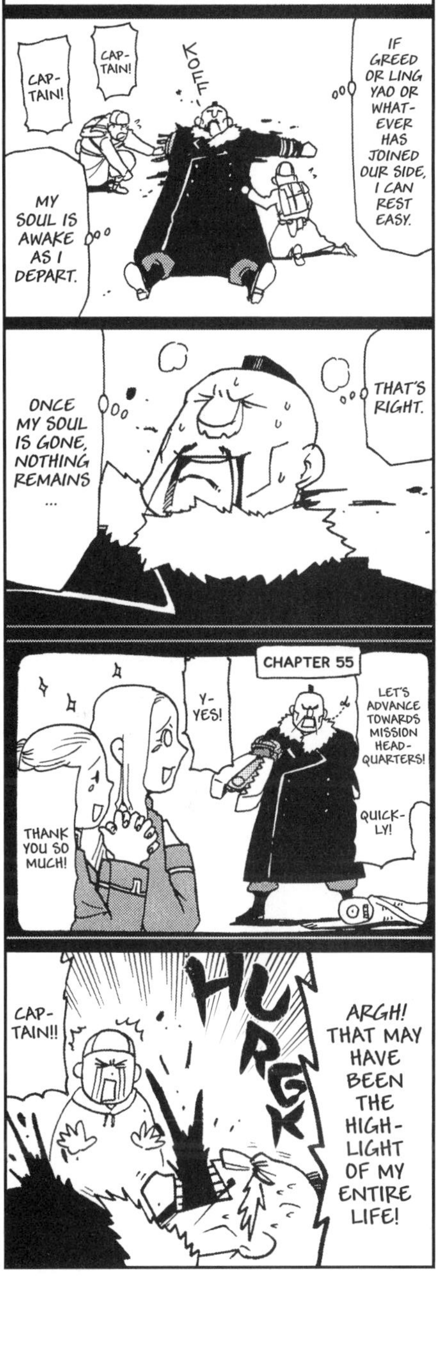
IF GREED OR LING YAO OR WHAT-EVER HAS JOINED OUR SIDE, I CAN REST EASY.
KOFF
CAP-TAIN!
CAP-TAIN!
MY SOUL IS AWAKE AS I DEPART.
THAT'S RIGHT.
ONCE MY SOUL IS GONE, NOTHING REMAINS ...
CHAPTER 55
LET'S ADVANCE TOWARDS MISSION HEAD-QUARTERS!
QUICK-LY!
Y-YES!
THANK YOU SO MUCH!
ARGH! THAT MAY HAVE BEEN THE HIGH-LIGHT OF MY ENTIRE LIFE!
HURGK
CAP-TAIN!!

OLD MAN FU'S DEATH

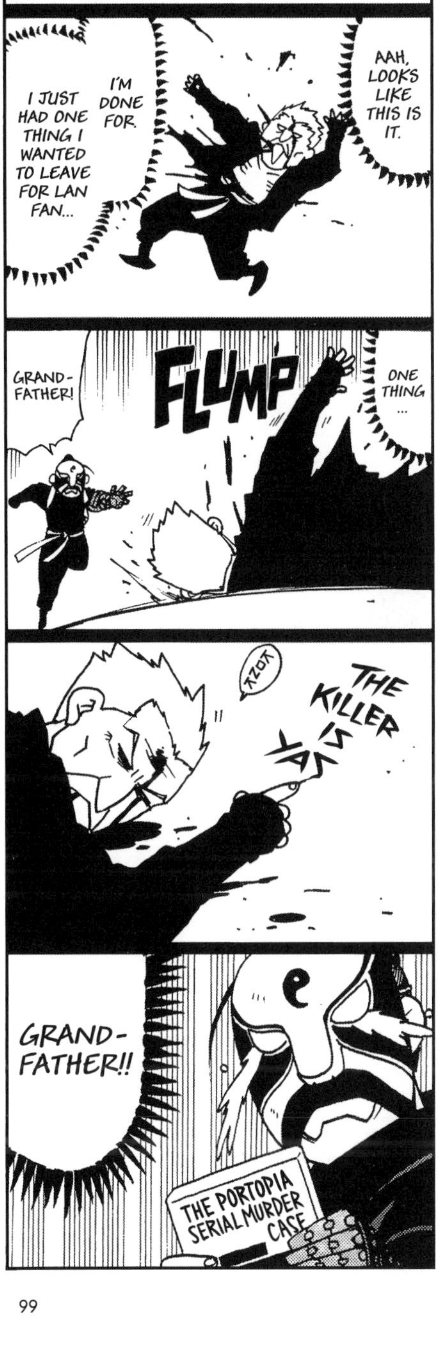
AAH, LOOKS LIKE THIS IS IT.
I'M DONE FOR.
I JUST HAD ONE THING I WANTED TO LEAVE FOR LAN FAN...
ONE THING ...
FLUMP
GRAND-FATHER!
THE KILLER IS YAS
GRAND-FATHER!!
THE PORTOPIA SERIAL MURDER CASE

YOUR NAME

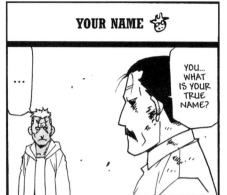

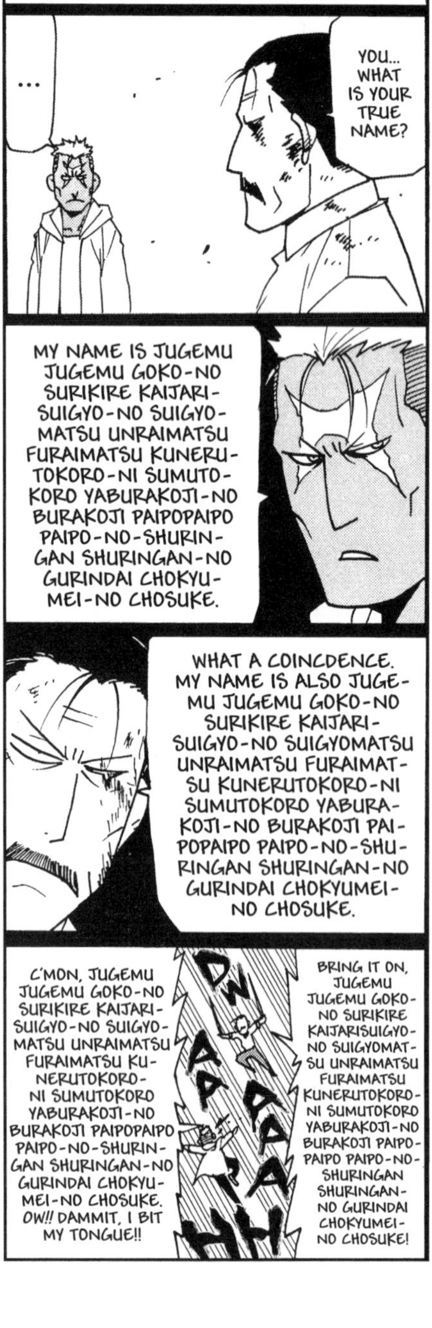

YOU... WHAT IS YOUR TRUE NAME?
...
MY NAME IS JUGEMU JUGEMU GOKO-NO SURIKIRE KAIJARI-SUIGYO-NO SUIGYO-MATSU UNRAIMATSU FURAIMATSU KUNERU-TOKORO-NI SUMUTO-KORO YABURAKOJI-NO BURAKOJI PAIPOPAIPO PAIPO-NO-SHURIN-GAN SHURINGAN-NO GURINDAI CHOKYU-MEI-NO CHOSUKE.
WHAT A COINCDENCE. MY NAME IS ALSO JUGE-MU JUGEMU GOKO-NO SURIKIRE KAIJARI-SUIGYO-NO SUIGYOMATSU UNRAIMATSU FURAIMAT-SU KUNERUTOKORO-NI SUMUTOKORO YABURA-KOJI-NO BURAKOJI PAI-POPAIPO PAIPO-NO-SHU-RINGAN SHURINGAN-NO GURINDAI CHOKYUMEI-NO CHOSUKE.
BRING IT ON, JUGEMU JUGEMU GOKO-NO SURIKIRE KAIJARISUIGYO-NO SUIGYOMAT-SU UNRAIMATSU FURAIMATSU KUNERUTOKORO-NI SUMUTOKORO YABURAKOJI-NO BURAKOJI PAIPO-PAIPO PAIPO-NO-SHURINGAN SHURINGAN-NO GURINDAI CHOKYUMEI-NO CHOSUKE!
DWAAAAAHH
C'MON, JUGEMU JUGEMU GOKO-NO SURIKIRE KAIJARI-SUIGYO-NO SUIGYO-MATSU UNRAIMATSU FURAIMATSU KU-NERUTOKORO-NI SUMUTOKORO YABURAKOJI-NO BURAKOJI PAIPOPAIPO PAIPO-NO-SHURIN-GAN SHURINGAN-NO GURINDAI CHOKYU-MEI-NO CHOSUKE. OW!! DAMMIT, I BIT MY TONGUE!!

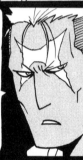

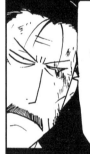

OLD, SO OLD

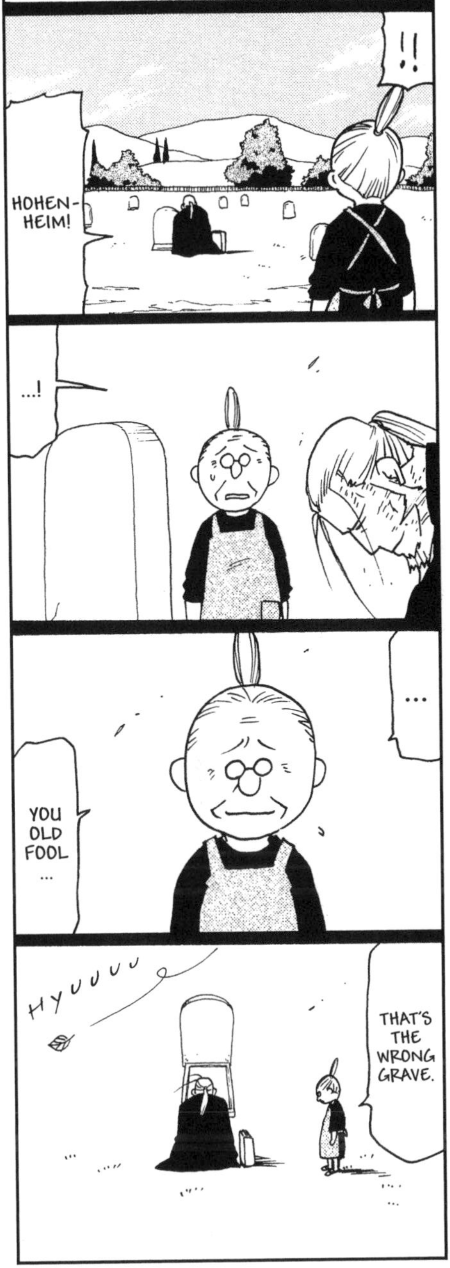
!!
HOHEN-HEIM!
...!
...
YOU OLD FOOL ...
HYUUUU
THAT'S THE WRONG GRAVE.

THE BEING WITHIN PRIDE

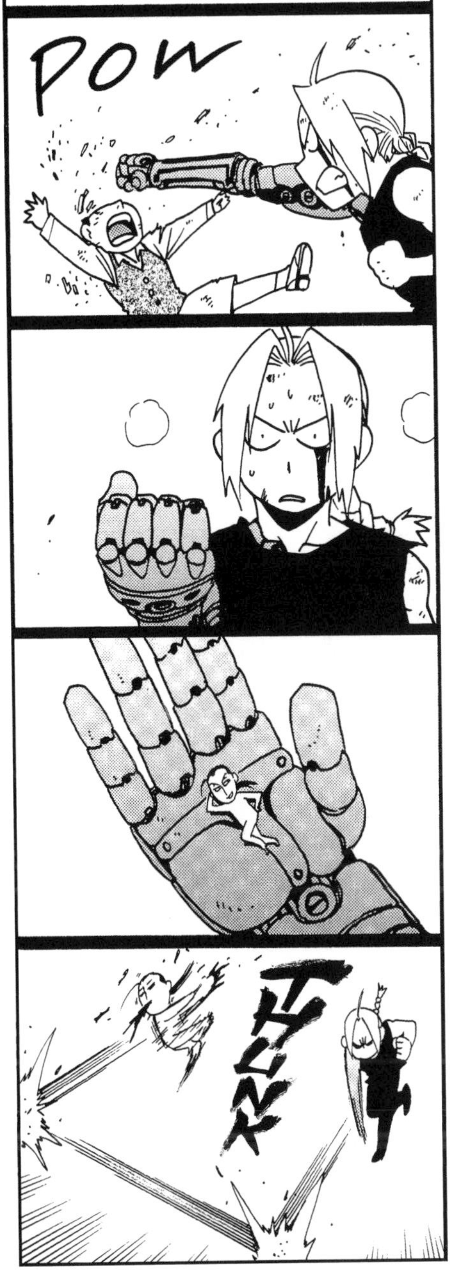
POW
THUNK

Brotherhood DVDs
Volume 16, November 2010

THE POWER OF A GOD

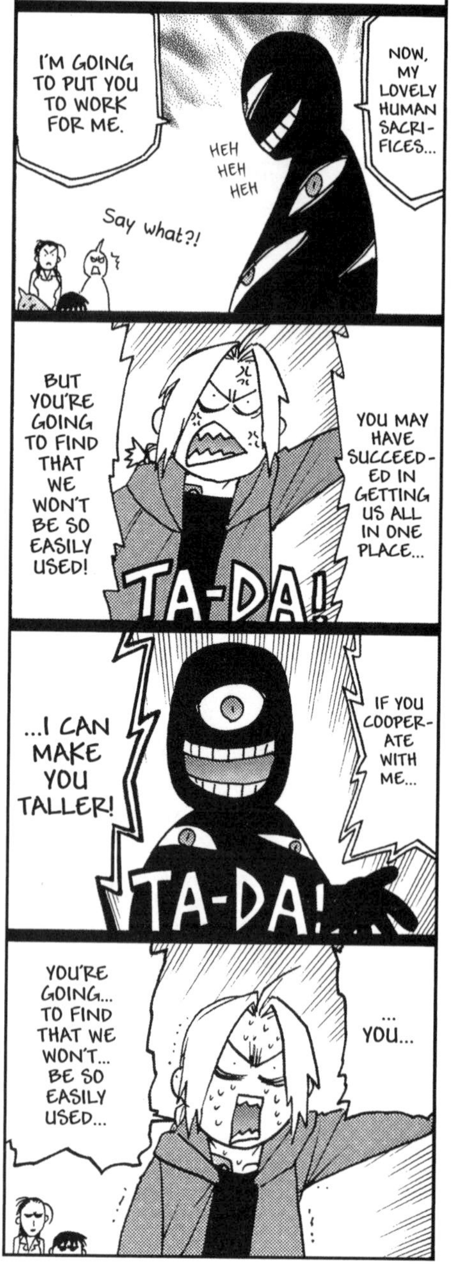
NOW, MY LOVELY HUMAN SACRIFICES...
I'M GOING TO PUT YOU TO WORK FOR ME.
HEH HEH HEH
Say what?!
YOU MAY HAVE SUCCEEDED IN GETTING US ALL IN ONE PLACE...
BUT YOU'RE GOING TO FIND THAT WE WON'T BE SO EASILY USED!
TA-DA!
IF YOU COOPERATE WITH ME...
...I CAN MAKE YOU TALLER!
TA-DA!
...YOU...
YOU'RE GOING... TO FIND THAT WE WON'T... BE SO EASILY USED...

HISTORY'S MOST PATHETIC BATTLE

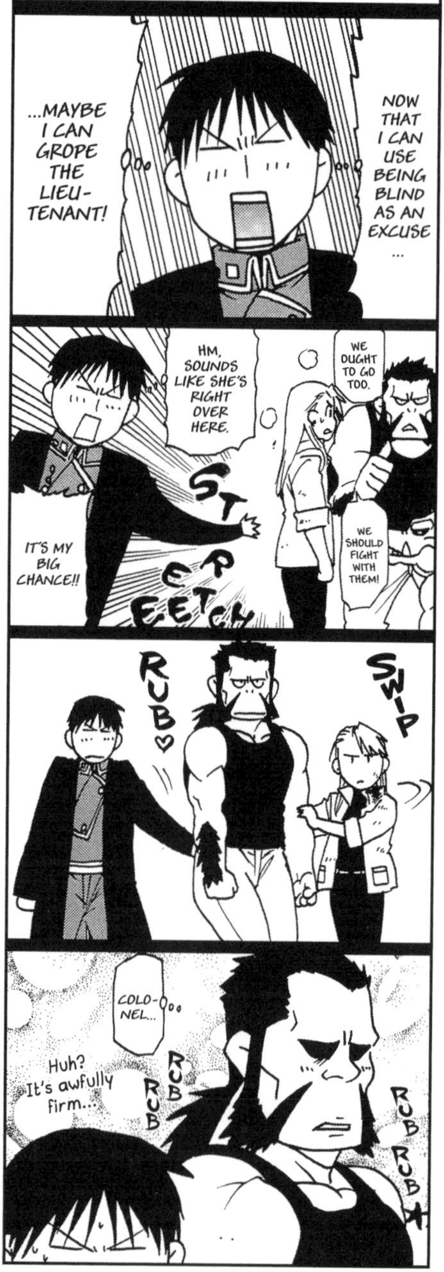
NOW THAT I CAN USE BEING BLIND AS AN EXCUSE...
...MAYBE I CAN GROPE THE LIEUTENANT!
WE OUGHT TO GO TOO.
HM, SOUNDS LIKE SHE'S RIGHT OVER HERE.
WE SHOULD FIGHT WITH THEM!
STREEETCH
IT'S MY BIG CHANCE!!
SWIP
RUB
RUB RUB
RUB RUB
COLONEL...
Huh? It's awfully firm...

FRONT LINES OF FASHION

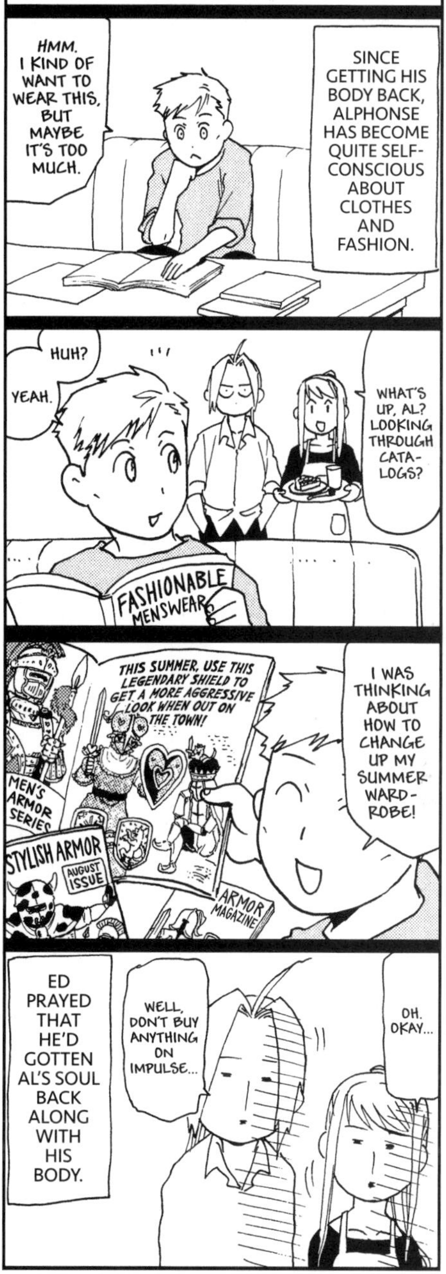
SINCE GETTING HIS BODY BACK, ALPHONSE HAS BECOME QUITE SELF-CONSCIOUS ABOUT CLOTHES AND FASHION.
HMM. I KIND OF WANT TO WEAR THIS, BUT MAYBE IT'S TOO MUCH.
WHAT'S UP, AL? LOOKING THROUGH CATA-LOGS?
HUH?
YEAH.
FASHIONABLE MENSWEAR
I WAS THINKING ABOUT HOW TO CHANGE UP MY SUMMER WARD-ROBE!
THIS SUMMER, USE THIS LEGENDARY SHIELD TO GET A MORE AGGRESSIVE LOOK WHEN OUT ON THE TOWN!
MEN'S ARMOR SERIES
STYLISH ARMOR
AUGUST ISSUE
ARMOR MAGAZINE
OH. OKAY...
WELL, DON'T BUY ANYTHING ON IMPULSE...
ED PRAYED THAT HE'D GOTTEN AL'S SOUL BACK ALONG WITH HIS BODY.

Brotherhood DVDs
Fullmetal Alchemist Festival 2009 in Pacifico
Yokohama Event Bonus, November 2009

WE LOVE YOKOHAMA!!

WE GET TO HOLD AN ANIME EVENT AT THE PACIFICO YOKOHAMA CONVEN-TION CENTER!
BRING ME, BRING ME!
WOO-HOO!
WHEN I THINK OF YOKOHAMA, I THINK OF THE LANDMARK TOWER.
I RECOM-MEND SEEING THE AKA-RENGA WARE-HOUSES.
NAW, IT'S ALL ABOUT THE YOKO-HAMA BAYSTARS!
MARI-NOS SOC-CER!
CHINA-TOWN!
LALA-PORT SHOP-PING!
BUT YOU KNOW, PACIFICO YOKOHAMA IS RIGHT BY THE OCEAN, SO...
...THAT MOIST WIND FROM THE SEA IS INTENSE!
SHUMAI
YEAAARGH!!
WE'RE GONNA RUST!!

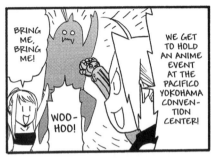

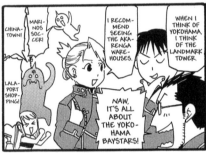

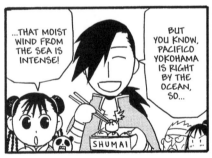

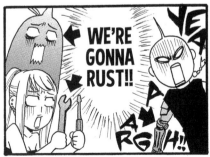

OTHER PRODUCTS

ALCHEMISTS ARE AMAZING

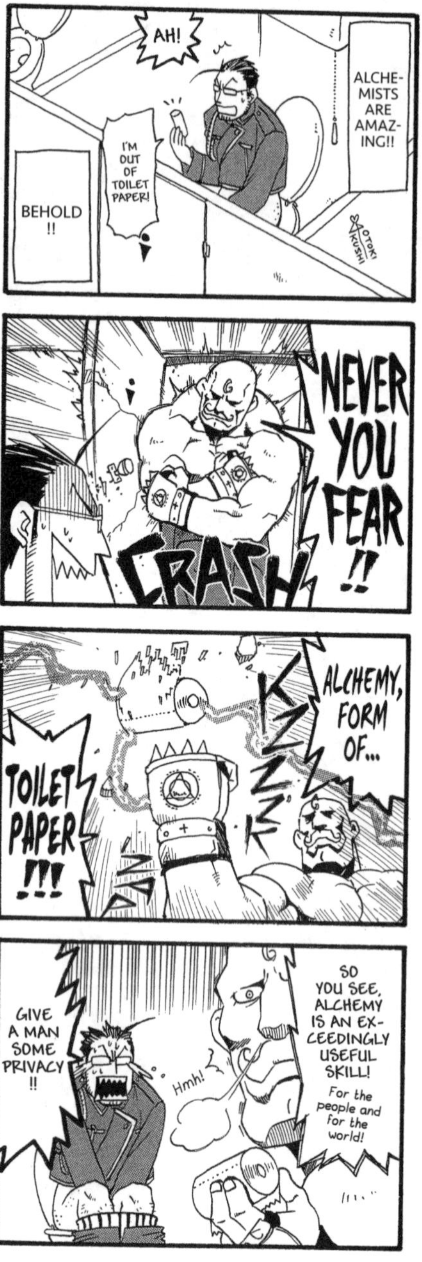
ALCHE-MISTS ARE AMAZ-ING!!
AH!
I'M OUT OF TOILET PAPER!
BEHOLD!!
OTOKI KUSHI
NEVER YOU FEAR!!
CRASH
ALCHEMY, FORM OF...
TOILET PAPER!!!
SO YOU SEE, ALCHEMY IS AN EX-CEEDINGLY USEFUL SKILL!
For the people and for the world!
Hmh!
GIVE A MAN SOME PRIVACY!!

HEY, MA'AM, YOU LISTENING?

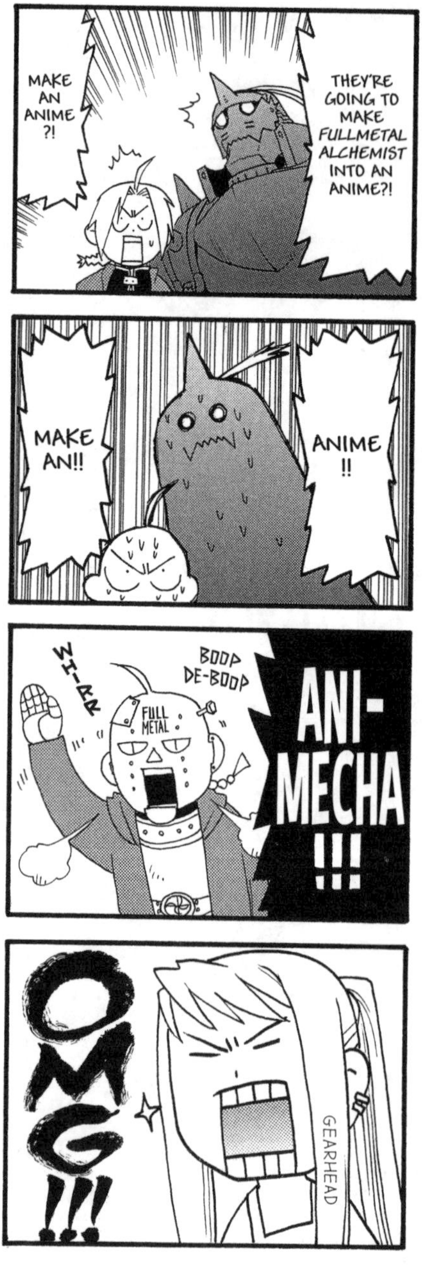
THEY'RE GOING TO MAKE FULLMETAL ALCHEMIST INTO AN ANIME?!
MAKE AN ANIME?!
ANIME!!
MAKE AN!!
ANI-MECHA!!!
BOOP DE-BOOP
WHIRR
FULL METAL
OMG!!!
GEARHEAD

HOW'S THE COLONEL BEEN LATELY?

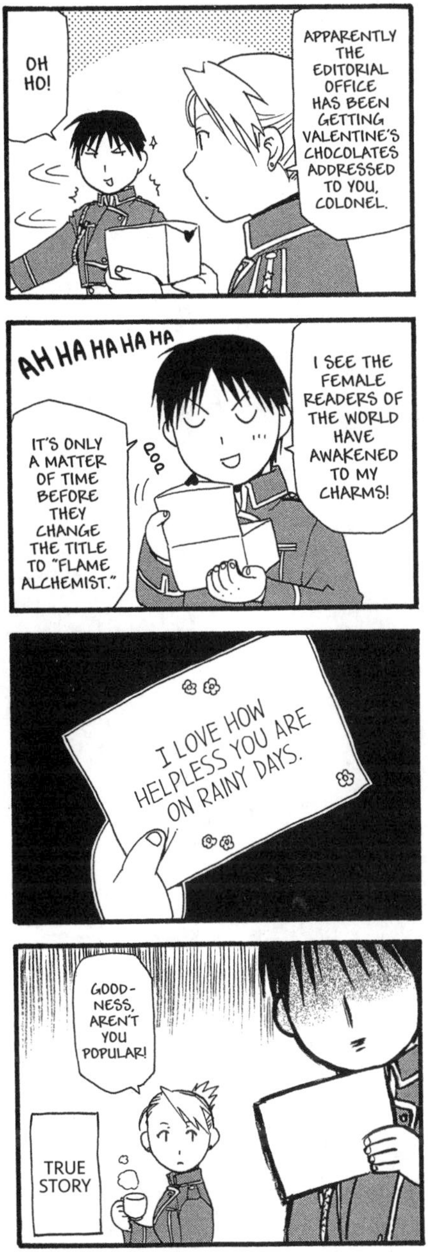
APPARENTLY THE EDITORIAL OFFICE HAS BEEN GETTING VALENTINE'S CHOCOLATES ADDRESSED TO YOU, COLONEL.
OH HO!
AH HA HA HA HA HA
I SEE THE FEMALE READERS OF THE WORLD HAVE AWAKENED TO MY CHARMS!
IT'S ONLY A MATTER OF TIME BEFORE THEY CHANGE THE TITLE TO "FLAME ALCHEMIST."
I LOVE HOW HELPLESS YOU ARE ON RAINY DAYS.
GOOD-NESS, AREN'T YOU POPULAR!
TRUE STORY

WHATEVER HAPPENED TO ROSÉ?

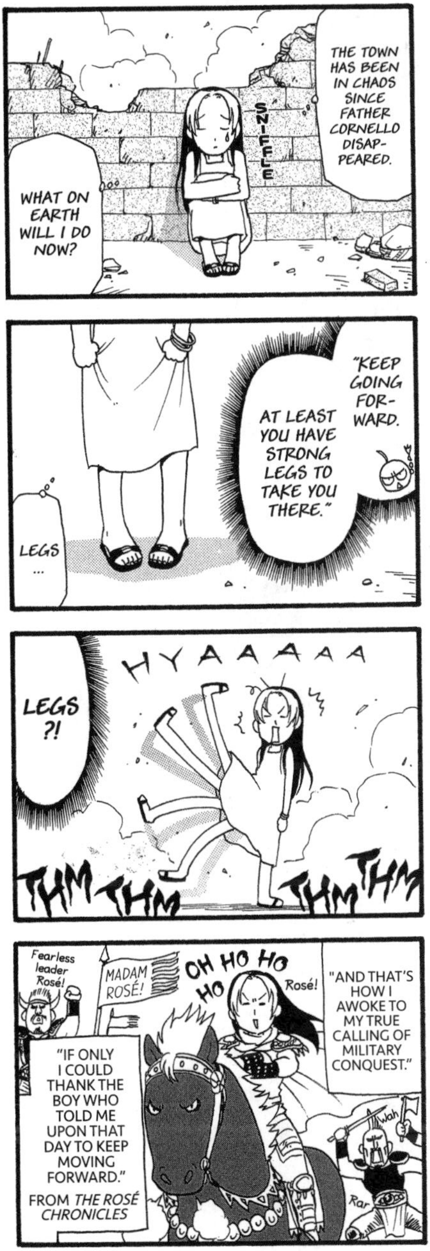
THE TOWN HAS BEEN IN CHAOS SINCE FATHER CORNELLO DISAPPEARED.
SNIFFLE
WHAT ON EARTH WILL I DO NOW?
"KEEP GOING FORWARD.
AT LEAST YOU HAVE STRONG LEGS TO TAKE YOU THERE."
LEGS ...
HYAAAAA
LEGS ?!
THM THM THM THM
"AND THAT'S HOW I AWOKE TO MY TRUE CALLING OF MILITARY CONQUEST."
Rosé!
OH HO HO HO
MADAM ROSÉ!
Fearless leader Rosé!
"IF ONLY I COULD THANK THE BOY WHO TOLD ME UPON THAT DAY TO KEEP MOVING FORWARD."
FROM *THE ROSÉ CHRONICLES*
Wah
Rar

Other Products
Shonen Gangan, May 2003,
Second Anniversary Character Contest

NEW COMMEMORATIVE ALBUM FLYING OFF THE SHELVES!
~THE SONG OF THOSE IN THE SHADOWS~

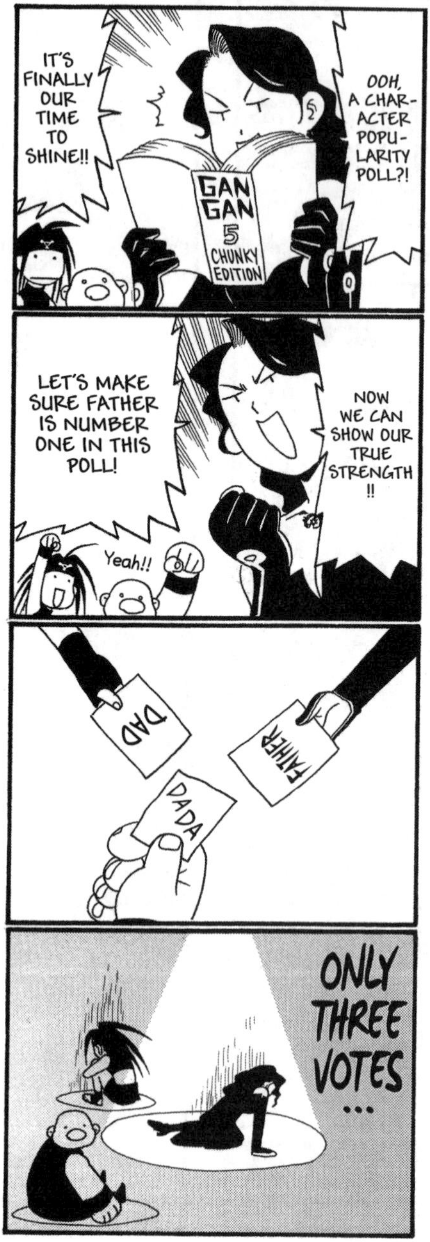
OOH, A CHARACTER POPULARITY POLL?!
IT'S FINALLY OUR TIME TO SHINE!!
GAN GAN 5 CHUNKY EDITION
NOW WE CAN SHOW OUR TRUE STRENGTH!!
LET'S MAKE SURE FATHER IS NUMBER ONE IN THIS POLL!
Yeah!!
FATHER
DAD
DADA
ONLY THREE VOTES...

FAREWELL, ELRIC BROTHERS!

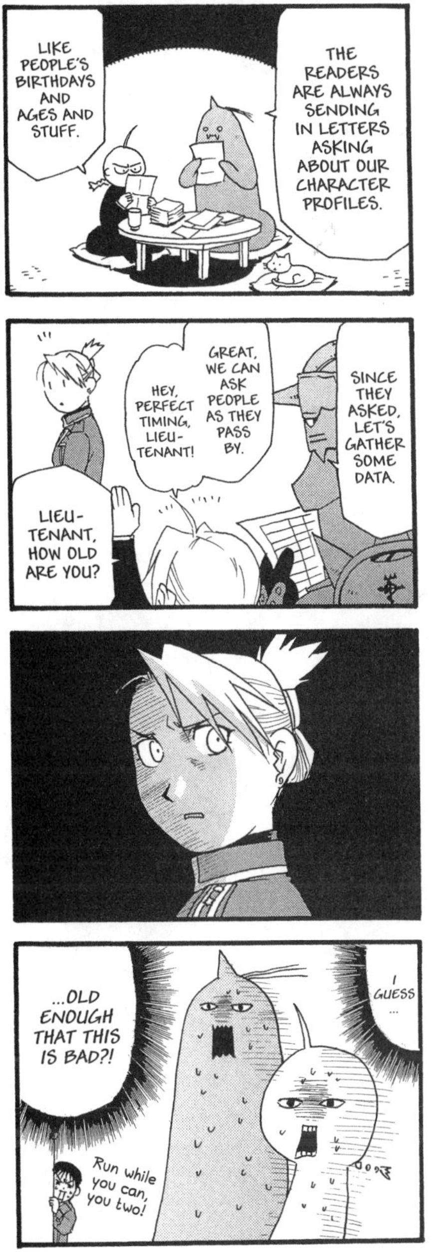
THE READERS ARE ALWAYS SENDING IN LETTERS ASKING ABOUT OUR CHARACTER PROFILES.
LIKE PEOPLE'S BIRTHDAYS AND AGES AND STUFF.
SINCE THEY ASKED, LET'S GATHER SOME DATA.
GREAT, WE CAN ASK PEOPLE AS THEY PASS BY.
HEY, PERFECT TIMING, LIEU-TENANT!
LIEU-TENANT, HOW OLD ARE YOU?
I GUESS...
...OLD ENOUGH THAT THIS IS BAD?!
Run while you can, you two!

ANOTHER TOWN BITES THE DUST

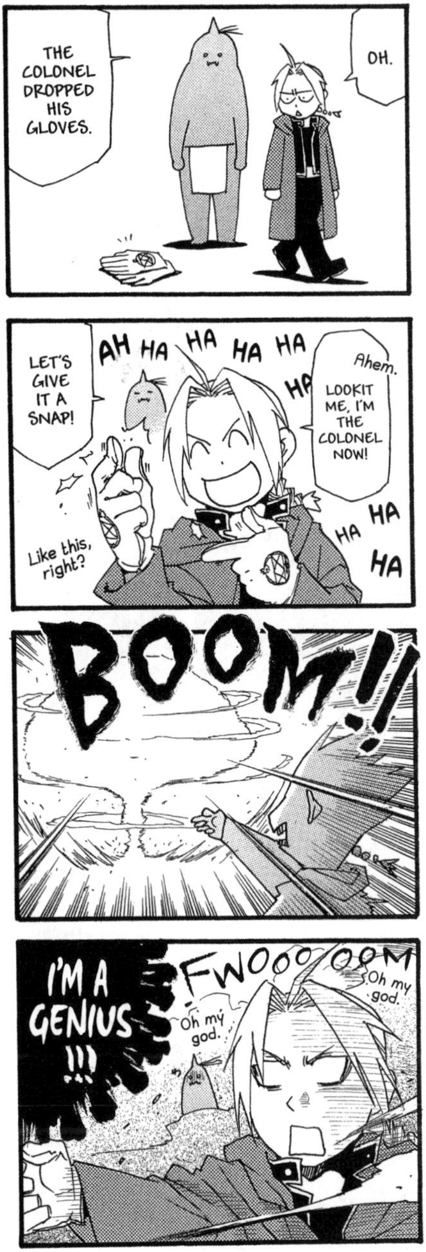
OH.
THE COLONEL DROPPED HIS GLOVES.
Ahem.
LOOKIT ME, I'M THE COLONEL NOW!
AH HA HA HA HA HA
LET'S GIVE IT A SNAP!
HA HA HA
Like this, right?
BOOM!!
FWOOOOOM
Oh my god.
Oh my god.
I'M A GENIUS!!!

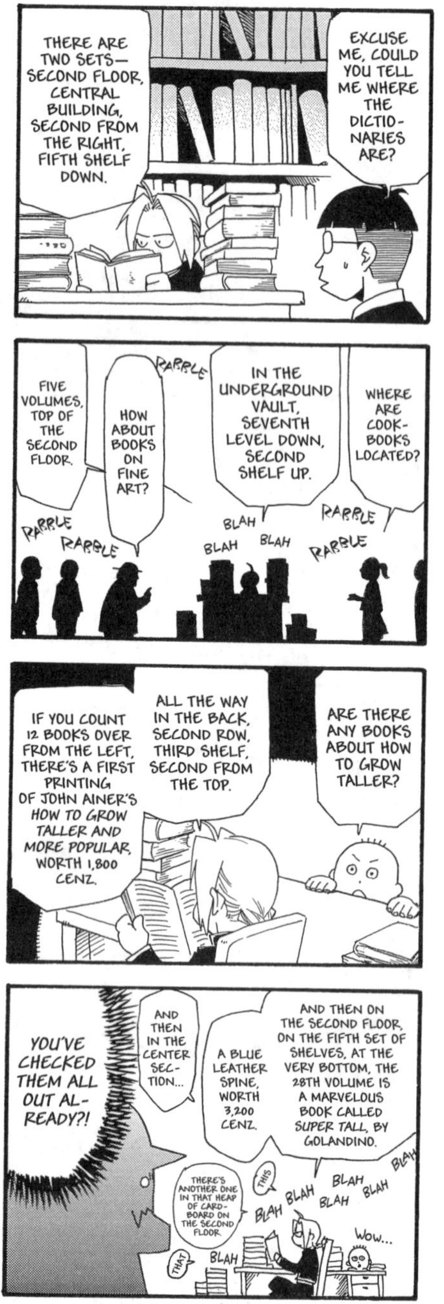
EXCUSE ME, COULD YOU TELL ME WHERE THE DICTIONARIES ARE?
THERE ARE TWO SETS—SECOND FLOOR, CENTRAL BUILDING, SECOND FROM THE RIGHT, FIFTH SHELF DOWN.
WHERE ARE COOKBOOKS LOCATED?
IN THE UNDERGROUND VAULT, SEVENTH LEVEL DOWN, SECOND SHELF UP.
RABBLE
HOW ABOUT BOOKS ON FINE ART?
FIVE VOLUMES, TOP OF THE SECOND FLOOR.
RABBLE
BLAH
BLAH
BLAH
RABBLE
RABBLE
RABBLE
ARE THERE ANY BOOKS ABOUT HOW TO GROW TALLER?
ALL THE WAY IN THE BACK, SECOND ROW, THIRD SHELF, SECOND FROM THE TOP.
IF YOU COUNT 12 BOOKS OVER FROM THE LEFT, THERE'S A FIRST PRINTING OF JOHN AINER'S HOW TO GROW TALLER AND MORE POPULAR, WORTH 1,800 CENZ.
AND THEN ON THE SECOND FLOOR, ON THE FIFTH SET OF SHELVES, AT THE VERY BOTTOM, THE 28TH VOLUME IS A MARVELOUS BOOK CALLED SUPER TALL, BY GOLANDINO.
A BLUE LEATHER SPINE, WORTH 3,200 CENZ.
AND THEN IN THE CENTER SECTION...
YOU'VE CHECKED THEM ALL OUT ALREADY?!
BLAH
BLAH
BLAH
BLAH
THIS
BLAH
THERE'S ANOTHER ONE IN THAT HEAP OF CARDBOARD ON THE SECOND FLOOR
WOW...
BLAH
THAT

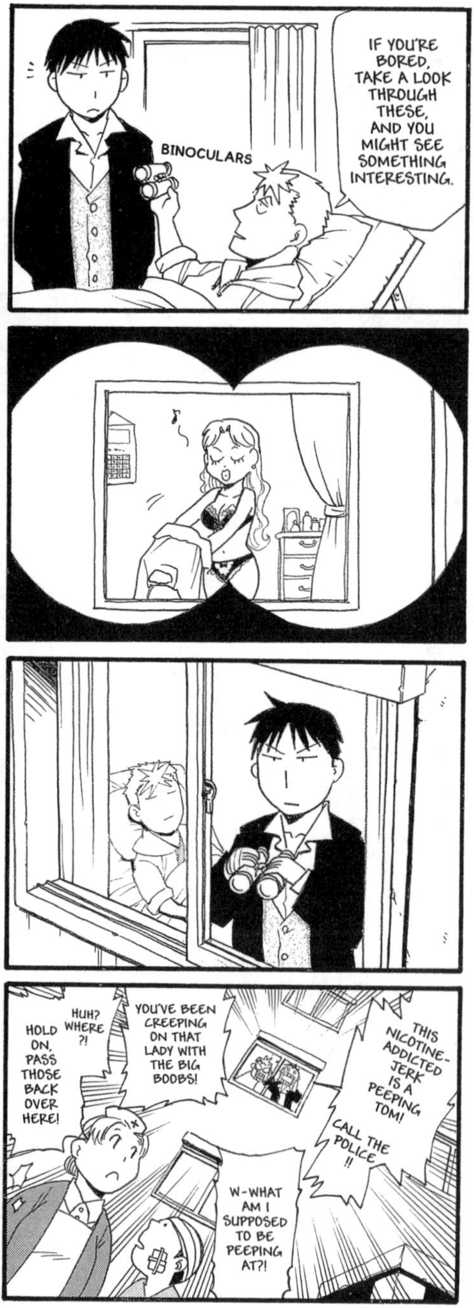
IF YOU'RE BORED, TAKE A LOOK THROUGH THESE, AND YOU MIGHT SEE SOMETHING INTERESTING.
BINOCULARS
THIS NICOTINE-ADDICTED JERK IS A PEEPING TOM!
CALL THE POLICE!!
YOU'VE BEEN CREEPING ON THAT LADY WITH THE BIG BOOBS!
HUH? WHERE?!
HOLD ON, PASS THOSE BACK OVER HERE!
W-WHAT AM I SUPPOSED TO BE PEEPING AT?!

Other Products

Shonen Gangan Magazine Bonus Gift, November 2003

HOW TO USE A SIGNING BOARD
NRRA-AAGH!
NAAAAAH!
RUB RUB RUB RUB
SWOOP
TOTAL HEIGHT...
170 CM!!
NICE TRY.
KLONK

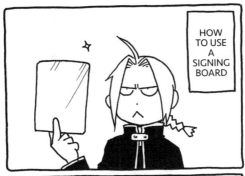

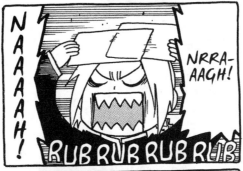

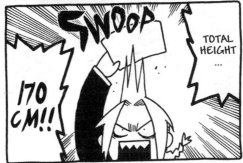

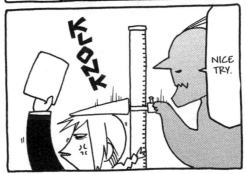

MR. ENVY, MR. ENVY!

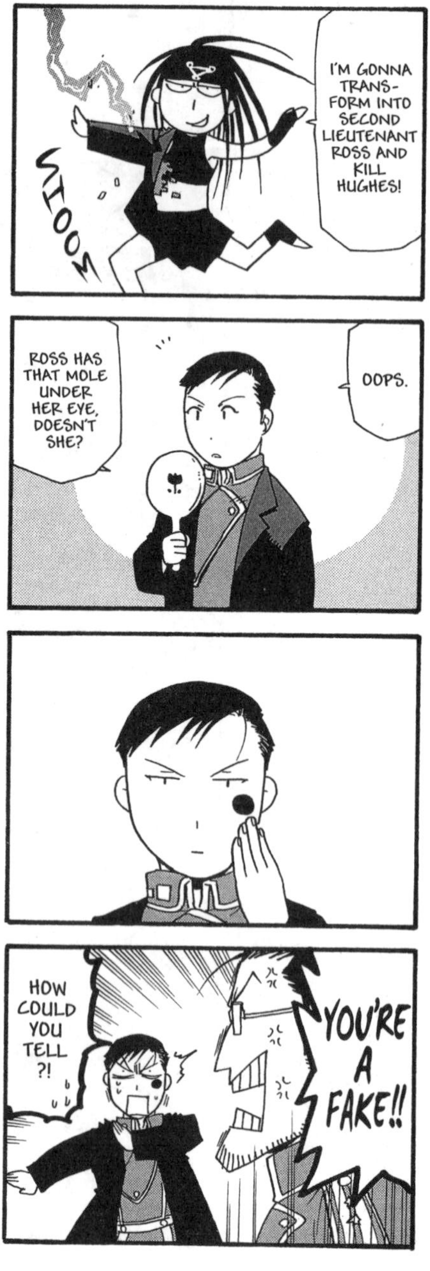
I'M GONNA TRANSFORM INTO SECOND LIEUTENANT ROSS AND KILL HUGHES!
WHOOM
ROSS HAS THAT MOLE UNDER HER EYE, DOESN'T SHE?
OOPS.
YOU'RE A FAKE!!
HOW COULD YOU TELL ?!

OUCH

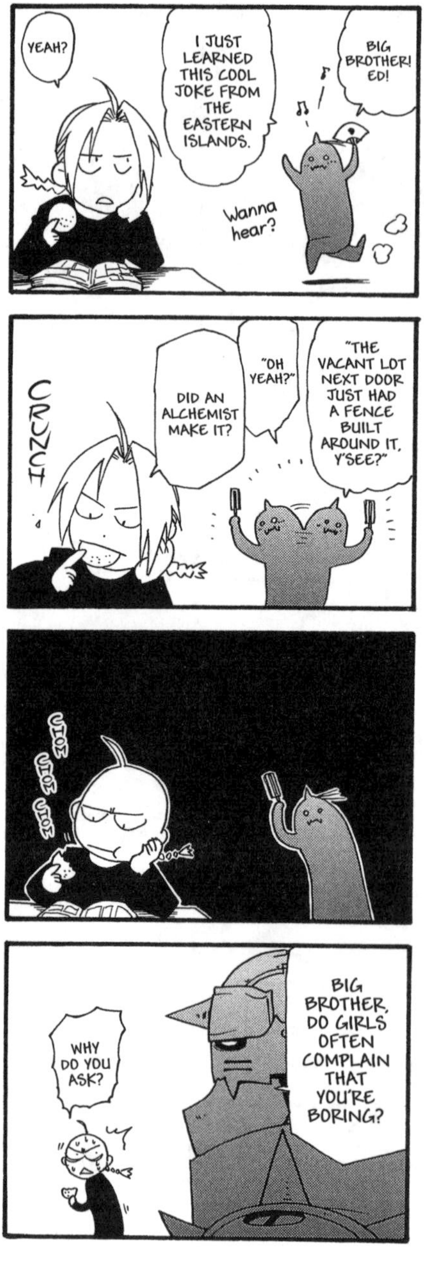
BIG BROTHER! ED!
I JUST LEARNED THIS COOL JOKE FROM THE EASTERN ISLANDS.
Wanna hear?
YEAH?
"THE VACANT LOT NEXT DOOR JUST HAD A FENCE BUILT AROUND IT, Y'SEE?"
"OH YEAH?"
DID AN ALCHEMIST MAKE IT?
CRUNCH
CHOM CHOM CHOM
BIG BROTHER, DO GIRLS OFTEN COMPLAIN THAT YOU'RE BORING?
WHY DO YOU ASK?

WHOLESOME MANGA

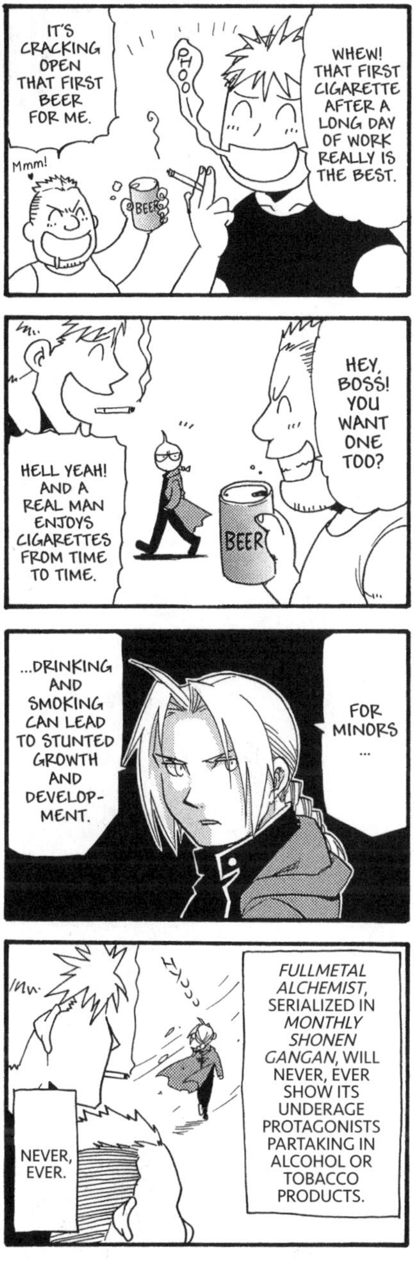
WHEW! THAT FIRST CIGARETTE AFTER A LONG DAY OF WORK REALLY IS THE BEST.
PHOO
IT'S CRACKING OPEN THAT FIRST BEER FOR ME.
Mmm!
BEER
HEY, BOSS! YOU WANT ONE TOO?
BEER
HELL YEAH! AND A REAL MAN ENJOYS CIGARETTES FROM TIME TO TIME.
FOR MINORS...
...DRINKING AND SMOKING CAN LEAD TO STUNTED GROWTH AND DEVELOPMENT.
FULLMETAL ALCHEMIST, SERIALIZED IN MONTHLY SHONEN GANGAN, WILL NEVER, EVER SHOW ITS UNDERAGE PROTAGONISTS PARTAKING IN ALCOHOL OR TOBACCO PRODUCTS.
NEVER, EVER.

GRAND FINALE

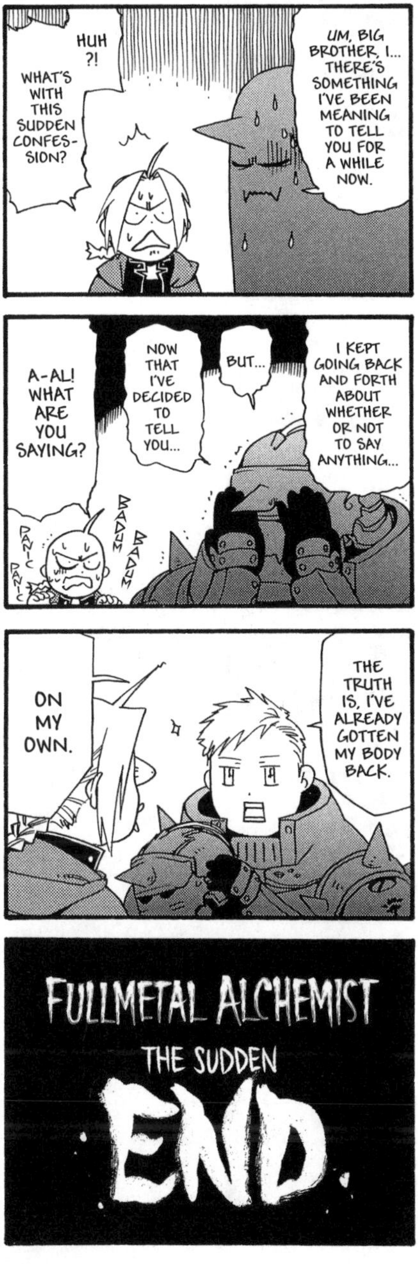
UM, BIG BROTHER, I... THERE'S SOMETHING I'VE BEEN MEANING TO TELL YOU FOR A WHILE NOW.
HUH ?!
WHAT'S WITH THIS SUDDEN CONFESSION?
I KEPT GOING BACK AND FORTH ABOUT WHETHER OR NOT TO SAY ANYTHING...
BUT...
NOW THAT I'VE DECIDED TO TELL YOU...
A-AL! WHAT ARE YOU SAYING?
BADUM BADUM
PANIC PANIC
THE TRUTH IS, I'VE ALREADY GOTTEN MY BODY BACK.
ON MY OWN.
FULLMETAL ALCHEMIST
THE SUDDEN
END.

SAFE SEARCHING

BIG BROTHER, WHAT'S THAT YOU'VE BEEN LOOKING AT SO INTENTLY?
UH. WELL, I'M RESEARCHING THE PHILOSOPHER'S STONE ON THE INTERNET.
HELLO! GOOD AFTERNOON!
I'M THE WEB SEARCH FAIRY!
POOF
IF YOU'RE A FAIRY, DOES THAT MEAN YOU GRANT WISHES?!
WILL YOU GIVE US INFORMATION ON THE PHILOSOPHER'S STONE?
MMM... NOPE!
INSTEAD, I'M GOING TO REVEAL YOUR SEARCH HISTORY!
HOW TO GET TALLER
MILK CONQUEST
HOW TO BE POP
WITH GIRLS
EIGHT
TRETCHES
EXY PICTURES
DULTS ONLY
AARGH!!!

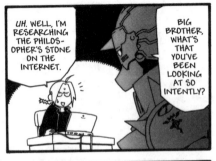

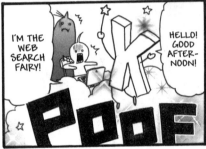

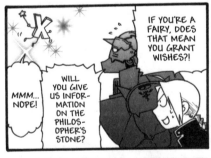

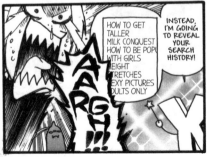

AWKWARD ALCHEMIST

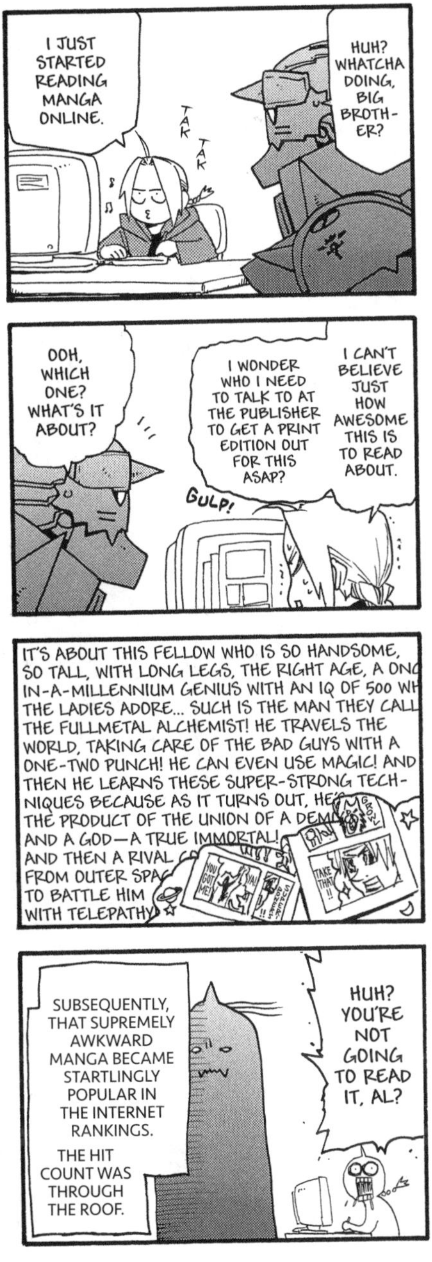
HUH? WHATCHA DOING, BIG BROTHER?
TAK TAK
I JUST STARTED READING MANGA ONLINE.
I CAN'T BELIEVE JUST HOW AWESOME THIS IS TO READ ABOUT.
I WONDER WHO I NEED TO TALK TO AT THE PUBLISHER TO GET A PRINT EDITION OUT FOR THIS ASAP?
GULP!
OOH, WHICH ONE? WHAT'S IT ABOUT?
IT'S ABOUT THIS FELLOW WHO IS SO HANDSOME, SO TALL, WITH LONG LEGS, THE RIGHT AGE, A ONC IN-A-MILLENNIUM GENIUS WITH AN IQ OF 500 WH THE LADIES ADORE... SUCH IS THE MAN THEY CALL THE FULLMETAL ALCHEMIST! HE TRAVELS THE WORLD, TAKING CARE OF THE BAD GUYS WITH A ONE-TWO PUNCH! HE CAN EVEN USE MAGIC! AND THEN HE LEARNS THESE SUPER-STRONG TECHNIQUES BECAUSE AS IT TURNS OUT, HE'S THE PRODUCT OF THE UNION OF A DEM AND A GOD—A TRUE IMMORTAL! AND THEN A RIVAL C FROM OUTER SPA TO BATTLE HIM WITH TELEPATHY
YOU GOT ME!
TAKE THAT!!
HUH? YOU'RE NOT GOING TO READ IT, AL?
SUBSEQUENTLY, THAT SUPREMELY AWKWARD MANGA BECAME STARTLINGLY POPULAR IN THE INTERNET RANKINGS.
THE HIT COUNT WAS THROUGH THE ROOF.

AWKWARD LURKER

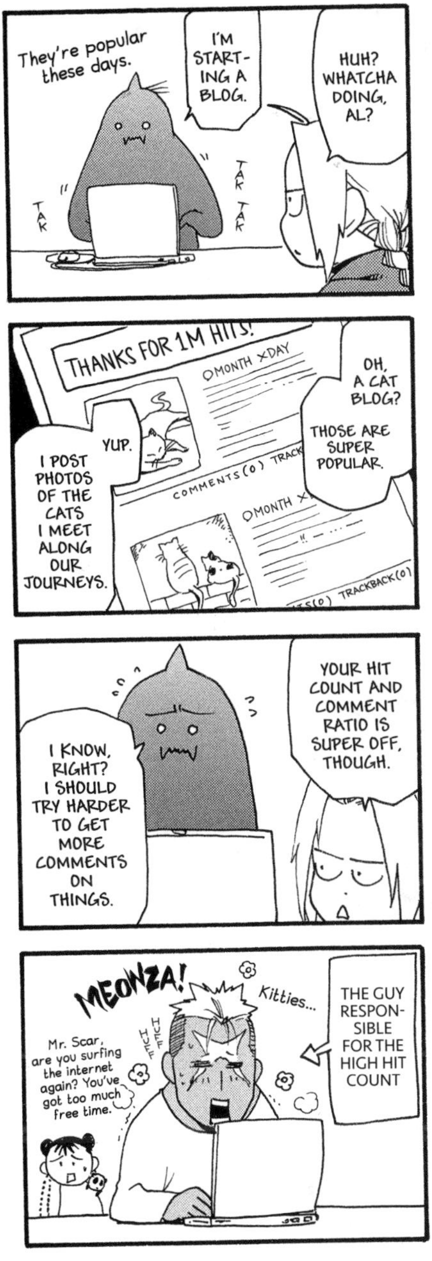
HUH? WHATCHA DOING, AL?
I'M STARTING A BLOG.
They're popular these days.
TAK TAK TAK
THANKS FOR 1M HITS!
○MONTH ×DAY
COMMENTS(0) TRACKBACK(0)
OH, A CAT BLOG?
THOSE ARE SUPER POPULAR.
YUP.
I POST PHOTOS OF THE CATS I MEET ALONG OUR JOURNEYS.
YOUR HIT COUNT AND COMMENT RATIO IS SUPER OFF, THOUGH.
I KNOW, RIGHT? I SHOULD TRY HARDER TO GET MORE COMMENTS ON THINGS.
THE GUY RESPONSIBLE FOR THE HIGH HIT COUNT
Kitties...
MEONZA!
HUFF HUFF
Mr. Scar, are you surfing the internet again? You've got too much free time.

SELF-AGGRANDIZING MANGA (FROM UNDER THE BOOK JACKET)

FULLMETAL ALCHEMIST IS A SHONEN MANGA.
BUT IT'S KIND OF LOW ON THE KEY ELEMENTS OF THE GENRE.
LIKE "HARD WORK."
CAN'T HELP THAT. WE STARTED OFF AT LEVEL 100.
"FRIENDSHIP"... YOU AND I DON'T HAVE TOO MANY FRIENDS.
DON'T SAY THAT ...
"COOL PROTAGONISTS"...
WELL, YOU'RE A LITTLE PUG-NOSED—
NOM NOM
COMRADES, MAYBE?
THEY'RE ALL OLD GEEZERS.
SHUT UP!!
HA! WE MAY NOT HAVE MUCH IN THE WAY OF HARD WORK OR FRIENDSHIP.
BUT THERE'S A SPECIAL APPEAL WE HAVE THAT THEY ALL LACK!
REALLY?! WHAT'S THAT?
MONEY AND INFLUENCE.
THIS MANGA'S A BAD INFLUENCE.
You could have at least said "brotherly love."
STATE ALCHEMIST

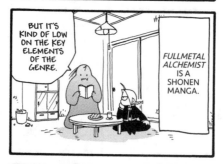

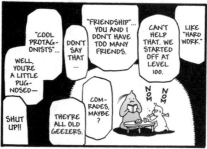

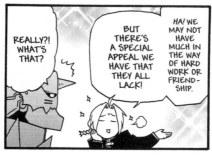

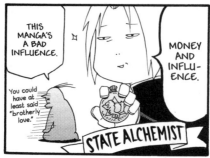

BONUS

FULLMETAL MASTERPIECE THEATER

BEAUTY AND THE BEAST

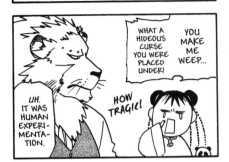

WHAT A HIDEOUS CURSE YOU WERE PLACED UNDER! YOU MAKE ME WEEP...
HOW TRAGIC!
UH. IT WAS HUMAN EXPERIMENTATION.
TO BE ALONE AND FRIENDLESS, DEEP IN THESE MOUNTAINS ...!
YO, HEINKEL! WE CAME OVER TO HANG OUT!
HEY.
TO STRUGGLE THROUGH LIFE WITH THAT UNSIGHTLY FORM!
NAW, THIS BODY'S PRETTY GREAT. I'M LIKING IT.
TO NEVER BE ABLE TO REGAIN YOUR HUMAN FORM UNTIL YOU CAN ATTAIN TRUE LOVE!!
How cruel!!
Wah!
NAW, I CAN GO BACK AND FORTH AS I PLEASE.
SHRINK

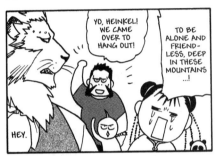

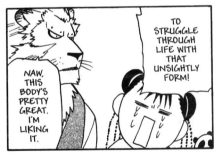

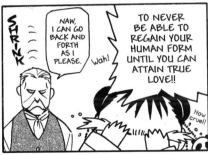

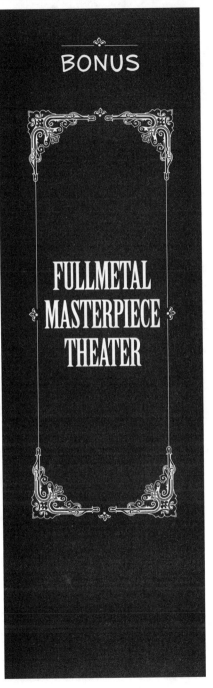

SWOLE-ERELLA

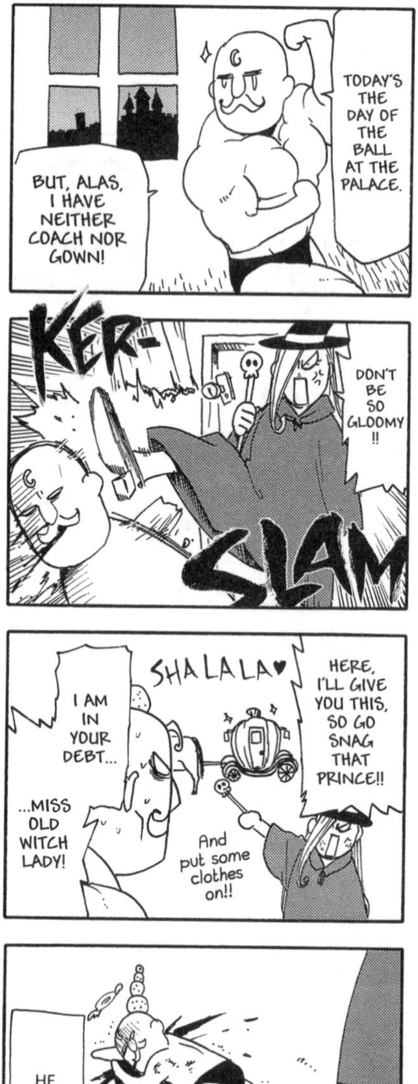
TODAY'S THE DAY OF THE BALL AT THE PALACE.
BUT, ALAS, I HAVE NEITHER COACH NOR GOWN!
DON'T BE SO GLOOMY!!
KER-
SLAM
HERE, I'LL GIVE YOU THIS, SO GO SNAG THAT PRINCE!!
SHALALA♥
I AM IN YOUR DEBT...
...MISS OLD WITCH LADY!
And put some clothes on!!
HE DIDN'T MAKE IT TO THE BALL.

RED RIDING HOOD

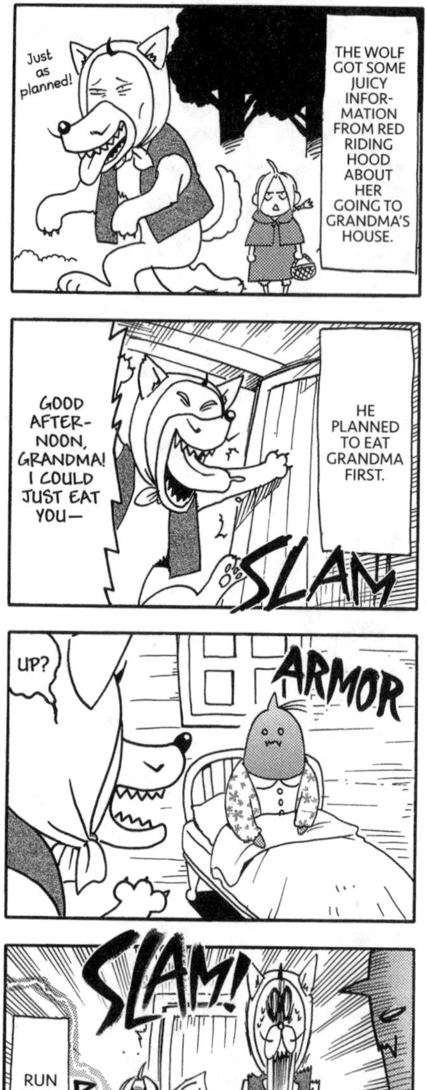
THE WOLF GOT SOME JUICY INFORMATION FROM RED RIDING HOOD ABOUT HER GOING TO GRANDMA'S HOUSE.
Just as planned!
HE PLANNED TO EAT GRANDMA FIRST.
GOOD AFTERNOON, GRANDMA! I COULD JUST EAT YOU—
SLAM
ARMOR
UP?
SLAM!
CHAK
BZZT
RUN WHILE YOU CAN, MR. WOLF!

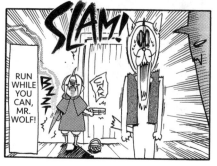

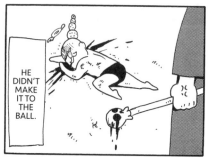

INCH-HIGH SAMURAI

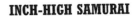

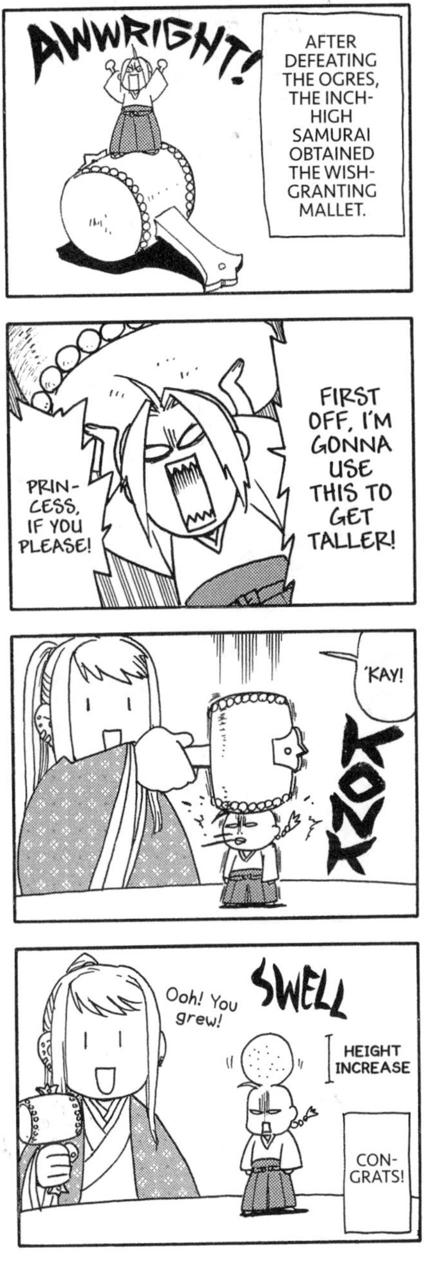
AFTER DEFEATING THE OGRES, THE INCH-HIGH SAMURAI OBTAINED THE WISH-GRANTING MALLET.
AWWRIGHT!
FIRST OFF, I'M GONNA USE THIS TO GET TALLER!
PRINCESS, IF YOU PLEASE!
'KAY!
KONK
SWELL
Ooh! You grew!
HEIGHT INCREASE
CONGRATS!

RED RIDING HOOD: PART 2

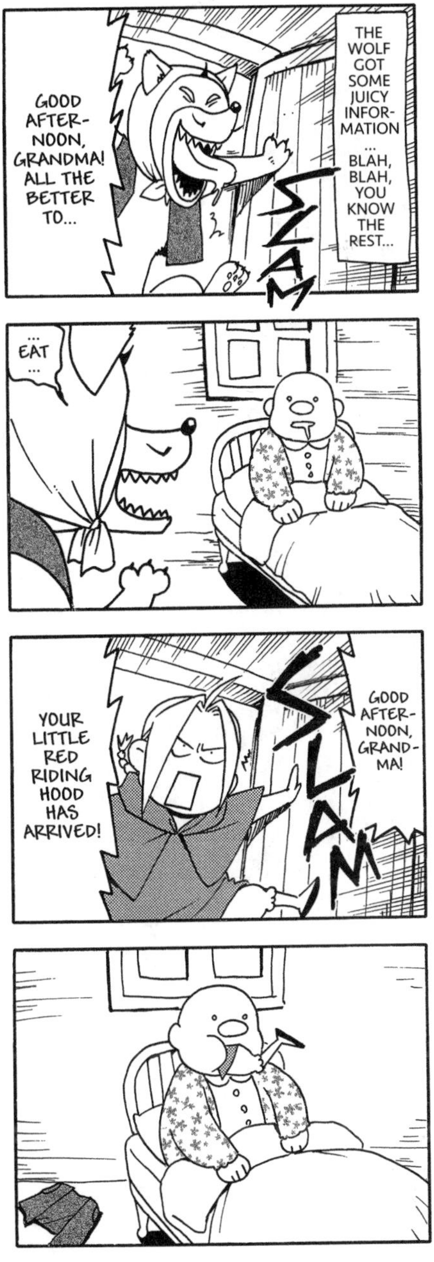
THE WOLF GOT SOME JUICY INFORMATION ... BLAH, BLAH, YOU KNOW THE REST...
GOOD AFTERNOON, GRANDMA! ALL THE BETTER TO...
SLAM
... EAT ...
GOOD AFTERNOON, GRANDMA!
SLAM
YOUR LITTLE RED RIDING HOOD HAS ARRIVED!

RUN, MELOS!

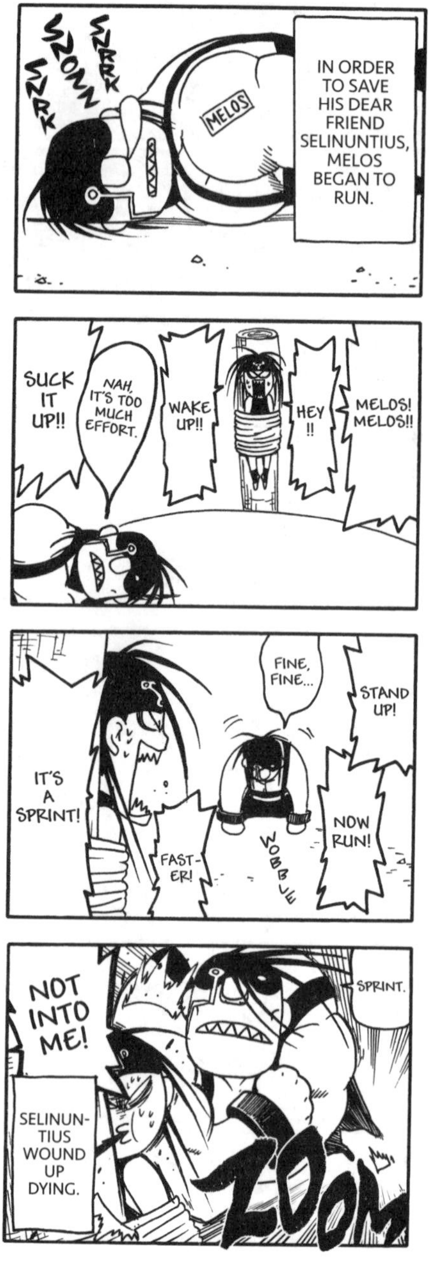
IN ORDER TO SAVE HIS DEAR FRIEND SELINUNTIUS, MELOS BEGAN TO RUN.
SNRRK
SNRK
MELOS
MELOS! MELOS!!
HEY!!
WAKE UP!!
NAH, IT'S TOO MUCH EFFORT.
SUCK IT UP!!
STAND UP!
FINE, FINE...
NOW RUN!
WOBBLE
FASTER!
IT'S A SPRINT!
SPRINT.
NOT INTO ME!
ZOOM
SELINUNTIUS WOUND UP DYING.

SPIDER'S THREAD

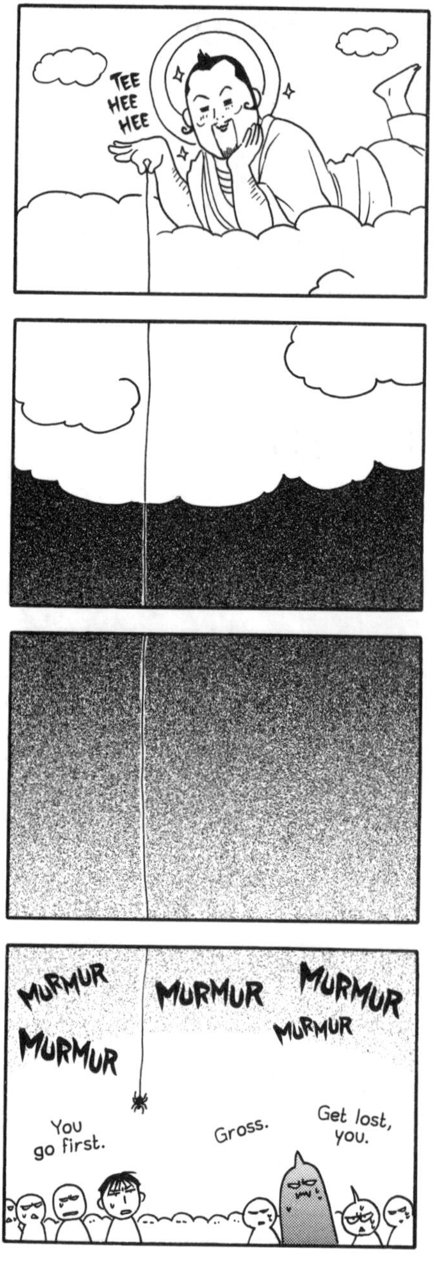
TEE HEE HEE
MURMUR
MURMUR
MURMUR
MURMUR
MURMUR
Get lost, you.
Gross.
You go first.

NORTH WIND AND THE SUN

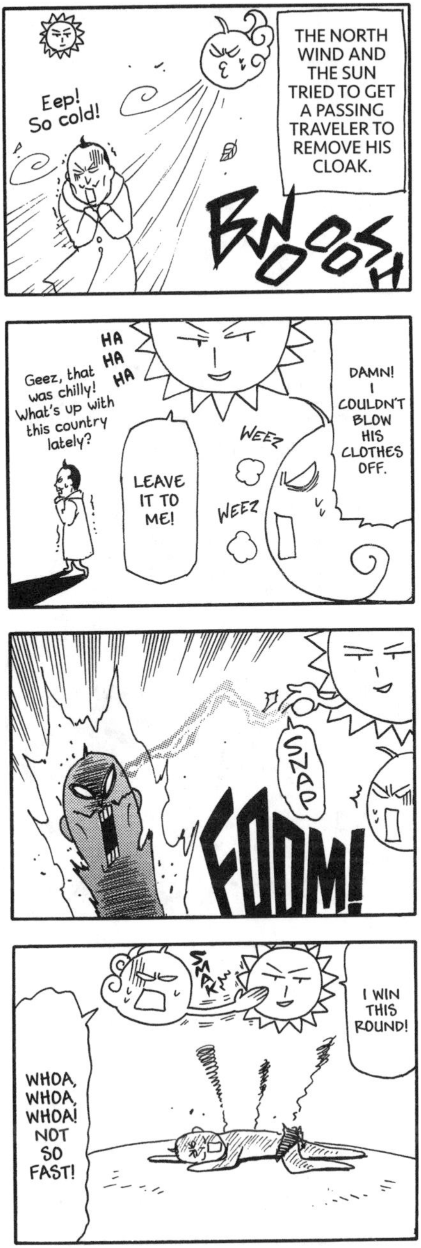
THE NORTH WIND AND THE SUN TRIED TO GET A PASSING TRAVELER TO REMOVE HIS CLOAK.
BWOOOSH
Eep! So cold!
DAMN! I COULDN'T BLOW HIS CLOTHES OFF.
WEEZ
WEEZ
LEAVE IT TO ME!
HA HA HA
Geez, that was chilly! What's up with this country lately?
SNAP
FOOM!
I WIN THIS ROUND!
SMAK
WHOA, WHOA, WHOA! NOT SO FAST!

THE GOLDEN AXE

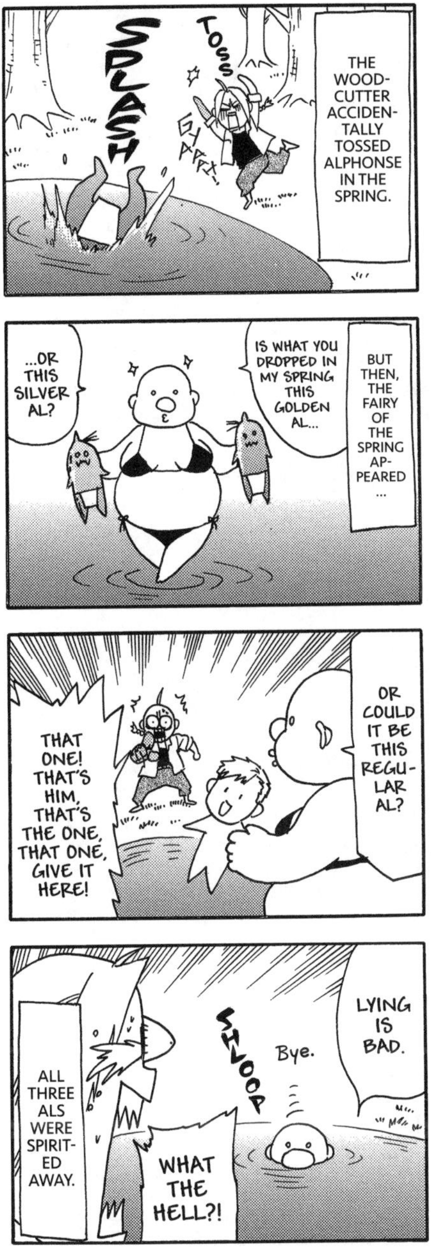
THE WOOD-CUTTER ACCIDEN-TALLY TOSSED ALPHONSE IN THE SPRING.
TOSS
SPLASH
BUT THEN, THE FAIRY OF THE SPRING AP-PEARED ...
IS WHAT YOU DROPPED IN MY SPRING THIS GOLDEN AL...
...OR THIS SILVER AL?
OR COULD IT BE THIS REGU-LAR AL?
THAT ONE! THAT'S HIM, THAT'S THE ONE, THAT ONE, GIVE IT HERE!
LYING IS BAD.
SHLOOP
Bye.
WHAT THE HELL?!
ALL THREE ALS WERE SPIRIT-ED AWAY.

THE COLONEL'S FUTURE

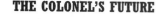

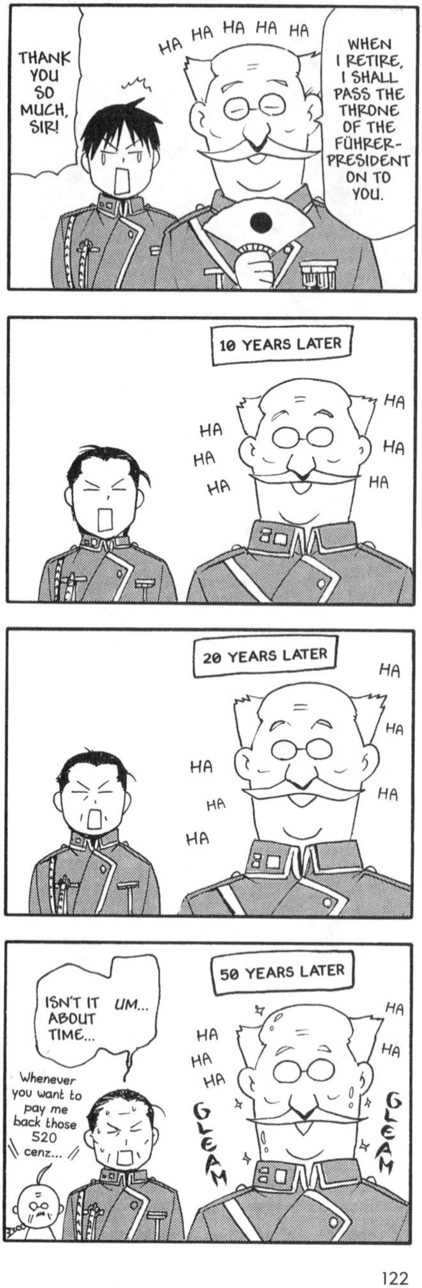
WHEN I RETIRE, I SHALL PASS THE THRONE OF THE FÜHRER-PRESIDENT ON TO YOU.
HA HA HA HA HA
THANK YOU SO MUCH, SIR!
10 YEARS LATER
HA HA HA
HA HA HA
20 YEARS LATER
HA HA HA
HA HA HA
50 YEARS LATER
HA HA
HA HA HA
GLEAM
GLEAM
UM...
ISN'T IT ABOUT TIME...
Whenever you want to pay me back those 520 cenz...

AL'S FUTURE

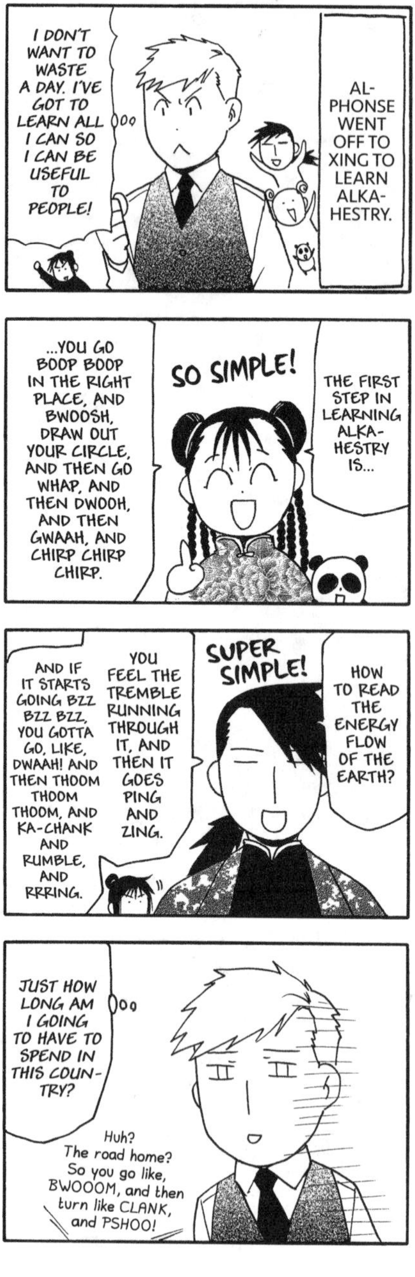
AL-PHONSE WENT OFF TO XING TO LEARN ALKA-HESTRY.
I DON'T WANT TO WASTE A DAY. I'VE GOT TO LEARN ALL I CAN SO I CAN BE USEFUL TO PEOPLE!
THE FIRST STEP IN LEARNING ALKA-HESTRY IS...
SO SIMPLE!
...YOU GO BOOP BOOP IN THE RIGHT PLACE, AND BWOOSH, DRAW OUT YOUR CIRCLE, AND THEN GO WHAP, AND THEN DWOOH, AND THEN GWAAH, AND CHIRP CHIRP CHIRP.
HOW TO READ THE ENERGY FLOW OF THE EARTH?
SUPER SIMPLE!
YOU FEEL THE TREMBLE RUNNING THROUGH IT, AND THEN IT GOES PING AND ZING.
AND IF IT STARTS GOING BZZ BZZ BZZ, YOU GOTTA GO, LIKE, DWAAH! AND THEN THOOM THOOM THOOM, AND KA-CHANK AND RUMBLE, AND RRRING.
JUST HOW LONG AM I GOING TO HAVE TO SPEND IN THIS COUN-TRY?
Huh? The road home? So you go like, BWOOOM, and then turn like CLANK, and PSHOO!

ED'S FUTURE

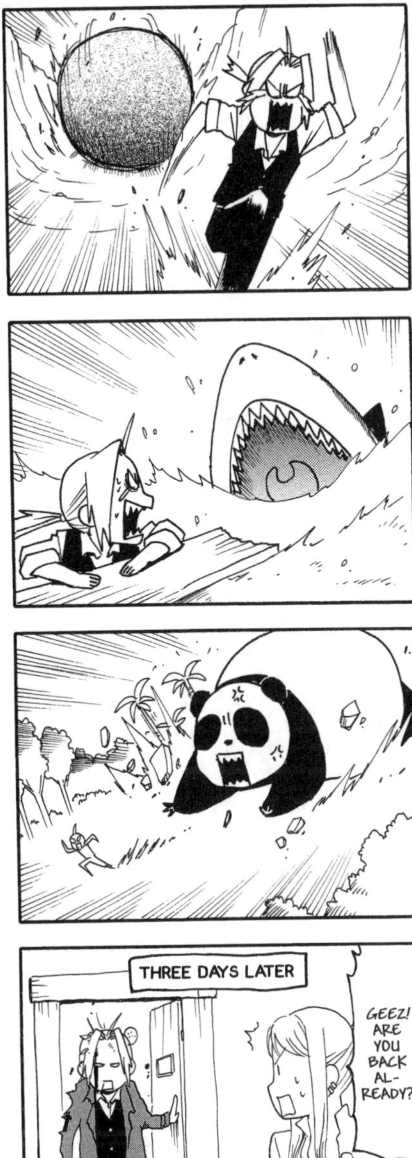
THREE DAYS LATER
GEEZ! ARE YOU BACK AL-READY?

YOKI'S FUTURE

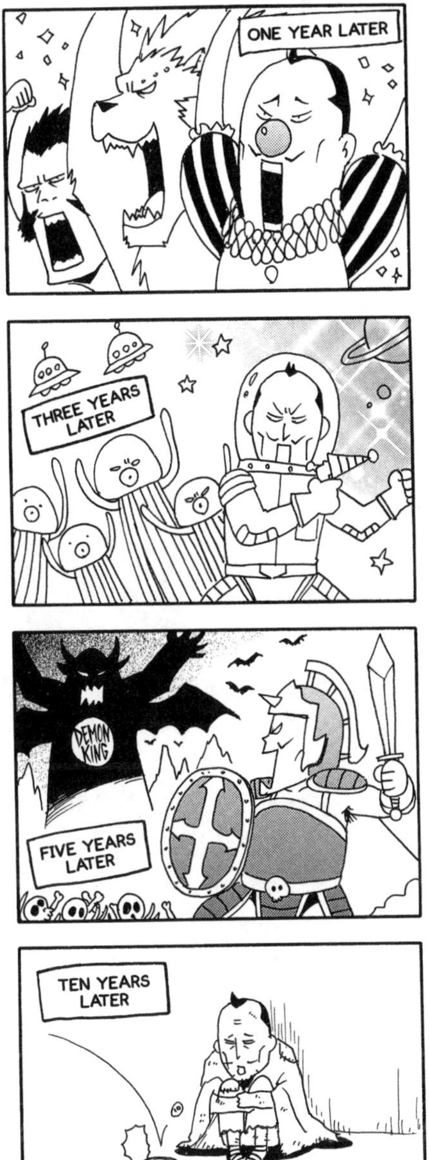
ONE YEAR LATER
THREE YEARS LATER
DEMON KING
FIVE YEARS LATER
TEN YEARS LATER
*THEN IT REPEATS.

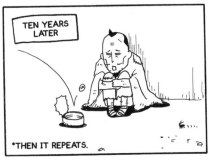

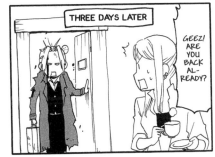

Other Products

The Land of Sand Tip-In Postcard, February 2003

BIG TEXT: WRITING A LETTER
SMALL TEXT: SCRIBBLE SCRIBBLE

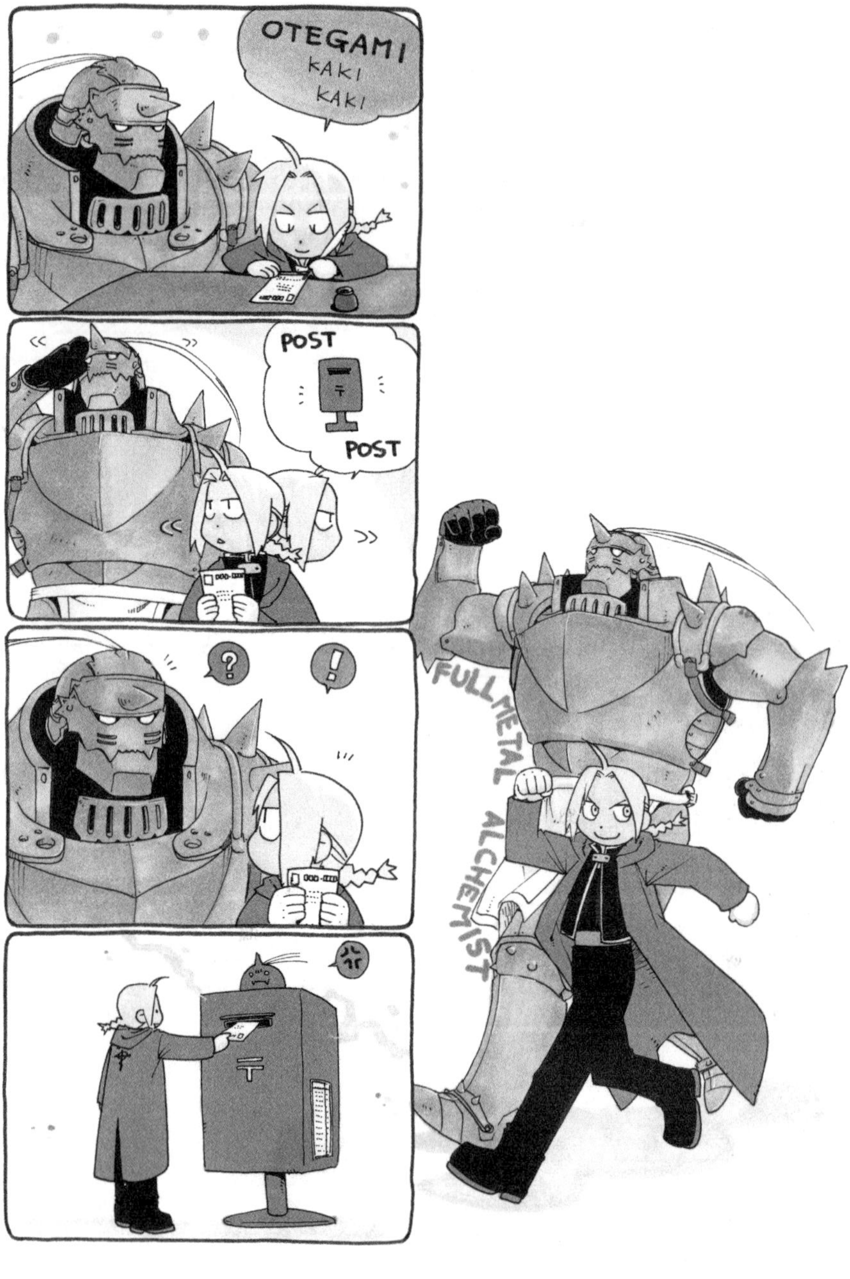

BONUS COMICS

YOU'VE GOTTEN SO ROUND

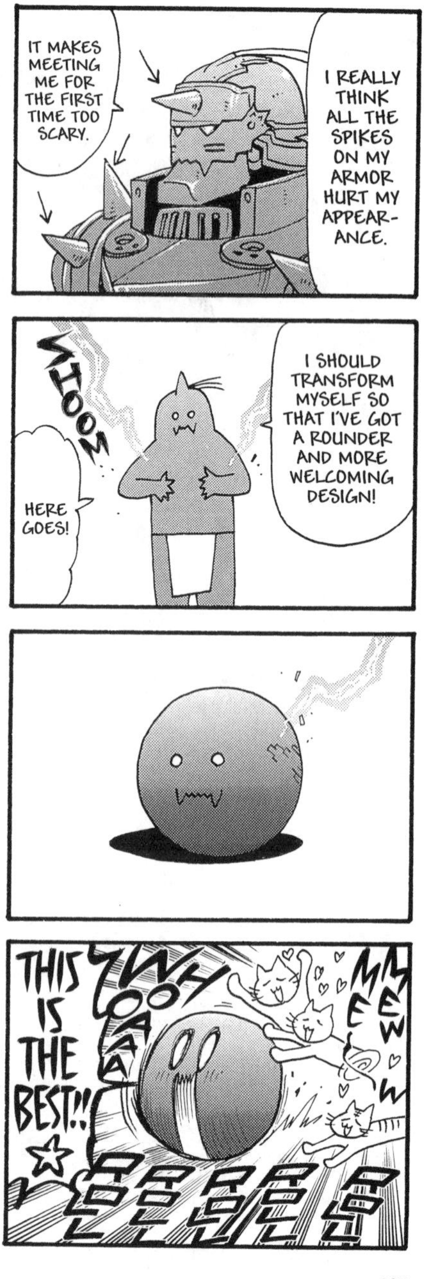
I REALLY THINK ALL THE SPIKES ON MY ARMOR HURT MY APPEARANCE.
IT MAKES MEETING ME FOR THE FIRST TIME TOO SCARY.
I SHOULD TRANSFORM MYSELF SO THAT I'VE GOT A ROUNDER AND MORE WELCOMING DESIGN!
SHOOM
HERE GOES!
MEW
MEW
WHOOAAA
THIS IS THE BEST!!
ROLL ROLL ROLL ROLL ROLL

TWO SERVINGS

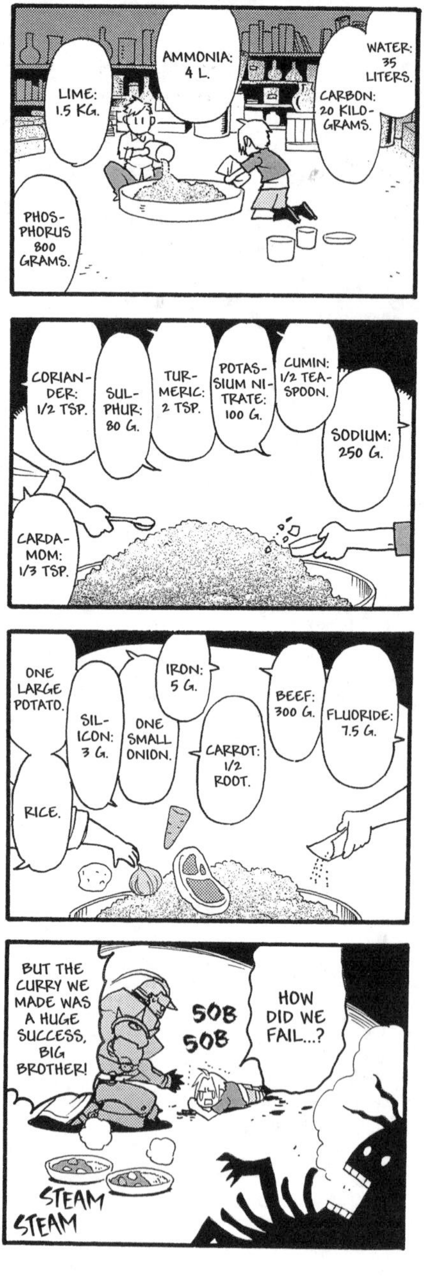
WATER: 35 LITERS.
CARBON: 20 KILOGRAMS.
AMMONIA: 4 L.
LIME: 1.5 KG.
PHOSPHORUS 800 GRAMS.
CUMIN: 1/2 TEASPOON.
SODIUM: 250 G.
POTASSIUM NITRATE: 100 G.
TURMERIC: 2 TSP.
SULPHUR: 80 G.
CORIANDER: 1/2 TSP.
CARDAMOM: 1/3 TSP.
FLUORIDE: 7.5 G.
BEEF: 300 G.
IRON: 5 G.
CARROT: 1/2 ROOT.
ONE SMALL ONION.
SILICON: 3 G.
ONE LARGE POTATO.
RICE.
HOW DID WE FAIL...?
SOB SOB
BUT THE CURRY WE MADE WAS A HUGE SUCCESS, BIG BROTHER!
STEAM STEAM

KILLING TIME

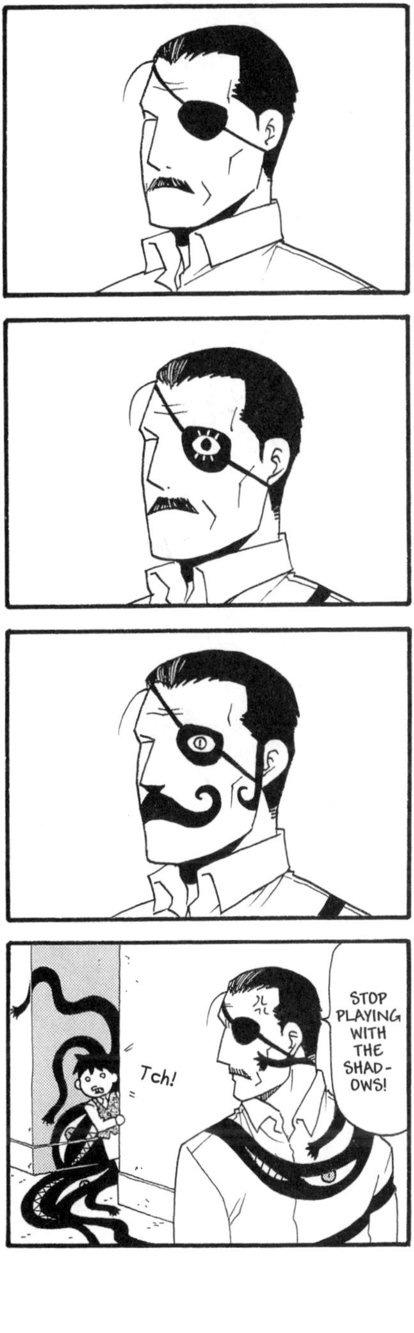
STOP PLAYING WITH THE SHADOWS!
Tch!

THE LEGENDARY HERO

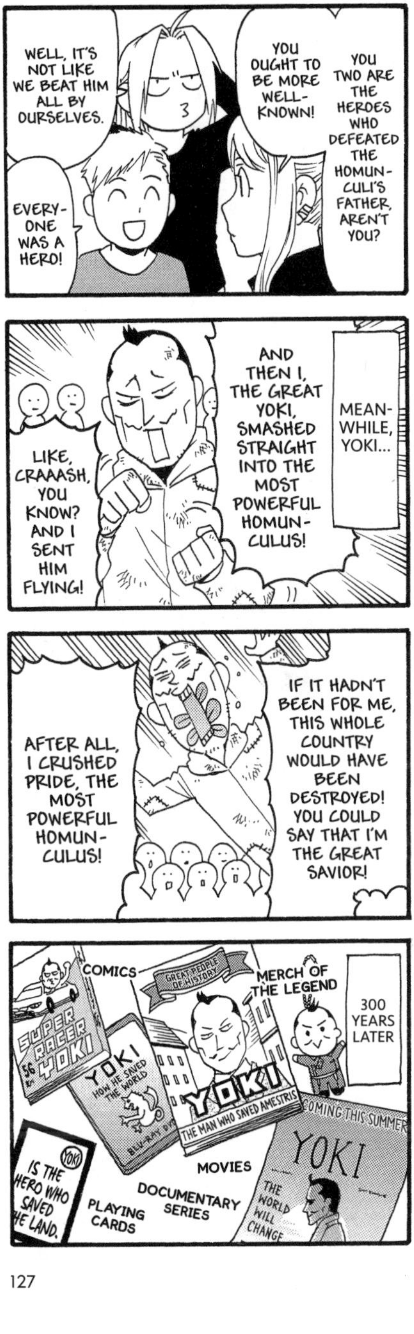
YOU TWO ARE THE HEROES WHO DEFEATED THE HOMUNCULI'S FATHER, AREN'T YOU?
YOU OUGHT TO BE MORE WELL-KNOWN!
WELL, IT'S NOT LIKE WE BEAT HIM ALL BY OURSELVES.
EVERYONE WAS A HERO!
MEANWHILE, YOKI...
AND THEN I, THE GREAT YOKI, SMASHED STRAIGHT INTO THE MOST POWERFUL HOMUNCULUS!
LIKE, CRAAASH, YOU KNOW? AND I SENT HIM FLYING!
IF IT HADN'T BEEN FOR ME, THIS WHOLE COUNTRY WOULD HAVE BEEN DESTROYED! YOU COULD SAY THAT I'M THE GREAT SAVIOR!
AFTER ALL, I CRUSHED PRIDE, THE MOST POWERFUL HOMUNCULUS!
300 YEARS LATER
MERCH OF THE LEGEND
GREAT PEOPLE OF HISTORY
YOKI
THE MAN WHO SAVED AMESTRIS
COMICS
SUPER RACER YOKI
56
YOKI
HOW HE SAVED THE WORLD
COMING THIS SUMMER
YOKI
THE WORLD WILL CHANGE
MOVIES
DOCUMENTARY SERIES
PLAYING CARDS
YOKI
IS THE HERO WHO SAVED THE LAND.

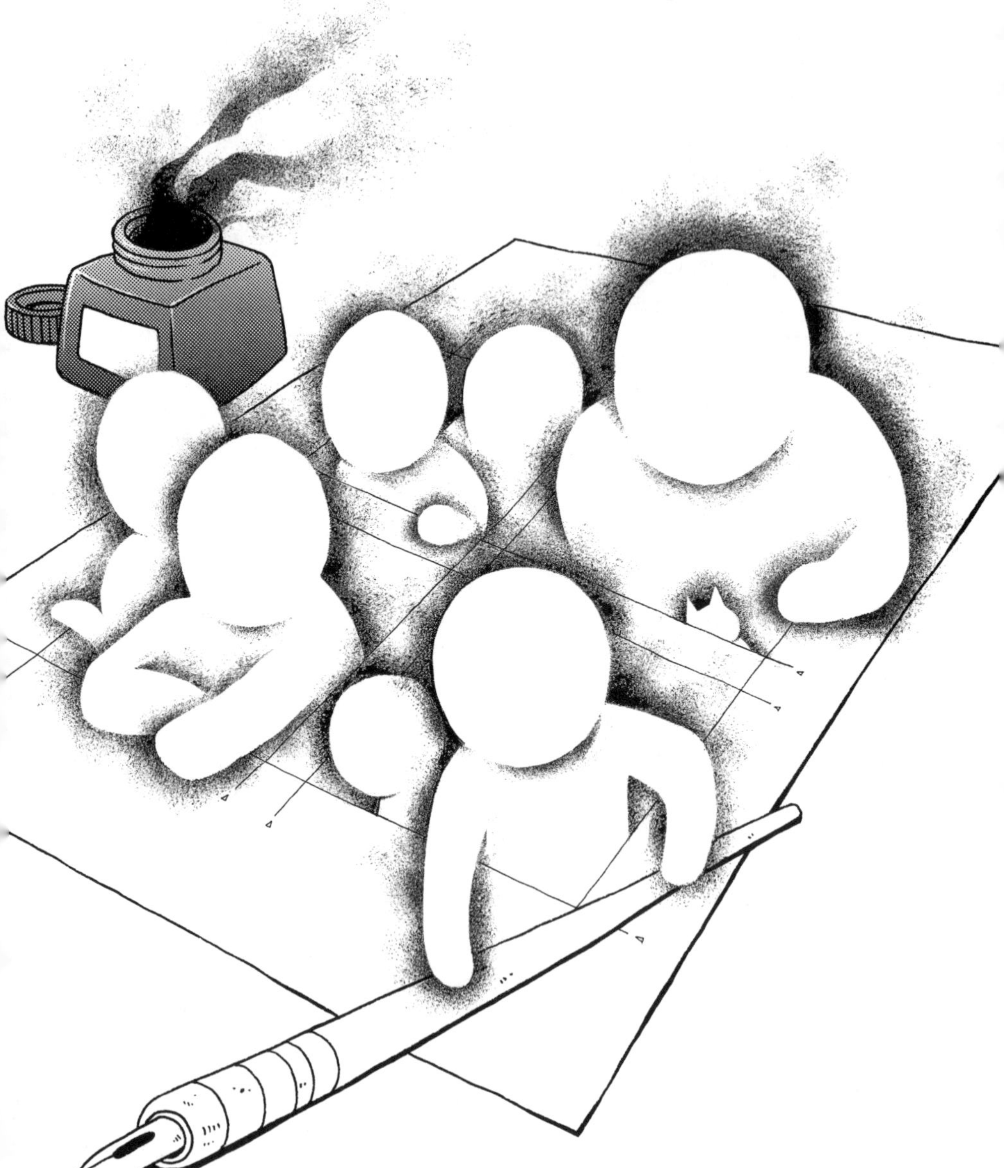

THERE'S A FULLMETAL ALCHEMIST LIVE-ACTION MOVIE COMING OUT!
YAAAY!!!
I MEAN, WE'VE ALREADY HAD DRAMA CDS, ANIME, GAMES AND WHATNOT...
IS THERE ANY FORM OF MEDIA WE HAVEN'T BEEN IN?
TAKA-RA-ZUKA?
!!!
LOOOOVE... IT IS FLAAAMES...

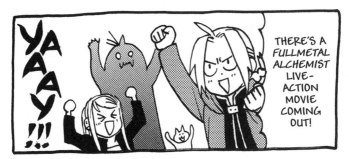

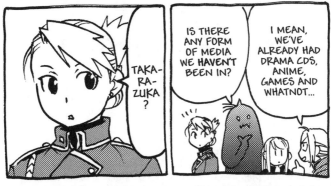

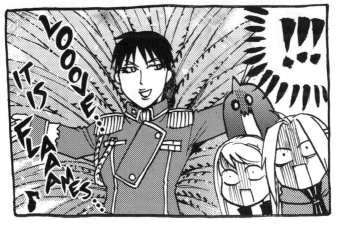

END

ABOUT THE AUTHOR

Born in Hokkaido, Japan, Hiromu Arakawa first attracted attention in 1999 with her award-winning manga *Stray Dog*. Her series *Fullmetal Alchemist* was serialized from 2001 to 2010 with a story that spanned 27 volumes and became an international critical and commercial success, receiving both the Shogakukan Manga Award and Seiun Award and selling over 70 million copies worldwide. *Fullmetal Alchemist* has been adapted into anime twice, first as *Fullmetal Alchemist* in 2003 and again as *Fullmetal Alchemist: Brotherhood* in 2009. The series has also inspired numerous films, video games and novels.

FULLMETAL ALCHEMIST
THE COMPLETE
FOUR-PANEL COMICS

Story and Art by HIROMU ARAKAWA

Translation: LILLIAN DIAZ-PRZYBYL
Touch-Up Art & Lettering: JEANNIE LEE
Design: ADAM GRANO
Editor: HOPE DONOVAN

FULLMETAL ALCHEMIST 4-KOMA
© 2017 Hiromu Arakawa/SQUARE ENIX CO., LTD.
First published in Japan in 2017 by SQUARE ENIX CO.,
LTD. English translation rights arranged with SQUARE
ENIX CO., LTD. and VIZ Media, LLC. English translation
© 2019 SQUARE ENIX CO., LTD.

Printed in the U.S.A.

Published by VIZ Media, LLC
P.O. Box 77010
San Francisco, CA 94107

10 9 8 7 6 5 4 3 2 1
First printing, March 2019

viz.com

ALCHEMY TORE THE ELRIC BROTHERS' BODIES APART. CAN THEIR BOND MAKE THEM WHOLE AGAIN?

FULLMETAL ALCHEMIST

FULLMETAL EDITION

STORY & ART BY
HIROMU ARAKAWA

A deluxe hardcover collector's edition of one of the most beloved manga of all time!

Fully remastered with an updated translation and completely fresh lettering, and presented with color pages on large-trim archival-quality paper, the **FULLMETAL EDITION** presents the timeless dark adventures of the Elric brothers as they were truly meant to be seen. Includes brand-new cover art and color insert, with behind-the-scenes character sketches from author **HIROMU ARAKAWA**!

FULLMETAL ALCHEMIST

       HIROMU ARAKAWA

HARDCOVER ARTBOOK COLLECTION OF OVER
300 ILLUSTRATIONS FROM *FULLMETAL ALCHEMIST*

This massive hardcover collection contains all the *Fullmetal Alchemist* color artwork by manga artist Hiromu Arakawa from 2001 to 2017, including the series' entire run and beyond! *The Complete Art of Fullmetal Alchemist* contains over 280 pages of gorgeous full-color illustrations, including all the original chapter title pages, the graphic novel covers for the single-volume and collected editions, portraits of the main characters, and promotional artwork. Includes an exclusive interview and a special step-by-step illustration creation discussion with Hiromu Arakawa.

VIZ

©2017
Hiromu Arakawa/
SQUARE ENIX

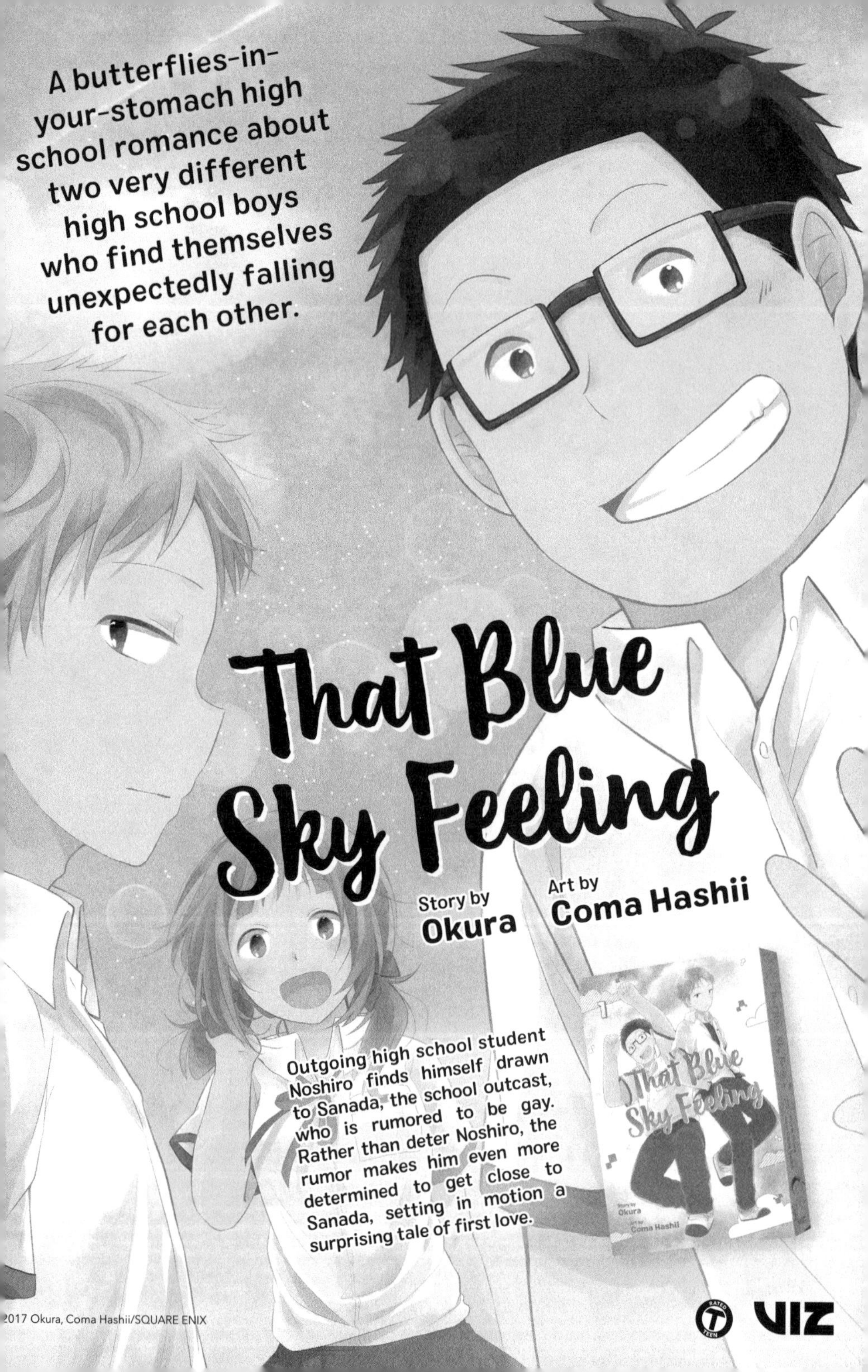
A butterflies-in-your-stomach high school romance about two very different high school boys who find themselves unexpectedly falling for each other.
That Blue Sky Feeling
Story by Okura
Art by Coma Hashii
Outgoing high school student Noshiro finds himself drawn to Sanada, the school outcast, who is rumored to be gay. Rather than deter Noshiro, the rumor makes him even more determined to get close to Sanada, setting in motion a surprising tale of first love.
That Blue Sky Feeling
Story by Okura
Art by Coma Hashii
2017 Okura, Coma Hashii/SQUARE ENIX
RATED T TEEN
VIZ

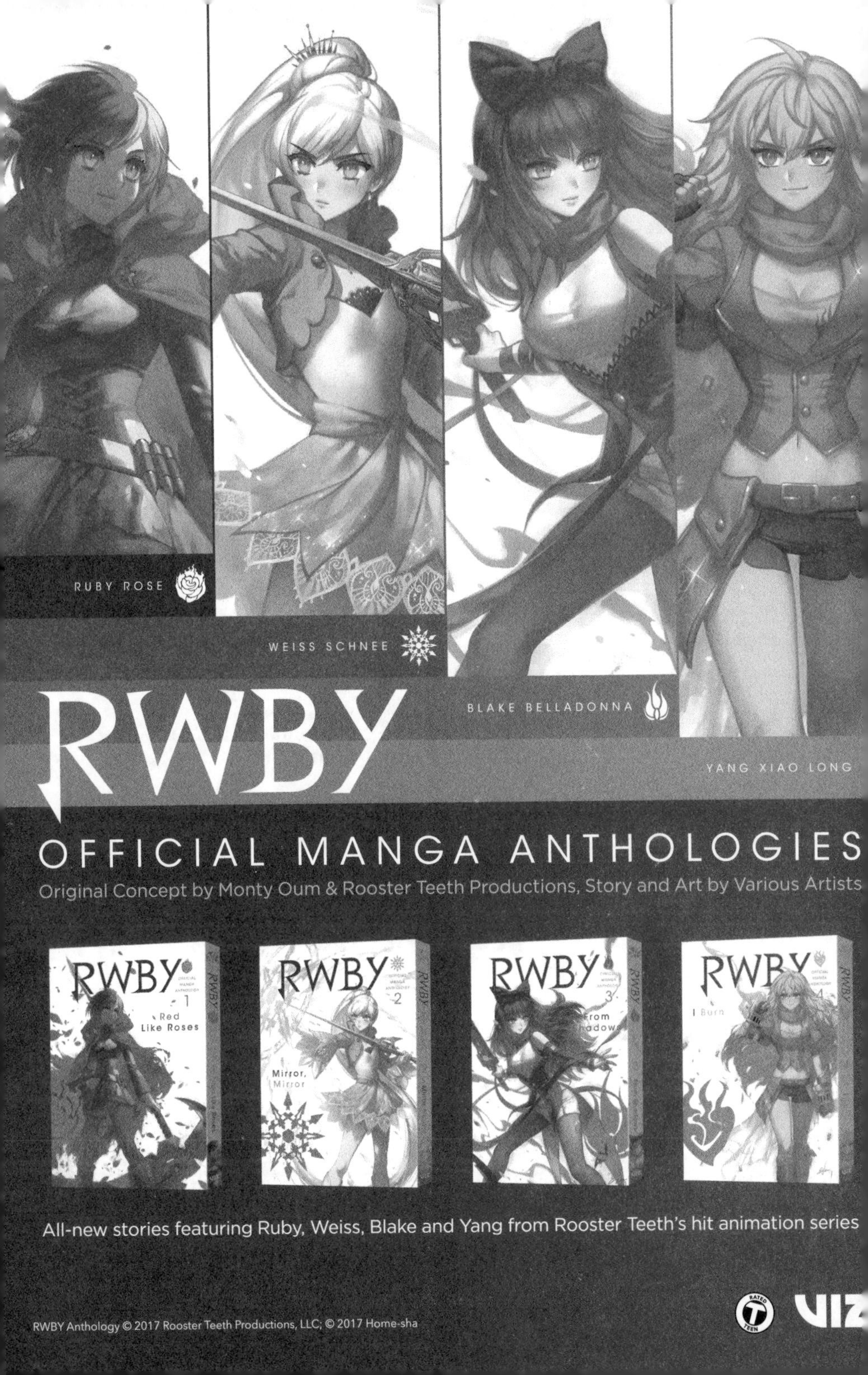
RUBY ROSE
WEISS SCHNEE
BLAKE BELLADONNA
YANG XIAO LONG
RWBY
OFFICIAL MANGA ANTHOLOGIES
Original Concept by Monty Oum & Rooster Teeth Productions, Story and Art by Various Artists
RWBY
OFFICIAL MANGA ANTHOLOGY
1
Red Like Roses
RWBY
2
Mirror, Mirror
RWBY
3
From
RWBY
4
I Burn
All-new stories featuring Ruby, Weiss, Blake and Yang from Rooster Teeth's hit animation series
RATED T TEEN
VIZ
RWBY Anthology © 2017 Rooster Teeth Productions, LLC; © 2017 Home-sha

This is the last page.

Fullmetal Alchemist: The Complete Four-Panel Comics reads right to left.